THE
CATHOLIC
MYTH

*The Behavior and Beliefs
of American Catholics*

ANDREW M. GREELEY

CHARLES SCRIBNER'S SONS

NEW YORK

Charles Scribner's Sons
Macmillan Publishing Company
866 Third Avenue, New York, NY 10022
Collier Macmillan Canada, Inc.

Library of Congress Cataloging-in-Publication Data
Greeley, Andrew M., 1928–
The Catholic myth: the behavior and
beliefs of American Catholics/Andrew Greeley.
p.   cm.
ISBN 0-684-19184-9
1. Catholics—United States—History—20th century.   2. Catholic
Church—United States—History—20th century.   3. Sociology,
Christian (Catholic)—United States—History—20th century.
I. Title.
BX1406.2.G698   1990
282'.73'0904—dc20
89-39259
CIP

Macmillan books are available at special discounts for bulk purchases
for sales promotions, premiums, fund-raising, or educational use.
For details, contact:

Special Sales Director
Macmillan Publishing Company
866 Third Avenue
New York, NY 10022

10 9 8 7 6 5 4 3 2 1

Designed by Jack Meserole
PRINTED IN THE UNITED STATES OF AMERICA

CONTENTS

ACKNOWLEDGMENTS

I thank Sean Durkin for his assistance in data processing, Mary Kotecki and Alice Rubio for their help with typing, and Daniel J. Herr for his perennial wisdom.

I am also grateful to the many colleagues with whom I have worked on projects through the years: James Coleman, Mary Jule Durkin, Joan Fee, Michael Hout, Kathleen McCourt, William McCready, William McManus, Philip Morgan, Peter Rossi, John Shea, Tom Smith, Teresa Sullivan, and David Tracy.

If everybody thought the same, there would be no need for sociological investigations. Sociologists are by definition interested in different ways of thinking.

—TATYANA ZASLAVSKAYA

THE
CATHOLIC
MYTH

1

THEY LIKE BEING CATHOLIC

ow, Father Greeley." Phil Donahue leaned forward eagerly, a snow leopard about to pounce on a victim. "Don't you think it would be better if all these dissenting Catholics left the Church? Wouldn't it be better for everyone if only those who agreed with the pope remained Catholic?"

"Who would pay the heat and light bills?" I asked, impatient, I fear, with the same old tired questions.

"Shouldn't all good Catholics agree in everything with the pope—birth control, celibacy, abortion, the ordination of women?"

What do you say to that sort of challenge? Four different issues, each with a different theological and cultural history: birth control is a subject on which the Church hesitated to make an issue in the nineteenth century. Celibacy is merely a matter of discipline. There are some cases—ectopic pregnancy, for example—when "Catholic abortion" is permitted. Women probably presided over the Eucharist in the early Church; the only theological argument against it is that it has not (apparently) been done since then.

Donahue, fangs bared, was not interested in theological or historical distinctions. He had his own simplistic paradigm and he wanted an answer that fit it—a paradigm which spelled DECLINE.

"Why should they leave?" I tried to parry his lunge.

"Because you can't be a good Catholic unless you agree with the pope, can you?"

"You stop being a Catholic," I replied, "only when you formally leave and join another denomination."

1

How to explain in a few moments two millennia of history in which pious Catholics, even saints, disagreed with the pope?

"Why don't they just leave?" Donahue demanded impatiently. Clearly he wanted them to just leave.

"Because"—I found a way out—"they like being Catholic."

He threw up his hands in disgust. "What does LIKING have to do with it?"

"Everything."

"What do you mean by that?" With a bit of a sneer.

"That would take a book to answer," I replied as the director behind the camera counted down the last five seconds of the interview.

I left quietly; Phil Donahue was, I think, frothing at the mouth. I had become so accustomed to banging my head against stone walls like his that I was not even mildly disturbed. Someday, I told myself, I would write a book to pry him and others away from their stone wall of ignorance.

In my heart that day I knew that even if I did write the book—this book in fact—he'd never read it. He already *knew* all that there was to know about American Catholics.

The interview had been a waste of time, like so many such are. The questions had been formed by a perspective about American Catholics that is utterly unrelated to the reality of Catholic life in America. Unless the perspective is changed and a different set of questions asked, the interviewer and his guest (whoever the guest might be) are forever doomed to chase will-o'-the-wisps in never-never land.

Like many other journalists who must become experts on the American Catholic Church in a few moments—with maybe a card or two of notes prepared by an associate producer—Phil Donahue was working with a "Catholicism in Crisis" paradigm. The changes in the Catholic Church had created a painful crisis of conscience for American Catholics. Either they would submit to Vatican rules or leave the Church, the latter an action that would create serious problems for their superstitious Catholic souls. The third possibility—that they would be Catholics on their own terms—simply did not fit into the paradigm with which such men and women approach the task of reporting on the Catholic Church.

There are two major forces that shape this paradigm. The first is American Nativism, the profound and powerful conviction that in some way it is impossible really to be a good Catholic and a good

American at the same time. Catholics are at last breaking with their superstitious past and becoming "just like everyone else." The "crisis" is the last dying gasp of immigrant Catholicism. All that will remain when it is over will be a Catholicism that is both independent of Rome and quite indistinguishable from mainstream American Protestantism. Every good American will sigh with relief that the indigestible has at last been digested.

The other cause of the "crisis" paradigm is the image that American Catholicism tried to produce for itself in the first half of the present century: in every way all Catholics always do what their leaders tell them to do. It was a foolish, even a frivolous myth, easily refuted by everyday parish experience. Moreover, it played into the hands of anti-Catholic bigotry.[1] The leadership of the Church, however, felt the need to prove again and again their loyalty to Rome and their integrity against the corruption of "non-Catholic" American culture.[2]

Both reasons for the "crisis" paradigm assume, however implicitly, that Catholic laity are ignorant and uneducated and they remain in the Church because of superstitious fear of hellfire.

At the beginning of this book I warn the potential reader that he must search his soul for traces of the Donahue paradigm. As long as you cling doggedly to it, I will have a hard time telling my story. I cannot shove aside your paradigm with facts and data unless you are willing to suspend it for a couple of hours and listen to my story. You must abandon your notion that Catholics are clinging to the Church by their fingernails and because of superstitious fear.

In fact, they are not clinging and they are not afraid. All the available empirical evidence establishes that they remain Catholic for the reason I gave Phil Donahue: *they like being Catholic.*

They have no intention of leaving the Church and becoming something else. No one will be able to drive them out.

Why, then, do they like being Catholic?

That's what this book is about. I intend to tell the fascinating, wonderful, and slightly daffy story of American Catholicism since

[1] Even today a quarter of Americans believe that Catholics do not think for themselves and do whatever their leaders tell them. The proportion goes to 30 percent among college-educated "liberals" in the northeastern region of the country.

[2] Even today the myth survives in the minds of such Catholic leaders as Cardinal Bernard Law and Archbishop Roger Mahoney, both of whom are convinced either—depending on the day you talk to them—that American Catholics still accept totally Vatican rule and rules or that they will return to such acceptance as soon as a catechism emerges that makes clear once again what the rules are.

the end of the Second Vatican Council, now twenty-five years old. I will describe how Catholicism is reshaping itself into new and intriguing forms for the next century and the next millennium. My story line is that, while as an institution the Catholic Church is in terrible condition, the Catholic community prospers—precisely because Catholics like being Catholic.

My central argument will be that Catholics differ from other Americans in that their imaginations tend to be more "sacramental" (or, to use David Tracy's word, "analogical"). By that I mean that Catholics are more likely to imagine God as present in the world and the world as revelatory instead of bleak. Much that is thought to be distinctively Catholic results from this distinctive style of imagining— the importance of community, institution, and hierarchy; the emphasis on ritual and ceremonial; the interest in the fine and lively arts; devotion to saints, angels, holy souls, and especially the Mother of Jesus; reverence for statues and images; the use of blessings, medals, and prayer beads.

My final recommendation will be that in the second quarter century after the Second Vatican Council it will be the task of the institution and its leadership—hierarchical, clerical, and intellectual—to rediscover the Spirit of God as She flourishes in their community and people.

Let me begin with some alleged facts about the current state of Catholicism in the United States.

Defections from the Catholic Church have increased since the Second Vatican Council. Moreover, because of the emphasis on religious unity in the ecumenical movement, Catholic opposition to religiously mixed marriages has declined and hence mixed marriages have increased.

The ordinary Catholic lay person is little affected by the theological controversies of our time or by the Roman repression of dissident theologians. A large number of elderly and conservative Catholics are bitterly opposed to the changes in the Church in recent years and in particular to the Mass in English. The decline of vocations to the priesthood is the result of the reluctance of young American men to take on the obligations of the celibate state.

There is little real anger among lay Catholics toward church leadership. Taking into account inflation and the demands of child-rearing and the decline of Sunday Mass attendance, Catholics are about as generous in their contributions to the Church as they ever were. Those who are most likely to leave the Church are the ones who dissent from its sexual teachings.

The Irish are the most conservative of American Catholics. While many Catholics may disagree with the pope, he is still a strong moral and spiritual leader in their eyes. The younger generation of American Catholics is drifting away from the Church and is not likely to return. The most important factor influencing religious behavior among American Catholics is the birth-control issue. Because of all the changes in the Church, American Catholics are not all that much different from American Protestants.

All of the above assertions are reasonable and sensible comments about the condition of the Catholic Church in the United States as it lurches into a new decade and toward the end of the century and the end of the millennium. You could propose them at a dinner party at night and encounter little argument. Have not such comments been made often on TV and, for example, in the pages of *Time?* They are unexceptional and unexceptionable.

They are also untrue.

That's right . . . they are all demonstrably false. There are few subjects in contemporary American life on which such arrogant and ignorant confidence is tolerated as has become acceptable when the subject is Catholicism and the Catholic Church. Consider the facts:

Since 1960 the proportion of those who are born Catholic yet no longer consider themselves Catholic has been constant (age distribution taken into account) at one out of seven. Mixed marriages have not increased. Since 1960 about one out of five Catholics has been in a religiously mixed marriage.

Twenty-five percent of American Catholics say their commitment to Catholicism has been weakened by the persecution of the theologians—the silencing of some and the expulsion from the rolls of Catholic theologians like the Swiss Hans Küng. Moreover, there is a strong relationship between Catholic attitudes toward such repression and financial contributions to the Church. The changes in the Church since the Second Vatican Council are supported by more than two-thirds of the Catholic population. The majority of men and women over sixty-five also support the changes. Eighty-seven percent approve of the English liturgy. The decline in vocations to the priesthood is the result of the failure of the clergy to attempt to recruit young men to their ministry.

Nonetheless, Catholics are bitterly angry at their leadership.

Since the only way Catholics can vote on what is happening in the Church is through their contributions, they have expressed their anger by cutting their financial contributions (as a proportion of income) in half since 1960, thus costing the Church $7 billion a year in revenue.

However, those who are thinking seriously of leaving the Church (about 6 percent) are not bothered by sexual teaching or even by the lack of concern about social justice, or the rights of women. They are rather disturbed by what they take to be the absence of spiritual and moral leadership. And, oh, yes, the Irish are the most liberal, politically and religiously, of American Catholics.

The pope's popularity has deteriorated badly since his most recent visit. In the aftermath of that visit and probably in reaction to the media emphasis on its costs, Catholic contributions in the areas he visited fell by a billion dollars. Despite this loss, projections based on life-cycle curves indicate that the younger generation will, by the time it reaches the age of its parents, achieve levels of devotional behavior similar to those of their parents.

The most important influence on the religious behavior of American Catholics is the religious behavior of their spouses. The second most important factor is the quality of Sunday preaching in the local parish. Nothing much else matters.

Finally, if religion is nothing more than sexual behavior, there might be some truth in the assertion that American Catholics are not much different from American Protestants—save for the fact that on many sexual matters Catholics are more liberal than American Protestants. However, religion is much more than sexual norms, and the American Catholic religious imagination continues to be different from the American Protestant religious imagination. The differences between Catholics and Protestants in some important matters may even be increasing.

Why do there seem to be contradictions in this batch of propositions? If Catholics approve most of the changes in their Church, why are they angry? If they are so angry, why haven't more of them left the Church?

If they haven't left the Church but are angry at church leadership, why haven't their children left?

This book will be concerned with answers to such questions. Briefly, Catholics are angry not at the changes but at the insensitivity and the incompetence of their leaders. They have not left the Church for the very simple reason I have put forward earlier—incomprehensible to most journalists who pontificate on Catholicism—that they like being Catholics. Their children remain Catholic because in our society you have to be something and Catholicism seems to them the most rational choice. *They, too, like being Catholic.*

I propose to the reader that there is nothing in the conventional wisdom about American religion, available in the elite media, in the graduate departments of the great universities, and in the leading seminaries and divinity schools of the country that will account for the turbulence and exuberance of the last quarter century of American Catholic history. One needs new perspectives on the nature of religion and on the nature of American religion to cope adequately with the always paradoxical and often apparently contradictory phenomena of Catholic history during the years since the end of the Second Vatican Council.

To briefly summarize my perspectives I will contend that to understand contemporary American Catholicism one needs to think of religion as imaginative and indeed poetic behavior and American religion as poetic behavior that confers identity. In such a situation it is utterly rational (even by the standards of free-market economy, rational-choice models) to continue to be Catholic no matter what the damn fools who are your leaders might do.

I use the term "damn fools" advisedly and in lieu of more scatological language.

My story will not be a sociological monograph, but it will be a story told by a sociologist who has intensively monitored the condition of American Catholicism for the last thirty years—before and after the Second Vatican Council. The primary strength of my story will come from sociological data and theory. I will go beyond the data to explain, reflect, speculate, recommend, and occasionally rage; but I will sharply distinguish between theory and fact on the one hand and opinion and recommendation on the other.

I will endeavor to spare the reader tables and charts, so dearly loved by us social scientists and so abjectly feared by many lay folk (in this case those who are not sociologists) who are (wrongly) intimidated by our apparatus. I promise the reader who is put off by our numbers and our charts that he will be able to read and understand this book without having to look at a single table or chart. I will keep the apparatus to a minimum and refer to technical works that validate my assertions for those who want more evidence and more details about methodology.

Most of the data on which this book is based have been collected in national probability samples of Americans. The interviews have been conducted by well-trained interviewers, subject to check for quality control, using carefully prepared questionnaires. The analyses have been carried out with the most approved methods of survey data analysis and have been subject to the scrutiny and criticism of my professional colleagues.

Everyone who makes an assertion has executed a survey of some sort. When Cardinal Law asserts that the Catholic laity welcome the repetition of the Church's birth-control teaching, he is basing his statement on conversations with a certain number of Catholic laity (unless he is picking this truth out of the blue sky—not totally improbable behavior for a cardinal). He has asked them questions, they have given him answers (or some equivalent form of interaction). He has summarized the answers and reports on them to us in his assertion.

The difference between the cardinal and me is not that I take surveys and he doesn't. Rather the difference is that I worry about random sampling, careful questionnaire construction, quality control, precision, and cautious reporting of the data and he doesn't.

I think I can say with some confidence that the technical aspects of the facts I report will not be questioned by competent social scientists. The monographs, articles, and memos which have recorded these facts have been reviewed by professional colleagues through the years and have stood the tests appropriate for careful and responsible work. No one who understands the tools of our trade will question, for example, the accuracy of my finding that only 70 percent of Americans of Hispanic origin are still Catholic (as opposed to 77 percent fifteen years ago). My interpretation as to the meaning of that finding (Catholic leadership has blundered in its response to Hispanic migration and the challenge of the fundamentalists) is less unassailable.

The facts themselves, however, are the result of the most careful and approved methods of random probability samples in national surveys and of standard advanced methods of data analysis.

I do not propose to defend either probability sampling or statistical analysis. They are modes of human knowing that educated men and women accept as valid—though many priests and most bishops reject them. To the latter I recommend that they enroll in courses in their local community colleges if they wish to catch up with educated Americans on the subjects of surveys and data analysis.

If the reader of this book is not prepared to accept the epistemology of survey research and my competence and integrity at it, then this would be just as good a place as any to stop.

Sociology is the study of patterns of social relationships and the values that generate these patterns—patterns that we now understand exist as pictures and images we call symbols before they are articulated in prose propositions. I propose as my guiding theme in this book that the symbols in the minds of Catholics are somewhat different from those in the minds of other Americans. Catholics "imagine" human communities, from the family on up, with somewhat different pictures than do other Americans. I will attempt to sustain this theme by testing it against data that measure human attitudes and behaviors in social relationships. My conclusion will be that the Catholic imagination is indeed different and that its appeal to Catholics, often despite the official pronouncements of church leaders, explains their loyalty to the Catholic tradition.

The theme is subtle and the analysis to sustain it will necessarily be intricate; for neither fact do I apologize.

There are a number of specifically Catholic objections to this form of knowledge which I perhaps ought to mention.

The Catholic Church is not a democracy and it does not make decisions by counting noses and taking surveys.

The Catholic Church is, too, a democracy, indeed the oldest democracy in the world (a point I will return to later). But regardless of what it is, the sociologist in exercising his professional skills is not (or at least should *not* be) attempting to deprive those with decision-making responsibility of their authority. He is rather providing factual information that they perhaps should consider in making their decisions. This distinction, which apparently is too subtle for most hierarchical minds, has not escaped Pope John II. In his "Exhortation on the Family" he notes that while it is certainly true that the social survey provides one useful means for uncovering the "sense of the faithful," it is not the only means available.

I would not and could not disagree. I must observe, however, that the pope has gone further in that statement to acknowledge the importance of the survey than any member of the American hierarchy.

The Catholic sociologist should report what human behavior ought to be and not what it is.

This second cliché—obscurantism at its most pure—denies the independence of empirical research. The only findings that are acceptable to the one who propounds this cliché are those that have already been preordained by ecclesiastical authority. The Catholic researcher *ought* not to report that Hispanics are leaving the Church but rather that they continue to be loyal to the Church. The objective world, from this viewpoint, has no reality of its own; it exists only to prove that church leadership is at all times correct.

Many readers will have a hard time believing that anyone could seriously propound such a position. I assure them that it is typical in church leadership: tell us what we want to hear, not what the facts show to be true. It is a position on which church leadership has no monopoly, but they are the only ones of whom I am aware who elevate it to a theological principle.

The sociologist who describes Catholic resistance to official teachings is in fact responsible for that resistance.

This third cliché—which is a derivative of the second—is a version of the old custom of blaming the herald of bad news for causing the bad news. "Catholics would not be practicing birth control," a prominent archbishop told me, "if it had not been for your work encouraging them to do so. You must bear a terrible burden of responsibility for the rejectioin of the birth-control encyclical."

It did me no good to reply that my book *Catholic Schools in a Declining Church* (Greeley, McCready, and McCourt, 1976) was published eight years after the encyclical and that it reported on data collected six years after it. Nor did it help to doubt that Catholic laity made decisions about their sex lives on the basis of a sociological report. Nor was I able to defend myself by saying that my colleagues described only what people were doing, not what they should be doing. By telling them what other people were doing, he insisted, you encouraged them to do it themselves. I did not clear myself of his charges by the defense that when 88 percent of a population reject an official teaching it is hardly a secret.

Again most readers will find it difficult to believe that such an argument could be seriously advanced by anyone but a fool. I assure them it was and is a serious position inside the Church. The American hierarchy, after our study of the priesthood that showed a *de-

cline in support for the birth-control position among priests as a result of the encyclical, has firmly rejected all proposals for serious social research. The reason? The Vatican blamed the bishops for the finding even more than they blamed us. If the bishops had not sponsored the survey, then priests would not have known that they were not supporting the pope's teachings!

It is not easy in an environment created by such a mentality to be a social scientist, especially if you are a priest and most especially if you are a priest who has no intention of ever not being a priest. I studied sociology to be of service to my archdiocese and to the rest of the Church. Not once has the archdiocese ever availed itself of my skills and, after the study of the priesthood twenty years ago, neither has the national Church. The problem with me is that I uncover facts that are unpleasant—that is to say, facts that upset the Vatican and hence cannot be true.

What you say is not true because it doesn't apply to my parish.

There is always a priest who rises at the end of a lecture or writes a letter and says that what I have reported is not true in his parish. His people, for example, are more generous than ever. Net of inflation? I ask. He's not sure what the inflation rate is. What proportion of their income? I ask. He doesn't have precise figures about the income in his parish. Maybe he's right. Maybe his people are giving more than the 2.2 percent that was the Catholic contribution rate in 1960 and more than the 1.1 percent that is the current rate. I'm never certain about that because he doesn't have any information on those matters. But it does me little good to say that I am not reporting about his parish and hence he need not feel that I am attacking him. I am reporting national averages.

Still he feels that he's attacked. Like the rector of Holy Name Cathedral in Chicago (and now a bishop) who objected vehemently (I almost said viciously) to my finding that Catholics are unhappy with the quality of preaching in their church. He and all his priests were good preachers, he insisted, and my finding was an assault on them. In fact, as some discreet inquiries revealed, they weren't all that good (Monsignor Blackie Ryan, my fictional cathedral rector he is not!), but I wasn't studying the cathedral parish and I wasn't assaulting anyone; I was merely describing average reactions.

More recently a monsignor from New York wrote to the Jesuit magazine *America* to protest my article on the decline of Hispanic Catholics because, as he said, he and many other priests had worked hard to learn Spanish and serve the Hispanic people well. After such work it was inconceivable that they could be leaving in such numbers.

I understood the monsignor's pain, but not his methods of data collection and analysis.

I doubt that many of those who read this book will react in any of the four ways I have described. It is nonetheless necessary that they know about these reactions that constitute the climate in the institutional Catholic Church today for the sort of research I do and for the story I'm going to tell.

Even though it is a story that, I will suggest, has an astonishingly happy ending—happier than any the leadership has a right to expect— it is still a story the leadership will reject in principle because it does not agree with what they want to hear, which is what they think the Vatican does not want to hear.

Their cowardice and corruption and dishonesty thus become not merely part of the context in which the story is told; they themselves become part of the story. Hence they must be mentioned in its prologue.

I will not try to hide my anger at the hierarchy, the clergy, and the scholarship of the American Catholic Church. No one can engage in three decades of serious study of American Catholicism and not be angry. Anger is part of the story, too, an essential part. American Catholics have not deserted their Church during the last quarter century. But their loyalty is not due to most of those who occupy the three leadership positions of bishop, priest, and "intellectual."[3]

I justify my anger at this trinity by the fact that perhaps never before in human religious history have such glorious opportunities been wasted by cowardice and ambition (in the hierarchy), by mediocrity, self-pity, and envy (in the clergy), and irresponsibility and amateurism (in the intelligentsia).

As I shall suggest in this book, the tenacity with which American Catholics have clung to their Church suggests that there is nothing that bishops, priests, and scholars can do that they have not already done that might drive the laity out.

Why such Herculean efforts have failed is also part of our story.

To conclude this introduction I must emphasize that my efforts will deal with attempts to describe Catholicism as it is manifested.

---

[3] I place the word "intellectual" in quotes because many of those who have posed as scholars within American Catholicism during the last quarter century have little valid claim to the title.

—In religious images
—Of ordinary people
—As they can be discovered by research into their attitudes and behavior

The Catholicism of my work will not be that which one can find in the *Patrologia Latina* and *Patrologia Graeca* of Migner or in the *Enchiridion Symbolorum* of Denzinger and his successors. These sources of propositional doctrine are excellent and authentic records of Catholic theology and teaching and adequate propositional statements for their times of Catholic teaching. They also are criteria against which imaginative Catholicism can be legitimately examined and judged.

My contention, however, is that image and experience and story come before formal religious doctrine and are likely to have more raw power than purely propositional teaching can possibly possess. Moreover, if the imaginative heritage is always subject to the critical reflection of formal teaching, so too must formal teaching listen to the experience of the Spirit at work in the world. Between experience and reason, between image and doctrine, between story and creed there will always be tension, but there will also be fruitful interaction.

Thus if this book is about image as prior to doctrine in time and power, it is in no sense to be understood to be against reasoned reflection or an intellectual critique of experience. Moreover, I am not a "modernist." I do not believe that symbols can mean whatever we want them to mean. While a symbol (or a story such as a parable of Jesus) can have many different and valid meanings, it also has a firm and solid structure of its own and there are other means that *cannot* be applied to it without doing it violence.

I am trying to identify those parts of the Catholic tradition that are broader than doctrinal propositions but not opposed to them, although they may on occasion be different from the emphases that the official Church may think important in a particular era of human history.

This "nonpropositional" tradition can be found in music, art, architecture, folklore, popular piety, pastoral customs, and similar sources. Thus the ceremonies that cluster around First Holy Communion (as it used to be called) are for the most part not contained in the official rituals, but are an important component of the religious experience of Catholics, both children and adults. The Christmas carols sung at Midnight Mass are hardly official church music, but they express much of the religious experience and imagery of the Catholic tradition of celebrating the birth of Jesus.

For most of the history of Catholicism one must guess at the religious imagination of Catholics from such sources. However, at the present time, because of the sample surveys, one is able to obtain more direct measures of how the Catholic imaginative tradition influences the experiences of its people, especially in the critical relationships of their religious lives, most particularly as we shall see in their relationship with their priests and their spouses and their God.

2

ON A SUNNY
AFTERNOON IN
BERKELEY

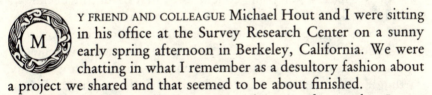Y FRIEND AND COLLEAGUE Michael Hout and I were sitting in his office at the Survey Research Center on a sunny early spring afternoon in Berkeley, California. We were chatting in what I remember as a desultory fashion about a project we shared and that seemed to be about finished.

Mike had been a promising young assistant professor when I came to the University of Arizona in 1979. Now he was a tenured associate professor at the University of California/Berkeley. Later he would become full professor and chairman of the Department of Sociology. We shared religious and sociological faith—Catholicism and empiricism—and were working on an article about church attendance in the United States. I had been working on a book for Harvard University Press on religious change in America since social surveys had begun and could find relatively little change to report. Since Mike knew much more than I did (or ever will) about advanced mathematical models, I sought his help in analyzing the patterns of American church attendance. We had discovered that Protestant churchgoing had not changed in forty years and that the only variation in Sunday devotion was a sharp Catholic decline between 1968 and 1975.

There wasn't much doubt as to why the Catholic decline had begun. It was a result of anger and frustration over the papal birth-control encyclical *Humanae Vitae* that had been issued in the summer of 1968. My analysis in the mid-1970s had established that fact; Mike and I redid that analysis using a newer and more sophisticated method and then replicated it with newer data from the National Opinion Research Center (NORC) General Social Survey (GSS). We were in the process of finishing our work on life-cycle curves that enabled us to project Catholic church attendance into the next fifteen years.

Since the GSS was repeated every year starting in 1972, it was possible to have information on each birth cohort in the sample at many different points in time. This fact permitted us to create a curve indicating the relationship with life cycle and religious behavior (devotion decreases from eighteen on and rises again from twenty-five to the middle forties) and then to ask whether the curves for any of the individual cycles were different at levels of statistical significance from the main curve. Since there was no significant variation, we concluded that there was no evidence that the present younger generation was less religious than its predecessors at the same age in life.

Thus we had two startling conclusions: first of all, the decline in Catholic weekly Mass attendance had stopped as abruptly as it had started. Second, a projection of these findings into the next fifteen years indicated that there was not likely to be any change in religious behavior at least till the end of the century. A third, perhaps equally startling conclusion, was inherent in these findings: the decline in Mass attendance that resulted from the encyclical *Humanae Vitae* was evenly distributed through the Catholic population and not confined to any single age group.

Not only were these findings not self-evident; they were not likely to be accepted by armchair experts on Catholicism inside and outside the Church. Nonetheless they were true and, since we published our article, have not been effectively faulted by anyone who has read them.

On that afternoon at Berkeley Mike and I were in the process of wrapping up the outline of the article. We had our story: the only statistically significant change in church attendance in the four decades of survey data was among Catholics and that only from 1968 to 1975; the decline occurred because of the birth-control encyclical and had stopped in 1975; projections into the future showed no significant differences between Catholics who were young at the present and their predecessors in the life cycle. We did not have an explanation, you will note, of why the decline had stopped. We were content with the general observation that the impact of *Humanae Vitae* on Sunday Mass going had come to an end. In truth I don't think we even considered the possibility of a more rigorous explanation.

I was shuffling through a pile of graphs I had brought up from Tucson, illustrations I planned to use eventually in the Harvard Press book. I noticed that two of them seemed virtually the same—the graph depicting the decline of Catholic church attendance from 1968 to 1975 and another one portraying the decline of Catholic affiliation with the Democratic Party during the same troubled era.

"Mike, these are the same curves."

"Mass attendance and party affiliation . . . do you think they're related?"

I reflected on the relationship between Communion reception and strong affiliation to the Democratic Party that seemed to follow marriage among young Catholics we had studied during the late 1970s.

"Probably not. But what if they are?"

"We'll never forgive ourselves if we don't check it out, will we?"

"It might be a real social fact," I said, thinking of the term used by Emile Durkheim, one of the founders of modern sociology, to describe a social relationship that was more than merely the sum of individual relationships. If you're lucky as a sociologist you might find one or two of those in a lifetime.

"It could be a coincidence," Mike warned.

"The encyclical and the 1968 Democratic Convention in Chicago happened within a month of each other," I replied. "The question is whether there is an accidental relationship or whether they are related by something more than a chance link in time. Did the people who left the party also stop going to church? Are the political independents the ones who have curtailed church attendance?"

At supper at Mike's house that night (with his charming wife, Flowe—née Mary Eileen—and his lively sons Jake, Ben, and Tim) and afterwards in the motel at which I was staying I knew for certain that the answer to that question would be yes.

I was absolutely certain that people who had left the party were also those who had left regular church attendance. How did I know? That's harder to explain. In the neighborhoods where I had grown up and in the parish where I had worked, political commitment and religious commitment had always seemed to go hand in hand. Then there was the story Pat Moynihan had told in *Beyond the Melting Pot* a quarter century before that afternoon in Berkeley.

"Ah," said Mrs. Finnegan to Mrs. O'Rourke, "have you heard what Councilman Murphy has done?"

"I have not. What is that wee gombeen man done now?"

"He's become a Raypublican, that's what!"

"Sure, he never has! Wasn't I after seeing him at Mass last Sunday!"

The story meant that for the Irish and for the other Catholic immigrants, the process of acculturation into American society had meant strong and strongly linked affiliations to their Church and their political party. That was not so surprising, was it? What Mike and I had sniffed in the data was something that a lot of people already knew.

But no one had ever pinned down precisely the facts of this relationship before: what had stopped the decline in Catholic church attendance in the United States when in other countries it had continued in reaction to the birth-control encyclical?

Some sort of underlying tenacity that inclined Catholics to cling to both their religion and their party, come what may, and despite the leadership of Pope Paul VI and George McGovern.

This "tenacity"—for want of a better word—was an important part of religion for all Americans. It explained why in the analysis I was doing for Harvard Press I could find so little change in American religion since 1940 despite all the talk among the media and academic elites about secularization. Belief in God, the divinity of Jesus and life after death, church attendance among Protestants, membership in church-related organizations, frequency of prayer, levels of religious intensity, denominational affiliation, rates of religious change and intermarriage—all had remained unchanged despite the enormous social changes of almost half a century. The only notable changes in religious behavior were the decline in Catholic churchgoing and a decline in the acceptance of the literal interpretation of the Bible. But the latter was almost limited to Catholics and especially to younger, college-educated Catholics—and was a change to a position on inspiration that had been taken by the Vatican Council.

"Modern Man," about whom the theologians wrote so much, existed only in the corridors of the divinity school faculty buildings. The ordinary lay people, whatever their denomination, were about as religious in 1985 as they were in 1940.

How could this be? some of the critics of the manuscript of the book had demanded. Didn't everyone know that religion was declining in America?

Now we had a hint of an explanation of how it could be true: Catholics could survive the traumas of the years after the Vatican Council with their religious affiliation mostly undiminished because of a religious loyalty. Religious loyalty was part of the warp and the woof of American culture. Hence, one might almost say *a fortiori*, other Americans would cling to their religious beliefs no matter what the scholars and the theologians might say about secularization.

My imagination churned all night long. I gave up trying to sleep (I've learned through the years that I should not try to work on either sociology or fiction after supper if I want to get much sleep). I remembered where my search for understanding of the American Catholic phenomenon in the "postwar world" (as we called it in the 1950s) had begun and the thirty-year course of its development. Maybe at last I had a handle on an explanation.

In the late 1940s and the early 1950s, Chicago had been infested by a horde of French "religious sociologists," men who had figured out the American Catholic Church the first week after their arrival. They were plainly shocked by the high levels of religious involvement among Americans, particularly American Catholics. After all, had not "secularization" virtually wiped out religion in France? How could Americans resist the inevitable trend of the modern world?

It didn't take them long to find an explanation. Catholicism in America was an immigrant religion. It helped the immigrants and their children survive the sufferings of adjusting to a new world and struggling up from the bottom of the economic ladder. However, the Frenchmen said confidently, once they had become successful and entered the mainstream of American life, they would leave the Church or at least leave regular religious practice as quickly as had their French counterparts.

I was not impressed by the "religious sociologists," but I took their point about the immigrant style of American Catholicism. It was a religious approach designed quite explicitly to protect the faith of the immigrants against the assaults of a society that was thought to be bent on depriving the immigrants of their Catholicism as a price of admission to the ranks of full-fledged Americans.

Moreover, it was also true that the Catholics who had returned from the war were swarming into colleges and joining the professional class. Even in 1950 I could see that most of my contemporaries were well on their way to the affluence that we began to believe was not about to be destroyed by a return to the Great Depression. As far as I could see these young men and women were not exactly leaving the Church. Indeed, if anything, they were more frantic in their participation in Catholic activities than their parents. Even then, a couple of years before my ordination, I wondered whether the Frenchmen had missed something.

In the curious designs of God, my first assignment as a priest was to a parish populated almost entirely by these postwar, college-educated, professional-class Catholics. I found no evidence to support the French theory. Quite the contrary: the parishioners were even more active in their parish than their predecessors had been in the Old Neighborhood. The French had missed one critically important point: professional-class Protestants were as religious as working-class Protestants. Assimilation into American society would have weakened the religious commitment of American Catholics, if and only if America were not a religious society.

Or so my instincts told me in the late 1950s after a couple of years at Christ the King parish in the Beverly district of Chicago. There was almost no empirical data to back up those instincts. My first book, *The Church in the Suburbs,* was a "data-free" attempt to write an agenda for the "professionalization" of American Catholicism. I realized quite clearly even then that I was working in a community that represented a turning point in American Catholic history: the end of the immigrant era and the beginning of the age of the college-educated. I didn't realize until the mid-1960s that another, equally decisive transformation was in process: the end of the counter-reformation and the beginning of the ecumenical age.

Many of the Catholic "liberal" intellectuals of the day (of the sort who wrote for *Commonweal)* were less sanguine than I was. They saw all kinds of evidence of drift away from the Church.

Thus even before I went to graduate school I was fascinated to the point of obsession about what was happening to the Catholic immigrant groups in this most recent phase of the assimilation process. Few priests shared my enthusiasm for the question because they didn't seem to think a change was occurring, despite the dramatic increase of professional-class parishes like Christ the King. Many of my contemporaries even to this day seem to think the seminary cliché is still true: the priest is the best-educated person in his parish.

One of my first goals when I went to graduate school in the autumn of 1960 was to begin to collect data so that I could monitor the change that I thought was taking place in the Catholic population. The first effort in what would become a lifetime project was my dissertation, based on a study of some 30,000 1961 graduates. There was no sign in that research that college-educated Catholic lay people were drifting away from the Church. Quite the contrary: they were even more likely to be at Mass every week than the typical American Catholic.

College students, however, were not the whole country. Peter Rossi (the director of NORC and one of my two mentors in sociology, the other being James Davis, who was also on the staff of NORC) and I launched a study of the American Catholic population in 1963 which focused on the impact of Catholic schools on the adults who had attended them as children. In the process, however, we had established a baseline, a benchmark for measuring future change in American Catholics. *The Education of Catholic Americans* was the first detailed sociological description of the American Catholic population—and providentially the study was done before the implementation of the changes of the Vatican Council. We would later be able to do a "before . . . after" portrait of the impact of the Council on American Catholics.

The "before" portrait depicted an increasingly affluent population that was still only one step away from the immigrant experience. Half of American Catholics were still immigrants or the children of immigrants, but now American Catholics of college age were more likely to attend college than their Protestant counterparts. Moreover, education and social and economic success correlated *positively* with religious behavior. Finally, the "hard" data refuted my French friends. American Catholicism had survived the movement away from the old immigrant neighborhood and was prospering. There was no reason to think it would not continue to prosper, especially since, as far as I could see, the changes that began to come out of the Vatican Council were popular with the Catholic people.

For the next eight years I monitored in various surveys Catholic behavior—religious, political, economic, and social. At first my optimism (which led one *Commonweal* editor to suggest that I wanted to be a bishop!) seemed justified. Warning signals began to sound, however, toward the end of the decade. The annual Gallup question about church attendance had actually shown an increase in Sunday attendance in the years immediately after the introduction of the English liturgy (of which 87 percent of our respondents approved despite *Commonweal*.) In 1969 and 1970, however, a sharp decline appeared in the Gallup statistics. In 1972 the first NORC General Social Survey showed an even sharper decline—a fall of fifteen percentage points in Sunday churchgoing from 1963. A comparable decline in other devotional behavior was recorded in the same year in a study we were doing at NORC on religious imagery.

I was surprised and shocked. What had happened? I wrote an article for *America* that I called "The End of American Catholicism?" and wondered whether the golden era was already over. That something was desperately wrong was by then obvious to many people. Nor was there much doubt as to the cause: the Vatican Council had somehow disillusioned or frightened or put off the Catholic laity.

In 1974 we redid the Catholic school study. The formal focus was on the question of whether Catholic schools continued to be important in a time of dramatic, not to say traumatic, change in the Church. But in the process I hoped we would find out why the Council had caused such a terrible crisis. The data analysis in that project was difficult and frustrating. The majority of Catholics were enthusiastic about the changes. Approval of the conciliar reforms correlated positively with devotional behavior. The Council thus seemed to have increased religious practice for American Catholics. Yet the declines were obvious everywhere—twenty-three points in Mass attendance, twenty percentage points in frequency of confession, and fifteen percentage points for support of priestly vocations in the family. Annual contributions to the Church diminished from 2.2 percent of income contributions to 1.6 percent. Only reception of Holy Communion had increased—doubled, in fact, from 12 to 25 percent receiving the Eucharist every week. If the Council was so popular, what else had happened to turn American Catholicism sour?

In the logic of social change analysis, one explains a change in one variable (such as Mass attendance) by a change in another variable that is correlated with the first variable. Consider the example of weight increases in twelve-year-old boys in the twelve months since their eleventh birthdays. One discovers that their height has increased, too, and that the correlation between weight and height is the same at both points in time. One would be justified in saying, therefore, that boys weigh more in part because they're taller. By such mathematical manipulation one can estimate the proportion of the change in weight that can be accounted for by the change in height. Having given up on a conciliar explanation for the declining devotional rates among American Catholics, I began to look for another explanation. What else had happened since 1965?

I recalled the many phone calls I received after I left Christ the King parish in 1965 from young people whom I had known in gram-

mar school or in the parish high club. With considerable embarrassment they would ask me about the use of the birth-control pill. Had
not the pope set up a commission? Was it not right to assume that if
a change were not possible, the pope would not have convened the
commission? Weren't priests now saying that lay people could follow
their own consciences on the matter? It was not that they didn't want
any more children, they just didn't want them now, since they already had two or maybe even three.

Could it be, I wondered, that the explanation of the decline in
Catholic practice was that Pope Paul VI had issued the encyclical on
birth control, *Humanae Vitae,* after many laity had already made up
their minds on the issue? It was obvious from our data that the
encyclical had not worked. In 1963 half the Catholic population had
accepted the birth-control teaching. In 1974 only 12 percent accepted
it. Might the encyclical account for the decline in religious devotion?

That was a chance question of the same sort that would explode
in my mind in Mike Hout's office ten years later. Maybe the Council
was a huge success. Maybe the encyclical had canceled it out. Maybe
if it had not been for the surge in devotion after the Council, the
decline after the encyclical would have been even worse. If one put
the decline in acceptance of papal authority and the decline in support
for the birth-control teaching into an equation, how much of the
change in the various devotional measures might be accounted for by
the sex and authority change?

The answer was that *all* of the change could be traced to the sex
and authority issue. The Council had been a success and the encyclical a disaster.

Response to this analysis was something less than enthusiastic. In
the *Time* cover story about our report *Catholic Schools in a Declining
Church,* there was an answering statement from Archbishop
Bernardin—then president of the American bishops—in which he
said that the Catholic Church does not make decisions by taking
polls. He cheerfully ignored our complete agreement with that position. We were not saying that the birth-control decision was wrong
or that the Vatican should reverse itself. We were merely pointing out
what its effects had been in the United States. However, by 1985 I
think acceptance of this account of the decline in the years immediately after the encyclical had become practically universal. Only the
bishops—and most of them only in public—have rejected the explanation.

Curiously enough, at the very time I was worrying about the

"end of American Catholicism" and working on the analysis of the 1974 "before . . . after" study, the decline stopped. In the years after 1975 both the GSS and Gallup studies showed that Catholic Sunday Mass attendance had stabilized at 50 percent. The erosion of devotional behavior had stopped as suddenly as it had started. Mike Hout and I knew on that spring evening in Berkeley that *Humanae Vitae* had begun the erosion, but we did not know what had put an end to it.

When I finally fell asleep that night on the shore of the bay I thought we were about to find out. Here, I was convinced, was the key to understanding the present condition of American Catholicism and perhaps of all American religion.

Before I could finish breakfast the next morning, Mike was on the phone.

"Were we right?" I demanded.

"Were we ever!" He chortled. "Would you believe that for Catholics who are strongly affiliated with a political party—doesn't matter which one—the decline in regular church attendance between 1972 and the present is only nine percentage points (from 66 percent to 57 percent) while the decline for the 'pure' political independents, those who do not lean to either party, is thirty-four percentage points (from 63 percent to 29 percent)?"

"The center doesn't hold!"

"Let's call our article that."

"Will this fit one of your Rasch models?"

"Let's try it!"

I wasn't quite sure then what a Rasch model was. But I knew it was a highly sophisticated technique developed by the Swiss statistician Georg Rasch (1960) on which Mike was working with our mutual mentor, Otis Dudley Duncan of the University of California at Santa Barbara. It was an extremely rigorous technique for determining whether there was really an underlying variable "out there in the real world" that explained the correlation between two other variables.

We were not arguing that political behavior affected religious behavior, or vice versa. Rather we were positing a latent common cause that must explain both, a common cause we called "loyalty." It was responsible in our model for the relationship between political and religious affiliation.

At the high end of the "loyalty" continuum is a disposition to stay with an institution even in the face of opposition from the leaders of the institution. At the low end is a disposition to disassociate oneself from the institution whose leadership endorses moral and political stands contrary to one's own convictions. People differ in their predisposition to make a choice to stay with an institution or to leave it when they disagree with the official position of that institution. The model suggested to us that if we could have measured the subjective and objective aspects of loyalty we would have found that the degree of attachment to the rituals, symbols, and community of the local parish is a primary constituent of the "loyalty" we had uncovered.

We speculated that such "loyalty" has been an "anchor" for many Catholics: it enables them to counteract the disorganizing pressure of dissension within the Church. The decline in church attendance stopped precisely when all those whose "loyalty" was not strong enough to resist this pressure had already cut down on their church-going (and contributions and other forms of religious behavior). It would require a very different kind of equally powerful shock wave to erode further the wellspring of communal loyalty that remains in the Catholic population.

In the conclusion of our article we asked, "To what are Catholics, in the present instance, loyal? Not to the pope, not to the official teaching, not to their bishop and his support of the pope. . . . We think that the disgruntled Catholics who score high on the loyalty dimension . . . stay with the Church because it is their birthright. In their hearts, they are as Catholic as the pope, whether he thinks so or not."

Whence comes this loyalty? Is it an irrational superstition that has somehow survived in the most industrialized nation in the world? Or is it a rational reaction in a society in which religion has always been important because one's religious affiliation has always been a crucial part of one's self-definition and social location in the society? In a society that is both religiously pluralistic and traditionally devout, may not loyalty be both a powerful force and a rational choice?

My friend Martin Marty of the University of Chicago Divinity School, who is almost always right, observed a number of years ago that the increase in second homes might finally destroy the long tradition of religious observance in America. Those who go away every weekend would be less likely to belong to a church and less likely to attend church because membership and attendance would have crossed the threshold of tolerable inconvenience.

Marty sold the tenacity of American religion short in that prediction. Second homes have increased, but neither church attendance,
nor church membership, nor (for Protestants) church contributions
have declined. Might we not consider the possibility of a model that
suggests that in a pluralistic and devout society such loyalty is eminently rational? Choosing for your own tradition, in other words,
makes perfectly good sense.

I cannot say that everyone makes a religious choice. Minimally,
however, in American society some 30 percent of the population
decide between their twenty-fifth birthday and their fortieth birthday
to become regular churchgoers. Ten percent of the population also
decide to move (back in most cases) from religious nonidentification
to religious identification. Perhaps many more make decisions, in
their early and middle twenties, about continuing their original religious identification and the devotional levels of their middle teens.

There are, then, many, many religious decisions and choices being made in America, even if these decisions are usually in favor of
one's own original religion and in favor of the levels of religious
devotion exhibited by one's elders when they were in their early and
middle forties.

In the United States more than four-fifths of those who are born
Catholic and more than nine-tenths of those who are born Protestant
or Jewish eventually opt for their own religious heritage. Why? I
would suggest that the reason for this is that in the calculus of benefits, the choice of one's own religion seems to most Americans,
finally, to confer the most benefits.

You have to be something. You don't want to be Jewish or Protestant, heaven (you should excuse the expression) knows. So, perhaps reluctantly and perhaps with a sigh of resignation, you end up
(on the average) being Catholic just as your parents were and to hell
with the leadership.

The choice, after all and when all is said and done, of the religion
of one's parents may suggest a certain addiction, a propensity to
choose the familiar because so much has been invested in the familiar,
perhaps a phenomenon not unlike the decision to remain with one's
original word processing program even if other programs promise
more benefits, because (quite rationally) it is calculated that the advantages of Word Perfect over Microsoft Word are not worth the
investment of start-up time required to obtain skill in the program.

George Stigler and Gary Becker (1977), in their discussion of
"consumption capital," ask why people who have developed a taste

in classical music (for example) sustain that taste even at times when it might not be "rational" in the economic sense to do so. They respond that the time and energy expended on developing the taste is considered to be "capital." Having "invested" in your taste for classical music, you are disinclined to give up the benefits of that investment. So, too, the "consumption" of a given religious heritage could be said to rise with exposure to the heritage. The more time and effort you have put into your religion, the less likely you are to give it up. Could one be said to be "addicted" (I use the term of the two distinguished authors) to one's religious (or one's word processing) heritage because one has acquired consumption capital in that heritage?[1] It's hard enough to learn one religion—its rituals, its protocols, its doctrines, why bother learning another when the extra benefit does not seem all that great?

I propose the following paradigm:

Most Americans (we need not debate how many exceptions there might be) are born into a religious tradition. Quite likely one could extend the assertion to say that most people in the world are born into some religious or quasi-religious heritage. There are five components to a tradition: A set of *symbols* that, *pace* Clifford Geertz (1968), purport to explain uniquely the real, to provide answers to problems of injustice, suffering, and death, the Christmas and Easter stories, for example. A collection of *rituals* that activate these symbols at crucial life-cycle turning points and inculcate the paradigms that the symbols can contain, Midnight Mass on Christmas and the Easter Vigil fire and water service, for example. A *community* that is constituted by and transmits these symbols and rituals. A *heritage*, a system of elementary beliefs based on the symbols, to pass on, should one wish, to one's children. Finally, a *differentiation* from those who are not born inside the heritage.

Let us consider next the schedule of benefits a person faces when considering a decision to affiliate with a religious tradition in the middle-twenties phase of the life cycle.

First of all, the community provides a pool of preferred people with whom we are inclined to interact: friends, marital partners, perhaps business or professional colleagues. Second, it offers familiar rituals for crucial turning points in one's life. Third, it supplies symbols, that express meaning when one is in a situation that requires

---

[1] George J. Stigler and Gary S. Becker, "De Gustibus Non Est Disputandum," *American Economic Review*, March 1977, pp. 76–90.

meaning. Fourth, it offers various social and organizational activities that confer advantages of various sorts on its members.

(I note here that the more actively one engages in religious activities—up to a certain point, perhaps—the more available these resources may become. There may also be a law of diminishing returns: Sunday Mass may find you a spouse, daily Mass may not notably enhance the chances of finding one.)

If you choose to give up your own tradition and opt for another, there will be a considerable cost in giving up these utilities. Other people may not respond to the most familiar interactive cues as do members of one's own tradition—they may, for example, put on hats when they enter church instead of taking them off. One may lose valuable relationship networks. One may have to learn new symbols and integrate them into one's personality orientations, not an easy task in adulthood, perhaps for many not even a possible task. One may have to engage in ritual behaviors with which one is not familiar and that one might even find distasteful. One may have to find new organizational activities with relative strangers.

Or one may have to live without symbols, rituals, and community. Or to try to do so.

"Why should I leave?" a young Catholic man asked me. "I like being Catholic. I'm proud of it. I'd be out of place as anything else. So I disagree with the pope and despise the jerk that's my pastor. Is it any more their religion than it is mine? I'd have to give up too much if I left."

What are the alternative benefits that would attract a person to choose a tradition other than one's own or, if it be possible, no heritage at all?

One attractive possibility is that such a choice would punish parents and church leaders at whom one is angry.

Another attraction is upward social mobility. If one is not a Catholic or a Jew, for example, one might have access to elite social positions or more esteem in elite circles. It was only in the last two decades, for example, that Catholics and Jews earned access to college presidencies.

One might also win freedom for oneself from what one takes to be the restraints, the superstitions, the repressions, and the tyrannies that are inherent in one's heritage and community. One can, for example, eat bacon for breakfast or, in the old days, meat on Friday. One can use the birth-control pill with a clear conscience. One need not take seriously what the local pastor or priest has to say. One can ignore the pope and refuse to be worried about Israel.

One is free to engage with a clear conscience in pleasurable practices on which one's religious tradition seems to frown or to embrace social and ethical concerns that do not preoccupy one's religious leaders—when was the last time the Catholic Church launched a campaign for good government?

By rejecting one's religious tradition one may obtain access to a particularly desired role opposite—a potential spouse in most cases—who would otherwise not be available.

How does one deal with the loss of such benefits if one chooses to stay within the heritage in which one is raised? (In the concrete this option—leave or remain—is the usual contact for religious choice.) One may choose to ignore the restraints and the liabilities that the tradition seems to impose. One can remain Catholic, devoutly Catholic in one's own estimate, and still practice birth control because one is able to appeal from a church leadership that does not understand to a God that does. (I presume that such behavior would be called "free-riding," a phenomenon that marks all religions, even Catholicism in the days since the decline of the Inquisition.)

This is the ordinary strategy in religious choice, I submit, since most Americans do indeed elect to remain in their own heritage. The choice becomes more desirable and hence more rational to the extent to which one is able, one way or another, to diminish the costs of the choice.

In more elaborate and intricate form such schedules of costs and benefits go into the calculus that constitutes rational religious choice. Some social scientists, believing that religion as such is irrational, may dismiss such a calculus. Such a dismissal, however, will not affect the decisions that others make. Nor will it provide the skeptics with symbols, rituals, and communities of their own.

In sum, the "familiarity" factor (or religious consumption capital)—broadly understood—explains why it seems rational, finally, for most people to opt for religion and for their own heritage.

To put the matter simply: Why is it rational for Americans to be more devout than the English or the French? Why is it rational for the Irish to be even more devout than Americans? (They are, be it noted, less likely to describe themselves as "very religious.")

There are two possible paths to follow: one may note that a "minority" religion, that is to say one that is not established or quasi-established, is probably, like Avis, going to try harder. It may offer more services (one thinks of parochial schools in this country) to attract and hold its members. It thus becomes increasingly rational to stay in your tradition and reap the extra benefits that the tradition confers because of its "minority" status (in America all religions are "minority" as the word is being used here). Moreover, there may well be a relationship between the degree of religious devotion and activity in which you engage and the services that the institution (in the interests of its own self-preservation) will make available to you: if you are not a devout Catholic, you may not be able to take advantage of the parochial schools.

In the "minority" or pluralistic situation, the Church may go out of its way to help you find a presentable marriage partner, more out of its way than it would in a situation where it has a near monopoly on available spouses. It is rational to take advantage of such a situation. But the variety and quality of the pool may depend to some extent on your willingness to engage in high levels of religious behavior.

I do not want to discuss at length the question of why large numbers of minority (in the usual sense of that word) group members do not desert their group when there seem to be ample benefits in doing so. I merely want to note that it seems to be true that for many within the minority group, the fact of being in a disadvantaged group merely intensifies the identification. Why such an "identity" is a benefit is an interesting question but beyond my concerns at the present. That it is a benefit in a pluralistic society seems obvious enough. ("Yes, I'm Jewish and proud of it.") That which strengthens identity is often estimated to be worth the cost.

So I propose that the combination of symbol, ritual, and community provides a partial "identity," a useful response to the question "What are you?" and an answer often stated with pride and even defiance. Such an answer signals to others and to oneself one's symbolic and ritual orientation and one's potential pool of preferred role opposites.

I finally propose by way of summary that a religion attracts loyalty and devotion from its members in proportion to the thickness of the differentiation—the importance of religious differences in creating a personal identity—and for two reasons. Ordinarily the religion will offer more services when its membership is sharply distinguished from the rest of society, and hence perhaps in jeopardy of defection. Moreover, paradoxically, and despite the fears of religious leaders of the risk of defection, the distinction from others that religion provides is a benefit itself for self-definition. Hence the more loyal one is to one's tradition, the stronger the distinction and the more proudly it is professed.

If your church does not perceive itself as threatened and your membership in it adds little to the identity into which you are born as a member of a society, if it does not differentiate you sharply from the rest of society, then there are lower costs in making your choice, and lower benefits in making the choice, and hence less payoff for you in engaging in actions or professing beliefs that would link you more closely to your church.

Concretely, in one-religion societies (either *de facto* or, in the case of established churches, *de jure*), the differentiation is thin and the efforts the church perceives as necessary to attract and hold members are minimal. Hence it is less rational to commit oneself to higher levels of religious behavior.

Catholics in the United States and in Ireland will be notably more devout, therefore, than Catholics in France or Italy or Spain. Protestants in Sweden will be notably less devout than Protestants in the United States or Canada or Ireland. Anglicans in the United States, Canada, and Ireland will be more devout than Anglicans in England.

As a crucial test case let us consider England, which is a notably less religious society than the United States (as survey data measure religiousness). One would hypothesize on the basis of these reflections that most if not all of the lower levels of "faith" and devotion will be an Anglican phenomenon and that Catholics and Protestants in England will not differ notably from Catholics in the United States in their levels of religious devotion.

Eighty-one percent of the population of Great Britain believe in God as opposed to 96 percent in the United States. Twenty-six percent of the people of Great Britain attend church every week as opposed to 44 percent in the United States. Fifty-seven percent of Britons believe in life after death as opposed to 70 percent of Americans.

But there is no difference between Catholics in the United States and Catholics in Great Britain and between Protestants in the United States and Protestants in Great Britain in belief in God and life after death and in church attendance. Forty-two percent of the Protestants in both countries go to church every week as do 50 percent of the Catholics. Approximately 70 percent of both religious groups in both countries believe in life after death. Ninety-eight percent of the Catholics in both countries believe in God, 94 percent of the Protestants. The lower levels of religiousness in this country are purely an Anglican phenomenon.

The reasoning in these last several pages represents a reflection on the linkage that Mike Hout and I noticed for the first time on that sunny afternoon in Berkeley. Loyalty holds Catholics in their Church despite what the leaders say and do and because loyalty seems an eminently rational choice in a society that has historically been both devout and pluralistic. Indeed the tenacity and the rationality of such loyalty make the words and deeds of leaders usually quite irrelevant when religious choice is at issue.

Even the tidal-wave shock of *Humanae Vitae* did not lead to higher defection rates for American Catholics, nor even a notable increase in those who never go to Mass. Rather it diminished somewhat the regularity of Mass attendance—a pretty tame shock wave when you consider it after the fact.

I do not want to suggest by my "economic analysis" that American religious devotion is, as many critics insist, either "unauthentic" or "culture religion." Because it is rational to be loyal to your heritage—sometimes in the face of enormous difficulties created by the leadership of that heritage—it does not follow that you are insincere or hypocritical. It merely follows that you happen to live in a society where major social forces support religion rather than oppose it. American history and culture support religion more than do the history and culture of any other industrial nation in the world (except Canada, which is very like the United States in this respect). More frequent religious behavior may produce either more religious sentiment or more routinized piety in the individual—or possibly both. The sorting out of these different effects, however, ought to be an empirical challenge and not a matter that is resolved by the *a priori* rationale of self-hatred: if it's American, it has to be bad.

Our discovery of the latent "loyalty" dimension of American religion on that sunny afternoon in Berkeley would probably not win a Nobel Prize in sociology if there were one. However, it is, I think I can say candidly, one of the most important findings in the sociology of religion in the last couple of decades. It may, finally, only confirm what everyone knows to be true, viz., Americans are loyal to their churches. However, in truth, I'm not so sure that everyone knew it before the fact. If they did, they would have predicted the resiliency of American Catholics under pressure in the late sixties and the early seventies.

Loyalty to a heritage that helps you to define yourself, then, is the first theme in the story of the New American Catholicism. The second theme, in the next chapter, will be found in a more detailed answer to the question Hout and I asked in 1985: to what are American Catholics loyal?

My answer to that is the poetry of Catholicism. Or, in the words of David Tracy of the University of Chicago Divinity School, the analogical imagination.

3

DO CATHOLICS
IMAGINE
DIFFERENTLY?

ATHOLICS are becoming just like everyone else," my host said mildly as he filled up my cup with Earl Grey tea. I was sitting in the office of a distinguished American editor and discussing a book he wanted me to write, a book about the current "crisis" in Catholicism. I had not said that the crisis paradigm was incorrect.

"You're becoming indistinguishable from the Methodists," he persisted. "When you give up your distinctive beliefs about sexual ethics and papal authority, you become middle-class Americans quite like all other middle-class Americans."

"No, we don't," I insisted.

"What remains?" he demanded.

"We imagine differently."

"Imagine differently?" He raised an eyebrow. "What do you mean by that?"

"Religion," I said, with the sinking feeling that I would have no chance to explain to him in the few minutes left my life work as a sociologist, "is imagination before it's anything else. The Catholic imagination is different from the Protestant imagination. You know that: Flannery O'Connor is not John Updike."

"Interesting," he murmured, sensing vaguely what I was talking about but pretty certain that he didn't want to try to sell the book about which we were talking.

As an editor he knew what imagination was and the different imaginative sensibilities of different writers. Maybe your religion could influence your imagination, but what could a Catholic priest—a man who was supposed to defend doctrinal propositions—mean when he said that religion *was* imagination?

"It's what my sociological research tells me," I tried to explain, "and it's what drove me to write novels."

"*Very* interesting," he sighed. "Someday you must explain it to me."

"It's Christmas and Passover," I said, rising to leave, "and all the other stories in which religion is encoded."

"*Most* interesting," he said as we shook hands at the door.

There are, as I have said, two underlying premises on which this book is based. Religion is imagery (or poetry) and American religion is loyalty to one's imaginative (or poetic) heritage. The latter premise, described in the preceding chapter, is not original with me. I first encountered it as a young priest in the mid-1950s when I read Will Herberg's wonderful book *Protestant Catholic Jew*, which provided me with the insights and the images that surfaced again in Mike Hout's office in Berkeley.

I cannot claim a monopoly, as far as that goes, on the notion that religion is imagination; but it is a perspective on which no other sociologist is working. It also represents my abiding concern in the sociology of religion and perhaps the most important theme in my own personal life. It is surely the reason I write fiction. If I am remembered at all as a sociologist, it will be as a sociologist of the religious imagination. My own faith, as well as my confidence in American Catholicism is, each in its own way, grounded in this paradigm of religion as imagination.

As I walked out of the building and down Sixth Avenue, I reflected on how much would have to be said on the religious imagination before my friend the editor, as intelligent and as sensitive a man as one could find in the New York publishing canyons, would know what I was talking about.

This preoccupation had begun when I was a graduate student at the University of Chicago in the early 1960s. Older than many of my classmates and so certain about my own religious commitment that nothing in the university environment was a threat to it, I had come to acquire the tools to study the changing state of American Catholicism. My problems rather had to do with styles of knowing. West Side Irish Catholic that I was, I had no trouble with the empirical techniques I was learning, or even with the sociological theorizing I was picking up from the giants of our tradition like Max Weber and Emile Durkheim. What bothered me was the philosophical logic of science, which seemed to underpin what most of my teachers did and which was implied in almost every journal article I read.

I was certain that I never learned anything by following the "scientific method" and I kind of suspect that no one else did either. My M.A. mentor, Harrison White, insisted in a statistics class one day that "science is the pursuit of truth, no holds barred."

Theory, data, and insight, I found myself deciding, work together in combinations that are fluid, unpredictable, and creative; science and art may not be all that different. Both did their critical work in a dimension of the personality that I had learned in the seminary to call the intellect and after ordination to name the creative intuition or the preconscious.

Now, three decades later, such thoughts are quite acceptable in a sociologist; Professor White was proof that they were not unacceptable even then—and did not he have two doctorates, one in astrophysics and the other in sociology?

But they were thoughts I had to formulate for myself in those days, especially since my sociological tastes were drifting toward survey research and mathematical models. Then, on a cold March afternoon in 1961—John Kennedy being on the banks of the Potomac and John XXIII on the banks of the Tiber—our regular teacher (and I don't even remember the course) was absent for some reason. A guest lecturer, a young anthropologist named Clifford Geertz, substituted for him.

Even in those days Cliff was a dazzling lecturer, matching powerful insights with literary elegance. He laid out for us a theory of "religion as a culture system" that would appear later as one of his most famous and seminal articles. The thesis was that religion is a set of symbols that provide explanations for the ultimate problems of life and templates for responding to those problems. As I listened to him, I struggled with one of the most important intuitions of my life: religion operates in the same area of the personality where artistic expression and scientific insight flourish. To say the same thing in different words, I discovered that religion was preconscious activity before it was anything else—it began in that edge of the personality where our consciousness faded off into unconsciousness. Religion had its origins in that borderland of consciousness where metaphors and stories, images and symbols, daydreams and fantasies occur.

I did not conclude that religion *was* fantasy. Rather I decided that humankind's quest for fundamental meaning began not in the rational intellect but in the same dimension of the self where we made up stories. Later I would come to see that storytelling was a raw and basic quest for meaning.

I hasten to add that because we are reflective creatures religion does not end in the preconscious. It is not irrational behavior. It merely begins in the prerational—the creative—self, that self which I suspect Saint Paul had in mind when he said that the Spirit speaks to our spirit.

Geertz's definition of religion has had an enormous impact on me: "Religion is a system of symbols which acts to establish powerful, pervasive, and long-lasting moods and motivations in men by formulating conceptions of a general order of existence and clothing these conceptions with such an aura of factuality that the moods and motivations seem uniquely realistic."

"Symbol" was the key word. Now I understood the myths of the ancient religions, even of the ancient Hebrew religion. They were not designed to provide historical truth as we know it, much less "instant replays"[1] of ancient events; rather they were stories that purported to explain, in vivid language that affected the whole human person, what life meant and how humans ought to live.

I had picked up some of this notion in the seminary where there had been hints in our Scripture classes that myths were not legends, much less lies, but religious stories. Only in the midst of my struggles at the university with the modes of human knowledge was I capable of the first step toward understanding the full implication of the insight that religion was symbol and story long before it became theology and philosophy and that the poetry of religion was not inferior to its prose but rather anterior to it and, in terms of the whole human person, in some ways superior to it.

As I rode up in the elevator to my hotel room in New York after my conversation with the editor, another and much more recent encounter flashed across my mind. I had been sitting at my PC in my summer house in Grand Beach looking out over Lake Michigan. My research assistant (and nephew; nepotism begins at home), Sean Durkin, arrived with a diskette crammed with data from the NORC General Social Survey. I stuffed the diskette into the A drive of my

---

[1] I would not have used that word in the early 1960s since in those days when Johnny Unitas and Lenny Moore were destroying my Bears, instant replays did not exist.

Compaq computer, transferred the data file to my hard disk, and feverishly called up the SPSSPC+ data analysis program.

"Important?" Sean, always cool, demanded.

"Twenty-five years of work." I accessed the data file without looking up.

"Yeah?"

"These data wil prove once and for all that religion is imagination before it's anything else." I instructed SPSS to produce a set of correlations.

Sean nodded sagely. "*Really* important."

Indeed yes.

Even as I write this book I continue to explore the wonders of that insight—not original with me surely but utterly decisive for my own life as a sociologist, eventually a storyteller, a priest, and a person.

In every scientific enterprise, theory, data, and insight romp playfully in the creative imagination—often with results that the scientist does not anticipate and in ways that later he cannot even trace. The process cannot be budgeted, the play cannot be scheduled. The spirit, like the Spirit, blows whither she will. Data, however, are essential for both testing the theory and inciting the spirit. However, since the sociology of religion was a professional backwater for which almost no funding was available, data are hard to come by and the spirit languishes or busies herself about other tasks.

I ask the reader to follow my romp with the spirit through the complexities of the sociology of the religious imagination for two reasons. The less important one is that this is the way science normally works.[2] The more important one is that the reader is as likely to be skeptical as was my friend the editor about both the importance of the religious imagination and about the differences between the Catholic and the Protestant imaginations. My assertion that Catholics imagine (somewhat) differently is neither readily comprehensible nor self-evidently true. I must slowly and carefully build up the evidence in order to persuade the reader that I am not talking nonsense.

After I heard Cliff Geertz's lecture and read all his writing (and wrote a book called *Unsecular Man* in 1972) I continued for years in my ordinary work of studying American Catholicism with survey

---

[2] More slowly in the human sciences than in the biological, chemical, or physical sciences because the subject matter is more complicated, and more slowly still in the sociology of religion because data are so hard to obtain.

research methods. In the back of my head, however, was the notion that someday it might be a good idea to try to find survey questions that applied Geertz's theories to the interests and concerns of survey sociologists.

The years went on, all too swiftly I suppose, often with only some small reflections on this new and, as I suspected, fruitful approach to the study of religion. There was so much else to do and so little data to study the religious imagination.

During those years I added the notion of religious experience to the concept of religious symbol. The symbols, I came to believe, are inherited from our religious heritage and dispose us to experiences that give greater power to the symbols. From Rudolph Otto and William James I learned that religion results from an experience of the holy or the sacred, both the overarching religious experiences which shape the great traditions and the ordinary experiences of hope renewal that affect the ordinary daily life of humans. If, therefore, one can find some way to measure the quality of the religious imagery in an individual's organism, one will have access to his ultimate "culture system" and be able to make meaningful predictions about the way she will respond to the issues of life.

While I was working on this track and testing and discarding items that might measure the religious imagination, I fell under the influence of the "story theologians," most notably David Tracy and John Shea, both of whom helped me to advance my understanding beyond the original starting point from which Clifford Geertz had put me into orbit. Religion, I began to understand, originated with experiences that renewed hope, was encoded in the personality by symbols that recorded traces of those hope-renewal/template-providing experiences, and was shared through stories that leaped from the imagination of the storyteller to the imagination of the listener (and thus triggered recollections of his/her own hope-renewal experiences). Moreover, it was shared with others who because they possessed the same symbolic repertory constituted a storytelling community.

Religion, both in the life of the individual and in the great historical traditions, was then experience, symbol, story (most symbols were inherently narrative), and community before it became creed, rite, and institution. The latter were essential, but derivative. One must reflect on one's experience of hope-renewal and critique the experience from the perspective of one's tradition. However, reflection and critique presupposed experience and story and lost all their power and vitality when they became deracinated from symbol and story.[3]

The followers of Jesus experienced the one who had died as still alive. They told the story of his life, death, and continued life to all who would listen in narrative symbols they had taken from their own heritage. The new Adam, the new Moses, the new David had been resurrected (a metaphor they adapted from the theories of the Pharisees) from the dead. Someday we, too, would also rise.

My lover and I (both fictions) have grown cold, we have a bitter quarrel, our love dies, we both have lost hope that there is any purpose or direction in our lives; then in the cold, icy cave that is the burial place of our love, suddenly, unaccountably our love explodes again, and we are reborn in a new life of hope and love. We rush to share our story with others who have experienced the same death and resurrection countless times, even as we have.

Such parallel systems of death and rebirth, correlating with each other (God's love revealed in Jesus and revealing itself again in our human love for one another) and illuminating each other, are at the heart of religion—and also provide opportunities for, even the reason for existence of, the storytelling communities we call churches.

Religious language, I finally understood, was all metaphorical language, whether it be the language of primitive myths or of the most abstract philosophy. Mythmaker and philosopher were both playing the same game—searching for comparisons by which they could describe experiences of a Reality (Goodness, Graciousness, the Reason for Hope) that was in truth beyond all description and yet demanded to be described.[4]

If we could gain access to the religious stories of survey respondents we would, I was convinced, know far more about the rest of

---

[3] I developed these ideas in my book *Religion: A Secular Theory*, which was published in 1982, twenty years after I had first heard Cliff Geertz's lecture and fourteen years after the publication of the paper based on his lecture. Looking back on it I lament the time it took to develop my own paradigm, but in my own defense I can plead that (a) I didn't know I was working on a paradigm, (b) data to test it were hard to come by until my fiction provided the funds to pursue every year serious data collection in the sociology of religion, and (c) the Spirit still blows whither she will and takes her own sweet time. The word "secular" in the title means that experience of hope-renewal is part of ordinary life and is not confined to or even related to the formal ecclesiastical institution. Religion is secular before it becomes ecclesiastical just as it is experience, image, and story before it becomes catechism and code.

[4] My sister Mary Jule Durkin, who is a theologian, and I teamed up to write a book that developed our thoughts on the religious imagination, *How to Save the Catholic Church*, published in 1985, in which the paradigm is described in much greater detail.

their values and behavior than we would by the usual measures of religion that survey questionnaires produced—church membership, church attendance, doctrinal beliefs.

Those whose religious imagination has a propensity to a warmer, affectionate, more intimate, more loving representation of ultimate reality will also be, I hypothesized, more gracious or more benign in their response to political and social issues. Those who have a graceful image of God, it might be expected, will be more graceful in their relationships with their fellow human beings. Even with appropriate measures of social and religious liberalism held constant, those with the more gracious image of God will be more likely to support racial integration, civil liberties, and the principles of feminism; more likely to oppose the death penalty, and less likely to vote for a Presidential candidate who is perceived as being less than gracious to the poor and to minorities. The way you picture God will affect the way you vote—even when party affiliation and political orientation are held constant.

I was finally able to test this theoretical expectation with a battery of survey items that I had developed through the years in the General Social Survey from 1985 to 1987. Respondents are asked to locate themselves on a seven-point continuum between four forced choices of how they picture God—father/mother, master/spouse, judge/lover, and king/friend. On the resultant scale, which I called the GRACE scale, high scores were those that were more likely to lean in the direction of mother, spouse, friend, and lover while low scores were more likely to lean in the direction of father, master, judge, and king.[5]

Five percent of all Americans placed themselves on the side of the continuum indicating that they were more likely to imagine God as "mother" than "father." Twenty-five percent saw themselves in the center of the continuum indicating that they picture God as equally "father" and "mother," and the remaining 70 percent viewed themselves on the "father" side of the continuum, 51 percent of all the respondents putting themselves at the extreme "father" end of the scale.

Forty-five percent of the respondents chose the "friend" segment of the scale. Twenty-eight percent located themselves equally distant between "friend" and "king," and 27 percent placed themselves at

[5] The paper reporting these findings was published in the journal *Sociology and Social Research* in April 1988.

the "king" side of the scale (18 percent chose the "king" extreme, 31 percent chose the "friend" extreme).

A high score on the GRACE scale does indeed correlate with social and political attitudes and behaviors. Those who were more likely to picture God as a "friend" and a "mother" were less likely both in 1980 and in 1984 to vote for Ronald Reagan. They were also more likely to oppose capital punishment, to support civil liberties, to advocate government help for blacks, to reject the notion that blacks ought not to push their way into white neighborhoods, and to support feminist attitudes on the women's labor force and political participation. All of the relationships were statistically significant.

Moreover, when one holds constant age, sex, education, and region, the GRACE scale continues to correlate with capital punishment, feminism, civil liberties, and the two racial scales continue to be statistically significant. The GRACE scale is a more powerful net predictor of attitudes in these five areas than region, sex, and age, though generally not as powerful as education. Thus the effect of the GRACE scale on political and social attitudes is not a function of any of the demographic variables normally considered in social research.

Those with high scores on the GRACE scale were eight percentage points less likely to vote for Ronald Reagan in 1980 and twelve percentage points less likely to vote for him in 1984.

Was this propensity to vote against Ronald Reagan a function not so much of religious imageries as of political orientation or party affiliation? In each category of party identification I found a statistically significant relationship between religious imagery and the propensity to vote against Reagan, a twelve-percentage-point difference for liberal Democrats, a seventeen-percentage-point difference for liberal independents, a fifteen-percentage-point difference for liberal Republicans, a fourteen-percentage-point difference for moderate Democrats, and an eleven-percentage-point difference for moderate independents.

Religious imagery did not overcome conservative political orientation but among those who describe themselves as liberal or moderate and as independents or Democrats, the quality of religious imagery does have a considerable effect on voting behavior. The "story" of one's relationship with God contained in religious imagery does indeed help to tell the story one writes in the ballot box.

The religious imagination, then, does contribute to people's social and political attitudes and behaviors, and its contribution cannot be reduced to either demographic or political orientation and identification factors. The final question that must be asked, however, is whether the religious imagination as measured by the GRACE scale is merely a form of religious liberalism. Obviously the people with the more gracious religious imaginations cannot be written off as fundamentalists because, as we noted previously, those denominations that are likely to be fundamentalist have low average scores in the scale. To test the possibility, however, that religious imagery is merely a mask for religious liberalism, regression equations were written in which education, political orientation, and attitudes toward the Bible were entered as variables. What impact, if any, on political and social attitudes and behaviors does religious imagery net of education, political orientation (liberal versus conservative), and attitudes toward the Bible (fundamentalist or not)?

As might be expected, education and religious and political liberalism do diminish somewhat the relationship between religious imagery and attitudes and behavior. However, even net of education, political orientation, and attitude toward the Bible, the religious imagination (as measured by the GRACE scale) continues to correlate positively with all the dependent variables used in the analysis.

Images of God as "friend" and "mother," in other words, are statistically significant and reasonably important correlates of political and social attitudes and behaviors.

I had stumbled a couple of steps forward in my attempt to understand better the religious imagination. Religion, I now saw, could be profitably approached as a predictor variable that is of some considerable importance in understanding social attitudes and behaviors. The way one pictures God does affect attitudes and voting patterns independently of sex, age, education, region of the country, political orientation, and religious fundamentalism. People's "stories of God" do relate to their stories of political and social life.

While I was wrestling with this theory of the religious imagination and striving to perfect measures for testing it (and starting to write the novels that my theory said ought to be written), I was influenced by David Tracy's second book, *The Analogical Imagination,* published in 1981. He was, it seemed to me, exploring the same question of differences between Catholics and Protestants investigated at the turn of the century by the two founders of modern sociology, Max Weber and Emile Durkheim.

Max Weber thought that the "communitarian" ethic (strong support and control of the individual by the community) of the former seemed to impede educational and economic achievement while the "inner-worldly asceticism" of the latter, with its emphasis on individual achievement, facilitated the success of the latter. Emile Durkheim believed, on the other hand, that the "individualism" of Protestants induced higher suicide rates among them while the "communitarian" constraints available to Catholics tended to reduce suicide rates.

The theories of these two giants certainly fit the pattern of religious emphasis of the two denominational traditions. For Protestantism the tendency has always been to emphasize the relationship of the individual with God while for Catholicism the tendency has always been to emphasize the individual relating to God as a member of a community. Suicide rates and educational achievement rates would be two manifestations (and perhaps not the most important) of fundamental orientations that permeate the two traditions.

Quite apart from achievement and suicide rates, then, the question remains whether at the end of the century that began with *The Protestant Ethic and the Spirit of Capitalism* and *Suicide,* the distinctive orientations of the two heritages persist.

Religion, I had come to believe, is a set of symbols that provide answers to issues of the ultimate meaning of life, symbols that explain imaginatively what the world is about and provide templates for shaping human response to the world and thus the shape of the world in which humans live. Religion is an imaginative "cultural system"—a collection of directing "pictures" through which humans organize and give meaning to the phenomena that impinge on their consciousness, especially insofar as these phenomena require some explanation of the ultimate purpose of life. While these "pictures" may produce theological and ethical codes, they are prepropositional and metaphorical. The codes are derivative, the superstructure built on an imaginative and preconscious infrastructure.

Therefore, I concluded, the fundamental differences between Catholicism and Protestantism are not doctrinal or ethical. The different propositional codes of the two heritages are but manifestations, tips of the iceberg, of more fundamentally differing sets of symbols. The Catholic ethic is "communitarian" and the Protestant "individualistic" because the preconscious "organizing" pictures of the two traditions that shape meaning and response to life for members of the respective heritages are different. Catholics and Protestants "see" the world differently (or "saw" it differently). These preconscious "worldviews" are not, of course, totally different, but only somewhat different, different enough to produce different doctrinal and ethical codes and different behavior rates (or to have once produced different rates).

The central symbol is God. One's "picture" of God is in fact a metaphorical narrative of God's relationship with the world and the self as part of the world. It was precisely at this point that Tracy's work made its major contribution to my own thinking. His goal in *The Analogical Imagination* was to study the "classics" of the two traditions (the works of men like Luther, Aquinas, and Calvin) to discover the underlying imagery that shapes these crucial works. On the basis of his study, he suggested that the Catholic imagination is "analogical" and the Protestant imagination is "dialectical." The Catholic "classics" assume a God who is present in the world, disclosing Himself in and through creation. The world and all its events, objects, and people tend to be somewhat like God. The Protestant classics, on the other hand, assume a God who is radically absent from the world and who discloses Herself only on rare occasions (especially in Jesus Christ and Him crucified). The world and all its events, objects, and people tend to be radically different from God.

The word "tend" in the previous paragraph is used advisedly. Zero-sum relationships do not exist in the world of the preconscious. The analogical and the dialectical imaginations exist side by side in the personalities of the authors of the classics, opposing but also complementing each other. Rarely does one encounter a religious imagination that is purely analogical or purely dialectical.

Tracy argues that two approaches to human society of the respective traditions are shaped by these imaginative pictures. The Catholic tends to see society as a "sacrament" of God, a set of ordered relationships, governed by both justice and love, that reveal, however imperfectly, the presence of God. Society is "natural" and "good," therefore, for humans and their "natural" response to God is social. The Protestant, on the other hand, tends to see human society as "God-forsaken" and therefore unnatural and oppressive. The individual stands over against society and not integrated into it. The human becomes fully human only when he is able to break away from social oppression and relate to the absent God as a completely free individual.

There are still Protestants who have no objection to their children marrying Catholics, so long as the wedding is not in a Catholic church. They have no particular objection to Catholic doctrine or Catholic people or even to their child perhaps becoming a Catholic, but they cannot tolerate the idolatrous blasphemy of the statues that are still to be found in Catholic churches. God ought not to be identified with such idols, and humans ought not to have to go through such intermediaries as saints to talk to God.

This reaction, more visceral than propositional, illustrates perfectly the differences between the two kinds of imagination—the dialectical, which sets God over against the world and its communities and artifacts; and the analogical, which sees God's self-disclosure in such creatures.

Tracy's analysis complements and adds to the earlier insights of Durkheim and Weber. One may continue to speak of a "Protestant" ethic, but now one must understand the ethic as a set of fundamental world-explaining and world-shaping interpretative pictures. In this sense, ethos, as Geertz has observed, is the flip side of mythos. Formal ethic codes are derivatives of interpretative pictures. The higher suicide rates and the higher achievement rates of Protestants in turn-of-the-century Europe are the result ultimately of different symbol systems, of different stories of God.

In this perspective the more "conservative" Catholic stands on morality and doctrine are not so much the starting point of the Catholic tradition as the results of images of society and religion that are latent beneath the formal teaching of the tradition. Because communities are pictured by Catholics as sacramental, threats to communities must be resisted both by a reassertion of the values that seem to protect the communities and by support for doctrinal notions on which the communities appear to have been based. The Protestant heritage, freed from such powerful concern about the preservation of traditional communities because it imagines the communities to be sin-filled and God-forsaken, can perhaps afford to be more flexible in matters of morality and doctrine and human relationships (so long as the traditional, community-protecting norms are observed).

Tracy's work provides useful background for reconsidering the insights of Weber and Durkheim, but the issue that remains is whether the two different imaginations still persist in an urbanized, industrialized, ecumenized world at the end of the century. Do Catholics still see the world somewhat more analogically than Protestants? Do Protestants still see the world somewhat more dialectically than Catholics? Do Protestants, therefore, still tend to emphasize individual values? Do Catholics still tend to emphasize communal values? Does the Catholic value orientation still reflect an image of God as present in creation? Does the Protestant value orientation still reflect an image of a largely godless creation?

To put the issue bluntly, since the Reformation ethic can fairly be assumed, at least at some high level of generality, to have shaped the spirit of modern capitalism, is the dominant social trend away from a communal ethic and toward an individual ethic? Do the combined forces of modernization, urbanization, industrialization, ecumenization, and religious homogenization threaten the analogical imagination with extinction? Has the Catholic imagination already become or is it in the process of becoming a casualty of the modern world?

If one wishes to formulate expectations of how the different imaginations would shape values, one might very tentatively express the following "predictions."

Catholics will be more likely than Protestants to value social relationships because they see not sin but sacramentality, however flawed, in such relationships. The analogical imagination, which pictures humans as integrated into social networks, networks that in fact reveal God, will stress those values and behaviors that contribute to the building up and strengthening of those networks. The dialectical imagination, which pictures the individual as struggling for his personal freedom against the sinful oppression of social networks, will stress those values and behaviors that contribute to the strengthening of personal freedom and independence from group control.

Catholics will be more likely than Protestants to value equality over freedom because equality makes for smoother social relationships. Moreover, because social complexity and diversity will also be seen as sacramental, Catholics will be more tolerant than Protestants of diversity in their communities; Catholicism, as James Joyce remarked, means "Here comes everyone."

Because Catholics view society as a community of communities they will be more likely than Protestants to advocate decentralization of control to the smaller communities; hence the famed Catholic principle of "subsidiarity"—nothing should be done by a larger and higher organization that can be done as well by a smaller and lower organization—is a philosophical articulation of the Catholic "image" of society.

Protestants will value in their children the virtues of initiative, integrity, industry, and thrift more than Catholics while Catholics will value loyalty, obedience, and patience. Protestants will be especially likely to deplore vices that diminish personal integrity, honesty, and sense of duty. Catholics will be especially likely to be offended by actions that seem to violate relationship networks— adultery, prostitution, suicide. Catholics will stress the importance of common background in the choice of marriage partners; Protestants will stress compatibility of individual interests and personal fulfillment. Catholics will emphasize more than Protestants institutional religion, religious devotion, and doctrinal orthodoxy. Catholics will be less likely to feel lonely and constrained by social relations than Protestants (which social relations they do not take to be oppressive). Since Protestants are more likely to emphasize personal responsibility (Weber's "worldly asceticism") than Catholics they will also be more likely to emphasize a "work ethic" than Catholics, who will be more likely to work because they have to than because they want to.

Finally, because Catholics picture God as revealing Himself in society, however flawed the revelation might be, they will be more likely to advocate social change so that the disclosure of God will be improved. Protestants, on the other hand, will be more likely to despair of society ever being anything but God-forsaken and sin-ridden and hence will be less optimistic about and less supportive of social change.

In describing these expectations of a communal ethic against an individualist ethic, an analogical imagination against a dialectical imagination, a religious vision that pictures God in society against one that pictures God as radically "other" from society, I was not predicting anything more than differences in emphases and tendencies. To predict that Catholics are more likely to be willing to accept heavy drinkers in their neighborhoods than are Protestants is not necessarily to say that the majority of Catholics will tolerate drunks and the majority of Protestants will not. Rather it would be altogether possible for the majority of both groups to reject such deviants but the Catholic majority, according to the prediction, would be smaller than the Protestant majority.

Catholics more than Protestants would emphasize the social and moral order that is created by human relationships and "natural" hierarchy. Protestants more than Catholics would emphasize contracts and laws that protect humans one from another. Catholics would thus tend to be more "conservative" than Protestants on ethical questions that impinge on family life and more "liberal" than Protestants on issues of government intervention to promote social welfare. Protestants would tend more than Catholics to urge respect for law and property, Catholics would tend more than Protestants to urge respect for authority and social relationships.

I now had my second set of expectations to test, often inchoate if not incoherent until data became available to challenge me. Moreover, I also had found a possible link between the two sets of expectations. If the Protestant and Catholic imaginations produced different pictures of God and of the world and different pictures of society that in their turn produced different value orientations, might not the differences decline if we could hold constant the image of God? Thus we could "prove" that the intervening variable between denomination and value was an image of God as present and of creation as good.

After pondering these possibilities and testing them in one way or another for several years, I finally saw their implications for the understanding of American Catholicism: Catholics liked being Catholic because, however insensitive and even stupid church leaders often were, Catholic images of God as present and the world as good and society as sacrament were benign and appealing. Why give them up?

> Wherever the Catholic sun does shine,
> There's music and laughter and good red wine.
> At least I've found it so.
> *Benedicamus Dominio!*

I now had to discover whether the differences between Catholics and Protestants in social and political values persisted, whether they could be explained at least in part by differences of religious imagery, and whether in fact they were diminishing. If the Catholic imagination persisted despite changes in religious practice and ethical norms, then that which was the raw and primal core of the Catholic heritage also persisted. Catholics not only continued to be Catholics because they imagined differently but because they liked their different imaginations and were disinclined to give them up no matter what their leaders did and said.

Moreover, if the religious imagination is acquired early in life (as I think the evidence suggests it is), it may be pretty hard to give it up, especially in a society like our own where such differences continue to be an important factor in providing self-definition and social location. Catholics, perhaps especially American Catholics, imagined differently in part because they couldn't help themselves. Their pictures of God as present and the world as good—flawed but still good—had been on the average absorbed early in life and were unchanged in later life because they were unchangeable.

My first attempt to determine whether this was a sensible line of reasoning involved the same survey material from which I drew evidence about the link between pictures of God and Presidential voting. Catholics indeed were more likely to think of God as a "mother," as a "spouse," and as a "friend." Moreover, Catholics also scored higher than Protestants on all the measures of political and social liberalism that I had used in that analysis. Might the differences in religious images account for the differences in political and social attitudes?

As a matter of fact, they did account for some of the differences. If I took into account that Protestants were more likely to be from the South (and hence more politically conservative) and that their religious imaginations leaned more in the direction of "father," "master," and "king," I could eliminate the differences in attitudes on civil liberties, racial justice, capital punishment, and feminism. Catholics were more likely to be in favor of civil liberties, feminism, racial justice, and the end of capital punishment in part because they were less likely to live in the South and in part because they had more GRACEful religious imaginations.

These findings, however, applied only to the United States. Might it not be possible that there was something special in the experience of Catholics in the United States that disposed them to both more benign images of God and more "liberal" social and political attitudes?

Just before I began to write this book, I gained access to two studies done at the same time in several different countries that enabled me to determine whether there are differences between Catholics and Protestants in values and attitudes, especially toward the role of government, which transcend national lines and which can be predicted by the theory of the religious imagination. The first data base was the International Study of Values (ISV) conducted in 1981. [6] I asked whether in six English-speaking countries (Great Britain, Ireland, Canada, Australia, New Zealand, and the United States) and two continental countries (West Germany and the Netherlands) there were differences between Catholics and Protestants in their values, net of the differences in national cultures, and whether these differences could be predicted by the theory of the differences between Protestant and Catholic religious imaginations.

I formulated seventy-five hypotheses, fifty-four of which were supported by the data (none of the others were supported in the

---

[6] These surveys, as all described in this book, were national probability samples of respondents who were interviewed personally. The scales were constructed from their answers to questions designed to measure their values and attitudes.

opposite direction).[7] In all countries, Catholics are more likely to emphasize "fairness" and "equality" while Protestants are more likely to emphasize "freedom" and "individualism" in the workplace. With the exception of those in Great Britain, Catholics are also more likely to advocate the strengthening of authority and of the family. And in the United States and Ireland, they are also more likely to say that if they didn't have to work five days a week they would devote themselves to the community and to a small business of their own.

In all five countries, Catholics are more willing than Protestants to accept political extremists of either the left or the right into their neighborhoods. Except in Australia they are also more likely to accept those with drinking and emotional problems.

In Ireland and Australia and to some extent in Canada (though not in the United States and Britain), Catholics are more likely than Protestants to have strong positions on issues of "life ethics" (abortion, extramarital sex, euthanasia, suicide, etc.). In all five countries, Protestants are more likely than Catholics to emphasize issues of "personal ethics"—lying, cheating, stealing, bribing. In all the countries but the United States, Catholics are more likely than Protestants to disapprove of "socially disruptive" behavior such as joyriding, union busting, fighting with police, and failure to report damage to another's car.

In all countries, Catholics are more likely than Protestants to report agreement on crucial issues with parents and spouses and to emphasize the importance of shared background (religion, politics, tastes) as conditions for successful marriage. Protestants, however, are more likely than Catholics to insist on the importance of sexual fulfillment and living apart from parents and in-laws as conditions for a successful marriage.

In four countries, Protestants were more likely to value industry and thrift in their children and Catholics more likely to value religious faith and a sense of loyalty and duty (with the exception of Ireland, where Protestants rate loyalty and duty higher than do Catholics). In all the countries, Catholics are more likely than Protestants to emphasize traditional family values; and in all countries but Ireland, Protestants are more likely than Catholics to be tolerant of "sexual revolution" behavior. In Ireland, Protestants disapprove of

[7] I reported the results of this analysis in a paper called "Protestant and Catholic: Is the Sacramental Imagination Extinct?" in the August 1989 issue of the *American Sociological Review*.

such behavior even more strongly than Catholics—which is strong disapproval indeed.

Finally, as predicted, Catholics are more likely to be devout and to be doctrinally orthodox while Protestants are more likely than Catholics to be satisfied with the response to their needs provided by their churches.

These differences, easily predictable from the theoretical orientation of the two imaginations—analogical and dialectical—demonstrate how useless it is to try to pin the labels "liberal" or "conservative" on either denominational heritage. On issues of sexual morality and family life Catholics are clearly more "conservative" (because of their imaginative predispositions, I contend). But on issues of social justice and neighborhood community they are just as clearly more "liberal." And on matters of "corruption" whether they are more "tolerant" or more "corrupt" probably depends on which denominational heritage provides the observer's perspective.

To make certain that these findings were not the result of the one survey, I was able to attempt to replicate them in an analysis of data collected in 1985 by the International Social Survey Project (of which NORC is a part). This latter survey measured attitudes toward the role of government in four of the countries that had been studied by the ISV—Britain, Australia, West Germany, and the United States.[8]

The findings of the second analysis were similar to those of the first: Protestants are more likely than Catholics to support obedience to laws; Catholics are more likely than Protestants to approve violent protests and to support freedom of publication; Protestants are more likely than Catholics to resist temporary arrest for suspects and criminals and to feel oppressed by the power structures of society. Catholics are more likely than Protestants to support government intervention in the economy, government ownership of industry, and equalization of income.

The Catholic attitude toward the role of government may seem paradoxical—on the one hand supportive of more intervention and on the other more likely to approve of violent resistance. Perhaps the reason is that the Catholic imagination inclines people to expect the government to be good, modestly and imperfectly good perhaps, but still good. When the flaws in government become intolerable those

[8] I reported this research in a paper called "Denomination and Political Values: A Cross-National Analysis," *Sociology and Social Research* 54: 485–502.

who believe government can be a positive good are more likely to take to the streets than those who take it for granted that governmental power is always evil.

Again "liberal/conservative" paradigms cannot cope with the Catholic propensity to support "liberal" policies of government intervention and egalitarianism and "conservative" policies in response to crime and criminals. However, a paradigm based on a theory of different "imaginations" (or "ethics") can easily account for and find consistency in the patterns reported in this paper: Catholics tend to picture society as supportive and not oppressive; Protestants tend to picture society as oppressive and not supportive.

In both surveys I redid the analysis for those under forty years of age (and hence those who came to maturity in the 1960s, with all their turbulence and revolution, or later) to see if there was any sign that the differences of religious imagination between Protestants and Catholics were declining, either because of secularization or post–Vatican Council "modernization." There were no important differences between the correlations and hence no sign of the demise of the analogical imagination. It continues to be alive and well and existing all over the world. Church attendance may be declining. Acceptance of Vatican moral teaching may be eroding (though acceptance, as we shall see, was by no means universal in the years before the Vatican Council), but the imaginative substratum on which Catholicism rests still seems rock hard.[9]

Does this different pattern of religious images affect religion as well as social and moral attitudes and values? The 1988 General Social Survey added a module of questions about religion which it hopes to repeat periodically. The items in this module enable one both to make predictions based on the theory of the analogical imagination about religion and to see if the correlations that measure those predictions

[9] There were not enough Protestants in each of the nations of these two analyses to separate them into various denominations. However, in both cases I did separate investigations—one of Catholics versus Protestants, excluding the Anglicans, and the other of Catholics versus other Christians, including the Anglicans. There were no differences in the findings. However much they may differ in other respects from reform Protestants, the Anglicans seem to be similar to them in the relationships between religious imagination and social and political values. In the United States, there are rarely enough cases in a national survey to separate Protestants into the various denominations, except for the general category of Baptist (who are 20 percent of the population) versus all other. Lutherans, for example, are 7 percent of the population and Episcopalians 3 percent—in a sample of 1,500; therefore, one can expect to find about a hundred Lutherans and 45 Anglicans, hardly enough to risk estimates unless one is able to ask the same questions over several years and pool the results.

can be accounted for at least in part by different images of God and the world. By analyzing the response patterns (through a technique called factor analysis, the details of which the nonsociological reader need not be concerned with) I found several clusters of religious values.

RELATIONSHIP WITH GOD. Because they are more likely to see God as an intimate other with whom one can disagree instead of a distant and absent God and because they believe that God, present in the world, is responsible for the world, Catholics are likely to score higher on a scale that measures anger toward God and doubts about Her.

DEVOTION. A cluster of responses emerged that emphasized being born again, reading the Bible, inviting someone else to accept Jesus as savior, and saying grace. Such devotions seemed clearly Protestant in their orientation.

MORAL RIGIDITY. Four items that stressed rigid moral decision-making constituted a single cluster, which seems to reflect a dialectical approach to reality. Hence Protestants were expected to score higher on it than Catholics.

DOUBTS. Four questions were asked about events that created doubt about religious faith. These also clustered on one scale. Since Catholics, we have hypothesized, are more likely to doubt, it is expected that they will score higher than Protestants.

FAITH. Four items were asked about phenomena that strengthened religious faith; they, too, clustered on a single scale. Since Catholics see the world and its events as revelatory, it was expected that they would score higher than Protestants on this scale.

LIFE DECISIONS. Two response clusters emerged in an analysis of four items about influences on life decision-making: one with emphasis on the Bible and church leaders, the second with emphasis on the self and others. It was expected that Protestants, with their stress on individual decisions and the Bible as road map, would score higher than Catholics on both these factors.

PERSONAL GOODNESS. Four questions were also asked about what constitutes the good person. All four clustered on the same scale. With the emphasis on following one's own conscience in this factor it was expected that it would also produce higher scores for Protestants.

ATTITUDES TOWARD SCIENCE. Two scales were developed from four questions about science, one emphasizing the positive aspects of science, the other the negative. Since Catholics are more likely to see the world as sacramental, they would be more likely to appreciate the scientific study of the world and score higher than Protestants on the positive scale and lower on the negative scale.

There were, therefore, ten variables to be tested for denominational difference. Once a difference was discovered, it then had to be asked whether the religious imagination items developed for the General Social Survey can account for some of the differences. Catholics are more likely than Protestants to see God as an intimate other—lover, friend, spouse, and mother—and the world and human nature as basically good, as the theory of the analogical imagination predicts they would. Does this difference account for at least some of the denominational value differences that exist in the General Social Survey?

On six of ten scales the predictions were accurate. Catholics are more likely to emphasize the presence of God. Protestants are more likely to emphasize reading the Bible and being born again. Catholics are less likely to be morally rigid and are also less likely than Protestants to rely on the Bible and on authority for moral decisions. Protestants are less likely to have doubts or to be angry at God than are Catholics. Catholics are less hostile to science than Protestants.

Moreover—and this is the critical point—when one takes into account images of God (score on the GRACE scale), the differences either disappear or are substantially reduced. The difference in religious behavior that exists between Catholics and Protestants can be accounted for by their different images of God, who is perceived as distant (father, judge, king, master) in the Protestant imagination and present in the Catholic imagination (mother, lover, friend, and spouse).

While social science correlations are generally not very large, the average correlation between religion (Protestant or Catholic) and the variables I studied was three times as high as the average correlation with gender and about as high as the correlation with education. The different imaginations do matter in modern society.

The theory of the analogical imagination thus makes it possible to predict differences between Protestants and Catholics and then to partially explain them by different images of God and creation that the two heritages transmit from generation to generation.

It was a long pilgrimage, twenty-seven years, from Clifford Geertz's lecture to the two multination analyses—a long, circuitous, and often unintentional journey. The two themes—religious imagery and the differences between the analogical and dialectical imaginations—converged only toward the end. Moreover, the implications of this convergence for an explanation of why American Catholics continue to be Catholic struck me only as I was finishing the multination analysis and preparing to write this book: Catholics remain Catholic because they like the Catholic imagination that perceives God as present and the world as grace.

The differences between the two show up in the Catholic reaction to the remodeling of their churches in recent years. Both pastors and architects are inclined to eliminate the "excesses" of older Catholic church decoration—statues are reduced to a minimum, the crucifix is replaced by a cross, stained-glass windows are eliminated or deprived of representational images, candles are banished, the atmosphere becomes chaste, bland, and utterly inoffensive to any Protestant who may happen in.

Catholics don't like it, especially when they are not consulted about the changes. To be told by the parish "liturgy committee" that now their church is "liturgically correct" makes no difference at all. They liked it the way it used to be and don't like it the way it is now. Moreover, it was their money that paid for the way it used to be and their money that was used without their consent to pay for the changes.

A woman of my own generation, the least anticlerical of persons, brought me over to her newly decorated parish church that she, astonishingly, did not like one bit.

"It's lovely," I observed.

"It's not Catholic," she countered.

"You're right; but it's such a nice Congregationalist environment."

"We're not Congregationalists."

You betcha.

The pastor and the architect usually dismiss such complaints as the naïve ignorance of the "preconciliar" mentality. However, the instinct of such people is sound. The church in the Madonna video "Like a Prayer," with its statues and stained glass and candles, stands for the Catholic tradition in a way a church that looks much like a Quaker meetinghouse cannot. The challenge for Catholic artists, barely understood thus far, is to create contemporary buildings that manifest the rich Catholic sacramental tradition and not ones that are "just like" the churches of other traditions.

While I was working on the book, I found another and perfectly delightful (to me at any rate) evidence of the Catholic imagination at work.

One of the preconscious paradigms that students learn in college and especially in graduate school is that which can be called "modernization" or "development": Under the impact of industrialization, urbanization, and "rationalization," human societies have been evolving from a condition in which most relationships are "primordial" to a condition in which most human relationships are "socially constructed." The "modernized" society will be more "rational" and less "archaic," more "scientific" and less "superstitious," more "bureaucratic" and less "familial," and more tolerant of diversity based on the old and outmoded social divisions.

This evolutionary "modernization" model persists as a presupposition of the collective unconscious of many social scientists, journalists, government administrators, and other presumably well-educated Americans: the more sophisticated and better educated a society is— the more "modern" it is—the less likely it is to be troubled by outmoded intolerances, all other things being equal.

Attempts to compare the "development" of social attitudes in countries in various stages of economic and social "development" are handicapped by the absence of international data and by the difficulty of holding constant cultural differences that are part of the matrix in which a culture and society are "developing." In comparing tolerance in Iran and the United States, to use an extreme example, one must somehow hold constant the Puritan origins of one society and the Islamic origins of the other, a virtually impossible task. How can one then falsify or verify the null hypothesis that, given the origins of both countries, Iran may have made more progress toward sophisticated and "rational" tolerance than the United States?

It might be possible, however, to look at a group of countries that share in some degree a common culture and see if there is a relationship between "development" and tolerance in those countries. In the English-speaking world, for example, are the more "advanced" countries the more "tolerant" of diversity and deviance? To put the matter more concretely, would not one expect Ireland, the least "developed" of the English-speaking countries, to score lower on measures of tolerance than Great Britain and the United States, which are among the most developed countries in the world?

The existing research literature on Ireland would agree that Ireland is an archaic, familial society, conservative, rigid, dominated by a reactionary Catholic Church. It is the most agricultural and most rural of the English-speaking nations, its GNP and educational attainment levels the lowest of any of these nations.[10] Many of the events that shaped the modern world—the Renaissance, the Industrial Revolution, the French Revolution—had only marginal impact on Irish peasant life. Ireland is the poorest and the most backward of the English-speaking nations—and hence the most likely to be reactionary and intolerant. Who would expect anything different?

One can examine these expectations in the data gathered in the International Study of Values from a question about whom one would reject as neighbors in representative samples of five English-speaking countries—Ireland, Britain, the United States, Canada, and Australia.

The question was worded "On this list are various groups of people. Could you please sort out any that you would *not* like to have as neighbors: People with a criminal record. People of a different race. Students. Left-wing extremists. Unmarried mothers. Heavy drinkers. Right-wing extremists. People with large families. Emotionally unstable people. Members of minority religious sects or cults. Immigrant/foreign workers." (Yes/no response.)

One would expect, on the basis of theory and past research, that the Irish respondents would score higher than respondents of other English-speaking nations on rejecting these undesirables, save perhaps with regard to those groups such as people of other races or immigrant workers who are rarely found in Ireland. In fact, the Irish turned out to be the most tolerant people in the English-speaking world, scoring either in first place for tolerance or tied for first in every single question. (They were especially likely to be more tolerant than their "betters" across the Irish Sea. The greatest differences in tolerance, moreover, concerned those deviant people of whom the Irish would be likely to have their own fair share or more than their fair share [the emotionally disturbed, heavy drinkers, and right-wing extremists].)

How can one account for such a dramatic reversal of expecta-

---

[10] It also has the highest per capita book-purchase rate in the world.

tions? How can one account for the striking finding that the Irish appear to be more tolerant than the British and the Americans? The Canadians and the Australians? What might have survived from archaic society which would sustain such tolerance (even if, as is possible, the present level might represent a decline from previous levels of tolerance)?

The most obvious difference about Ireland is that, even when one includes the Six Counties, it is an overwhelmingly Catholic country. For all its rigidities and flaws Catholicism has attempted to be a universal religion, a religion that means, in Joyce's words, "Here comes everyone." Might the Catholicism of Ireland account for the greater tolerance to be found in that country, as astonishing as such a suggestion may seem? Might the more "communal" or analogical religious imagination of Catholics, an imagination in which God reveals Herself in society instead of being absent from it as sinful and God-forsaken, encourage a greater toleration for diversity?

Might it be precisely the Sacramental Imagination that explains the difference?

When one takes into account (through statistical techniques) the fact that the Irish are Catholic, the differences between Ireland and the other four countries are diminished by half. Then when one takes into account the special nature of *Irish* Catholicism the difference goes away completely. The Irish are the most tolerant of the English-speaking people because they are Catholic and because they are *Irish* Catholic—in my terms because they possess the Sacramental Imagination that enables them to see God revealing Himself in everyone and because they have a special Irish variety of that imagination.

Unfortunately those who designed the ISV *(not* NORC) did not think it worthwhile to ask an ethnic question that would enable us to compare the mere Irish with the Irish Americans. However, other data prove that the Irish are the most tolerant of Gentile ethnic groups in America.

Some of my professional colleagues are inclined to dismiss this analysis as absurd. Doesn't everyone know that the Irish are racist bigots?

Only bigots know that, I reply, and that includes self-hating Irish bigots.

However, the important point for this analysis is that the theory of the Catholic imagination enabled me to predict the difference that emerged from the analysis and then to account for it.

Perhaps the most interesting item of the eleven measured is the attitude toward minority religious groups, of which there are plenty on both sides of the Six-County border and about which diversity terrorist violence continues in the Six Counties and occasionally in the Republic. Is this apparent tolerance for having others as your neighbors an Irish or a Catholic phenomenon or perhaps both? It appears to be both. The Irish, regardless of their religion, and British Catholics all differ significantly from English non-Catholics in this expression of religious toleration. There is more religious toleration (as measured by this variable) in violence-torn Ireland than there is in peaceful Britain.

While it is surely the least developed of the English-speaking countries, Ireland then would seem to be the most tolerant. Moreover, it is tolerant precisely because of its "archaic" religion of "Here comes everyone."

Social scientists may wish to examine their images of "development," of religion, and of tolerance.

And of Ireland.

An Irishman to whom I reported the even more astonishing finding that the mere Irish (as opposed to the Irish Americans) were more likely to approve of marriage ceremonies for gays (25 percent versus at the most 12 percent in other countries) expressed what I take to be the essence of Irish tolerance: "We don't give a fock what they do!"

On the weekend I write this chapter I read the following paragraph from the first page of a book:

"The contemporary American Church is so largely enculturated by the American ethos of consumerism that it has little power to believe or to act. . . . Our consciousness has been claimed by false fields of perception and idolatrous systems of language and rhetoric. . . . the Church will not have power to act or believe until it recovers its tradition of faith and permits that tradition to be the primal way out of enculturation."

The point here is not that I disagree with such propositions as analyses of either American culture or the situation of the Church in American society—though I consider them to be rubbish as social analysis—but that they are not analytic propositions at all. They are cries of the dialectical imagination against a sinful culture. I might almost say that a Catholic theologian could never write them; but these days some Catholic theologians have often rejected the metaphorical imagination of their heritage and no longer see human society and human culture as sacraments, however flawed, of God.

An authentically Catholic version of the problem might go like this:

"It is the task of the American Church to find out where God speaks, where the spirit blows, where grace is present in our culture, embrace these sacraments, correlate them with our heritage, and strive to deepen and enrich their impact on the rest of American life."

In their preconscious, usually implicitly, those who are raised Catholic in this country tend to find it very difficult to swallow the orientation of the first quote and very easy to accept the orientation of the second. One of the reasons Catholics were turned off—again on the threshold of their unconscious—by such recent Democratic candidates as George McGovern, Jimmy Carter, and Walter Mondale is that they were rubbed the wrong way by the "self-righteousness" (the term we would use) of those three evangelical candidates. "They're like Protestant ministers," many Catholic Democrats said to me.

These categorizations are unfair perhaps as intellectual statements, but they reveal raw and primal emotional reactions based on profoundly but not totally different imaginative styles.

In America you have to embrace some religion (only one out of every twenty persons does not) and you may as well stick with one whose imaginative style seems familiar and easy.

Ellen Foley in my novel *The Cardinal Sins* summed up the whole theme of this chapter, almost as though she knew what my research findings during the 1980s would be, when she said to Kevin Brennan, "I forgot about Father Conroy and Sister Caroline and First Communion and May Crownings and High Club dances and Midnight Mass. I want them all back, for myself and for my children."

Community, ritual, imagery—those are the forces that hold people in and draw them back. Often they are the very things that "progressive" clerics despise or eliminate, like the priest who canceled Midnight Mass at his parish because "too many people came"!

In a burst of false ecumenism, many Catholic clergy and theologians have repudiated or deemphasized precisely those aspects of the tradition that are most appealing and represent most powerfully the classic Catholic image of God as present in the world—angels, saints, souls in purgatory, statues, stained-glass windows, beautiful churches, and most of all Mary the Mother of Jesus.

There is no better manifestation of the Catholic imagination than devotion to the Mother of Jesus, as I will argue in detail in a subsequent chapter. It portrays quintessentially the Catholic picture of God as present in the world. It is the Catholic theme of the sacramentality of creation depicted most powerfully. Mary represents the mother love of God, the great historic Catholic insight that God loves us as a mother loves a newborn babe. Such a notion is so appealing that those who understand it, even dimly and preconsciously, will never give it up.

To anticipate: In our research on young Catholics, many of whom never went to May Crownings and most of whom never heard a Marian sermon, we found that the image of Mary is even more powerful for Catholics than the image of Jesus or of God. It correlates positively with political and social concern, pro-feminist orientations, warm relations with the opposite sex, and frequent prayer. There is no evidence that the image of Mary is the source of "antiwoman" sentiments as some radical feminists claim. Quite the contrary: for young Catholics just the opposite is the case. There is no more convincing proof that it is the appeal of the analogical imagination which binds Catholics to their tradition than the persistence of the Mary image and its positive impact on the lives of young Catholics.

Doctrine and rules do not attract Catholics to their Church. Images and stories do, often despite doctrine and rules and doctrinal formulators and rule-makers. In the United States, the analogical imagination has grown stronger among post–Vatican Council Catholics. While there is no difference between Protestants under forty and Protestants over forty on the GRACE scale, Catholics under forty are significantly more likely to imagine God as mother, lover, spouse, and friend than are Catholics over forty.

I have no desire to deny the importance of rules and doctrines. Nonetheless, while both rules and doctrines are important, they are essentially derivative, conclusions from and reflections on something more primary and primal—the experience of God and the stories that recount that experience (of which, as I have said, the Mary/Christmas story may be the Catholic symbol par excellence).

I think it fair to say that most Catholic leaders—bishops, priests, theologians, teachers—will not understand what I am saying and in fact will not want to understand it. They will dismiss the careful trail of theory, insight, and data which I have charted in these two chapters with shibboleths about "polls," about the Church not being a democracy, and about "steamy" novels. They will adduce brief and less elaborate explanations of why Catholics stay in the Church (or if they are on the left, of why Catholics are leaving despite my data, personal anecdotes about young people they know who have left).

One never persuades those who already know the answers and certainly not those who believe that it is the role of the good Catholic to do what their leaders tell them (whether you be a leader of the left or the right, a theologian or a bishop). Those who have no need to listen to the questions because they already know the answers could not even entertain the possibility that wisdom may come from listening to the questions and the spiritual needs that lurk behind the questions. Nor could they consider for even a second the possibility that their greatest resources are not their answers, not their technical training, not the courses they have taken, not their power, not their participation in the "magisterium but the poetry of their tradition of a God who is present and a creation which is sacrament and the intense loyalty of their people who link being Catholic to that tradition."

One last research finding to conclude this chapter on the religious imagination: Two different surveys taken the summer before the pope's 1987 visit to America, one by ABC News and one by Gallup, addressed themselves directly to the question of whether a Catholic respondent might leave the Church. Only 6 percent said they were thinking seriously of departing, only 2 percent that their departure was likely.

Who were those most likely to think of leaving? The disillusioned liberals, angry about the refusal to ordain women, the birth-control prohibition, the absence of concern about social justice? Or the conservatives, upset about change in the Church, liberation theology, and the pastoral letters of the bishops on nuclear weapons and poverty?

In fact, there was no relationship between convictions about these "mass media" issues and a propensity to leave the Catholic Church. Those who feel strongly on such matters stay in and continue to complain. The ones who think about leaving are the ones who feel that the Church, from the Vatican to their parish, is not responding to their spiritual needs.

Catholics stay in their Church because they like being Catholic, because of loyalty to the imagery of the Catholic imagination, because of pictures of a loving God present in creation, because of the spiritual vision of Catholics that they absorbed in their childhood, along with and often despite all the rules and regulations that were drummed into their heads. They leave, or think of leaving, because of the failure of church leadership to live up to that spiritual vision.

It is the poetry of Catholicism, then, that is the secret of its continuing appeal to American Catholics, an appeal so attractive and so deep that it has hardly been touched by the turbulence of the last quarter century. Loyalty and poetry, the themes of these two chapters and the basis for the rest of the book, hardly sound like powerful ties when we first hear the words, especially if we have grown accustomed to thinking of religion as rules and doctrines. The truth is that rules and doctrines exercise power only to the extent that they appeal to the religious experiences encoded in symbol and story.

4

"NOTRE DAME BEATS SMU"

s MICHAEL DUKAKIS anti-Catholic?" a friend demands the week before the election that occurs the day I begin this chapter.

"Certainly not!" I insist, assuming my role as a junkyard-dog Democrat—someone who would vote for the party even if it nominated a junkyard dog. "What would make you think that?"

"They haven't reached out to us at all. They've made no attempt to win over Catholic voters. Clearly they don't like us. Who was at Notre Dame to pose with Lou Holtz and the football team when they went to the top in the weekly football polls? George Bush, that's who. Why did no one on Dukakis's staff think of the same thing?"

"There are a lot of Catholics on his staff."

"Harvard Catholics."

I repeated my friend's question to a Dukakis supporter.

"Sure we tried to win back Catholics. We tried to appeal to all blue-collar voters, ethnic and not."

I try to explain to him that the majority of Catholics are no longer blue-collar. He looks at me as if I am crazy, as if I am saying the sun rises in the west.

"And there's the abortion issue," he adds. "Catholics turned us off on that one. We weren't going to win them back no matter what we tried."

I remark mildly that *New York Times* exit surveys show that abortion is an important voting issue for only 1 percent of Catholic voters. Again he gives me that "this-nutty-priest-is-off-the-wall" look. "It gets a lot of media attention."

"There are as many Catholic Democrats as black Democrats, each about 28 percent of those who are affiliated or leaning in the Democratic direction."

He frowns, trying to do some quick calculations in his head. "I don't think so."

"I ran the tables this morning."

"Well, they're conservative Democrats, especially those who have made a few dollars and moved to the suburbs."

"No, they are on the liberal half of the Democratic continuum. Forty-one percent of white Protestants, 31 percent of Catholics, and 30 percent of Jews describe themselves as 'conservative'; the rest are either 'moderate' or 'liberal.' "

He shakes his head in disbelief.

I shrug indifferently. I've been trying to tell this to Democratic politicians since 1970 with no discernible effect.[1] I tell them they'll keep on losing Presidential elections until they take the facts about American Catholics seriously. I now believe that they would rather lose than face up to the data about the social and political status of American Catholics.

I write this chapter the day after the Dukakis rout, reflecting that it could have been much worse. The ineffable Dan Quayle probably cost George Bush six percentage points in his plurality. With Bob Dole as his Vice Presidential candidate, Bush could have won 60 percent of the vote and forty-nine states. But the Democrats don't need to worry about the Catholic component of their coalition, right?

After a dip in the early seventies, the proportion of Catholics who identify with or lean in the Democratic direction has stood at three-fifths for the last decade and a half. Routinely between 60 and 65 percent of Catholics vote for Democratic candidates in congressional elections. The claim both of the elite that dominates the national Democratic Party and of conservative columnists like Pat Buchanan that Catholics are becoming more Republican and more conservative can stand the test of no attempts at empirical verification.

Nonetheless, if the Buchanan assertion and the three propositions described here were put to a vote by the Harvard faculty (whence the national Democratic Party draws its brains), I'm sure the over-

---

[1] In my book *Building Coalitions* (New York: Viewpoints, 1974).

whelming majority would hold that they are not only true, but so true as to be beyond any serious doubt.

The real truth is that while Catholics have not voted in majority proportions for any of the last four Democratic Presidential candidates, their shift away from McGovern, Carter, Mondale, and Dukakis has not been disproportionate—no greater than that of the rest of the country.

When ignorance exists despite easily available facts to the contrary and when that ignorance is destructive to the goals of those afflicted by it, then one must suggest that at some deep level of the personality that ignorance is bigotry.

How can one explain this unconscious bigotry that I submit affected Mr. Dukakis's staff though not necessarily the candidate himself? The Harvard elite and those like them who run the national Democratic Party are somehow embarrassed by Catholic Democrats. They need to believe that they are ignorant, superstitious, conservative "blue-collar, hard-hat ethnics." In 1970 Harvard economist John Kenneth Galbraith wrote an article for *The New Republic* in which he described the new Democratic coalition that would dominate American Presidential elections for the rest of the century—blacks, Hispanics, the poor, women, the young.

You'll note whom he left out. And to celebrate the purification of the party the 1972 convention —the one the TV commentators enthusiastically called the "most representative" political convention in American history—ejected George Meany and Richard Daley, the labor "boss" and the big city "boss." You've noted that Meany and Daley were both Catholic?

The Democrats were wiped out in that election and every other since, with the single exception of Jimmy Carter's paper-thin majority over the man who pardoned Richard Nixon. (George McGovern did carry Chicago, by the way.)

Mr. Galbraith apparently couldn't count. If you dump a group that numbers more than a quarter of your rank and file, you shouldn't expect to win. He has since written me to protest my interpretation of his 1970 article. He is not anti-Catholic, he insists, and his list of members of the coalition was not meant to be exhaustive. Funny, though, that we were the ones left out, wasn't it?

At the root of the powerful unconscious resentment of and bigotry against Catholic Democrats is the elite notion that it is somehow reactionary for religious affiliation to influence politics—not for Jews, perhaps, but certainly for Catholics. I cite as proof the fact that election surveys in the national press no longer report on religion as a variable—though subsequent analysis always shows that it is important.

As I walked home in the mild November evening last night from Rich Daley's suite at the Hyatt Regency, consoled that in Chicago and Cook County Democrats can still win, I reflected that it seems to be my destiny to try to report facts about American Catholics—facts proven beyond any reasonable dispute—to those who not only don't want to hear them but resolutely refuse to hear them.

There are, however, different degrees of resistance. It took the Catholic hierarchy[2] five years or so after my research on the rejection of the birth-control encyclical to accept the findings, even if they did it in off-the-record whispers. But those (Harvard-trained) elitists who refuse to believe that Catholics are still Democrats and still liberal on most social issues resist the facts with greater determination than do bishops.

I stood on the bank of the Chicago River looking at the reflections of the Michigan Avenue bridge in the quiet waters bathed in the glow of the white light reflected off the Wrigley Building. Rich Daley's father once hoped that people might be able to fish in the river during their lunch hour. Maybe someday . . .[3]

And maybe someday the myth of Catholics as simultaneously conservative and unsuccessful in American life would be abandoned by self-styled "liberals," Catholic and not. Naïf that I was when I began my research on American Catholicism, I had assumed that facts would sweep away misconceptions. I could not have been more wrong.

In the late 1950s when I was working as a curate in Christ the King parish in Chicago's Beverly district, there had been an outburst of "self-critical" literature about the failure of American Catholics to achieve either success or excellence in American society. There was special concern about the failure of Catholics to become seriously involved in the intellectual life of the country. Many explanations were advanced for these failures (for which empirical evidence from scholarly research—done by others—was given): emphasis on obedience and discipline at home and school, suspicion of science and learning, stress on financial gain over intellectual curiosity, large fam-

---

[2] With some exceptions as we shall see in a later chapter.

[3] As I would learn later from a special produced by WBBM anchor person Bill Kurtis, you can fish in the Chicago River now, even swim in it. Lake trout swim in the river as far as its entrance to the Sanitary District Canal.

ilies, recruitment of the most gifted into the priesthood, repression of creative flair. The Irish were the special targets of these scholarly and semi-scholarly attacks—written in most cases by authors with obviously Irish names.

A faculty member at a very distinguished university whose background is Irish Catholic but whose name does not reveal it wrote me about my findings on Irish success that he enjoyed it when his colleagues ridiculed my findings because he made more money than any of them and they did not realize either that he was Irish or that he was better paid than they were. I should be careful, he added facetiously, about letting the secret out.

In fact, many of the self-criticisms of the self-professed Catholic elite, I would realize later, were taken over from the conventional wisdom of American intellectual nativism, a wisdom that had been encoded in the report of the National Immigration Commission (the so-called Dillingham Commission) at the turn of the century and the subsequent restrictive immigration laws: the Irish were too fickle and too superstitious and too inclined to alcohol to be successful, the Italians were innate criminals, the Poles were unstable and ignorant. Catholicism and success in America were incompatible.

A new generation of Catholic scholars in the bright days after World War II looked at their own communities or rather the ones they'd left behind and decided that the criticisms they heard from their secular colleagues were probably true.

I assumed that the critics were right, but I also suspected that the reasons for the seemingly slow pace of Catholic social and intellectual progress were the recency of the Great Depression; the prosperity and educational attainment in Christ the King parish, I said to myself, are signs that in another generation there will be striking changes. My doctoral dissertation gave me an opportunity to test my explanation. NORC was studying the career plans of 30,000 June 1961 college graduates (in a sample that included some of the young people from my parish). The goal of the project was to determine whether enough young men and women were choosing medical and scientific careers (they were, by the way).

My piece of the action was to analyze the influence of religion on career plans. I could then determine why Catholics were less likely than others to choose graduate school and academic careers. "Find out," Monsignor[4] Bill McManus, superintendent of the Catholic

---

[4] Later Bishop, a role in which he will appear in a subsequent chapter.

schools in Chicago, said to me, "why our kids aren't going to graduate school."

The first hint that the change might not have to wait for another generation was that a quarter of the graduates were Catholic, the exact proportion of Catholics in the American population. Nonetheless, I prepared eighteen hypotheses to explain the failure of Catholic college graduates to choose graduate school and/or academic careers.

They all collapsed in the face of the data!

On a hot spring morning in 1961 I stopped by NORC to pick up the first cross-tabulation of graduate school plans (academic and professional) by religion—sheets spit out slowly on an old counter sorter that did not calculate percentages. Jim Davis, the director of the project and my mentor at the time, had scrawled across the top of my sheets, "Looks like Notre Dame beats Southern Methodist this year!"

Catholics were more likely than Protestants to choose graduate school and indeed academic programs in graduate school. The change that I thought lay in the future had already happened. It would continue. In 1961 Catholics were a quarter of the population and a quarter of the graduates. In 1988 they were almost 40 percent of the graduates—half again as likely to be college graduates as the national average.

Change? Hell, that's a revolution! And I was there!

I reexamined the studies on which the Catholic self-critics (mass masochists, as Edward Duff, S.J., would call them) based their charges. They described data that applied to the 1920s and the 1930s. But this was the 1960s. The world had changed, especially the part of the world in which American Catholics lived. There was, I noted in my dissertation, a neat two-proposition summary of the change: half of the Catholics in the United States were immigrants or the children of immigrants; Catholics of college age were as likely as anyone else to graduate and more likely to attend graduate school.

When the book version of my dissertation was published,[5] I was confident that the discussion of the state of American Catholicism would change from why we were doing so poorly to the question of what would happen now that we were doing so well. I was in for a big surprise. The roof fell in on me when my report emerged in the mid-sixties.

Commonweal, a "liberal," lay-edited journal for which I had a respect bordering on worship, launched a venomous attack (the be-

---

[5] *Religion and Career* (New York: Sheed and Ward, 1963).

ginning of a revulsion toward me that has persisted in that journal ever since). It launched a four-article symposium that shredded me if not my results. I was called a "naïve empiricist," and it was broadly hinted that I was unduly optimistic because I had ecclesiastical ambitions (a charge that *Commonweal* editors made explicitly off the record and behind my back: why else would anyone be optimistic about American Catholicism?).

I was dumbfounded. In a way, I still am. I've heard of killing the herald who brings bad news. But the one who brings good news?

The battle went on with scholars and nonscholars, Catholic and not Catholic insisting I was wrong: NORC's sampling techniques were deficient; Catholics might have begun graduate school but they wouldn't finish; those Catholics who had begun academic careers would not be successful; they certainly would not achieve either jobs in good universities or excellence in their fields.

I thought I had stumbled into Alice's Wonderland. No one produced contrary evidence. They were content with attack and personal vituperation. Even when their charges were refuted repeatedly, they still kept up the assault. More than a decade later a psychologist from Brigham Young resurrected all the old prewar data and in an article in the prestigious journal *Science* once more asserted the intellectual inferiority of Catholics; he ignored totally the considerable volume of literature that had by that time emerged (especially from NORC) proving the contrary. The editor of *Science* refused to print or even answer a letter of protest. An Italian-American scholar suggested that the high incomes I was by this time reporting for Italian Americans might be the result of their success in businesses like garbage collection. He was serious. Talk about self-hatred!

Thomas Sowell, the black economist, cited U.S. Census data to prove that the Irish were failures in America. When I responded that the survey showed that more than half the Irish in America were Protestant and that half generally lived in the South and in rural regions, had been in the country for at least five generations, and were in all likelihood descendants of Ulster immigrants who came before 1800,[6] Professor Sowell replied that it was inconceiv-

---

[6] In this assertion I was probably wrong. Many if not most of the southern Irish Protestants were descendants of Irish-speaking, marginally Catholic agricultural laborers who migrated before 1800 in search of land and drifted away from the Church, to which they had no strong ties, because of the total absence of priests. For the story of the Irish Protestants see my article "The Success and Assimilation of Irish Protestants and Irish Catholics in the United States," *Sociology and Social Research* 72:4, 229–36.

able to him that any Protestant would admit that he was Irish. To my reply that both George Wallace and Jimmy Carter made that claim he replied with an attack on NORC's sampling technique and suggested that we passed out our questionnaires in supermarket plazas.

I'm afraid that these exchanges are a fair sample of the quality of the debate. My modest suggestion that Catholics had caught up educationally, socially, and economically had unleashed the Furies. The emotional investment of many people in their conviction of the inferiority of Catholics was such that a question about that conviction became an attack on what was almost their religious faith.

The battle, mind you, was about an issue that could easily be resolved by looking at the affluent suburbs around the big cities or at one's colleagues on the university faculty. By 1980, 20 percent of the academic faculties at the best state universities were Catholic (progress at the elite private universities came more slowly). Yet the debate went on, as always without my adversaries feeling the need to produce any data of their own. Finally two Canadian scholars, R. L. Schnell and Patricia T. Rooke,[7] reviewed the literature of the debate (honestly, unlike the psychologist writing for *Science)* and concluded that there was not the slightest reason to question the intellectual parity of American Catholics.[8] That silenced the opposition, though occasionally someone will surface with new assertions about how "authoritarian" Catholicism interferes with the intellectual and creative development of its young people.

The battle, however, is not won. The term "blue-collar ethnic" is still a media shorthand for "Catholic," and still serves as a paradigm for the political elites, often with the adjectives "racist," "hard-hat," and "chauvinist" added.

One can patiently demonstrate, as I will try to do, that Catholics are less likely to be racists, more likely to be feminists, and more likely to favor disarmament,[9] and have no impact on the "blue-collar Catholic ethnic" stereotype.

[7] "Intellectualism, Educational Achievement, and American Catholicism: A Reconsideration of a Controversy, 1955–1975," *The Canadian Review of American Studies*, Vol. VIII, No. 1 (Spring 1977), pp. 66–76.

[8] They also observed the Church as an institution had not caught up with its population: there were no distinguished Catholic universities and little sign that the leadership of the Church valued intellectual excellence.

Tell me about it!

[9] And, as Professor James Wright has demonstrated, more likely to oppose the Viet Nam war from the beginning.

Only a fool would say that the Irish are the most successful and the most liberal Gentile group in America—even if it happens to be true.[10] Only an idiot would assert that the Catholic ethnics are more liberal than the typical American—even if the assertion happens to be accurate.

Let us, however, look at the facts, for those whose minds are open enough to consider them. In 1987 and 1988, the average white[11] Protestant income was $24,899, according to the General Social Survey. The average Catholic income was $28,367. Catholic income is 14 percent higher than Protestant income. One does not conclude that Catholics are therefore better than Protestants. One only concludes that they are not economically inferior.

In the mid-1980s,[12] 61 percent of the Catholics in the country were white-collar workers as opposed to 55 percent of the white Protestants; 21 percent of Catholics were professionals as opposed to 19 percent of white Protestants; 39 percent of Catholics had attended college as had 37 percent of white Protestants. (Remember that Catholics include Hispanics and white Protestants obviously do not include blacks.)

The college data are especially striking evidence for my assertion that there are twin revolutions taking place within the American Catholic population—the change from counter-reformation to ecumenical age and from immigrant to professional. In the beginning of

---

[10] For documentation of this folly see my book *The Irish: Their Rise to Wealth and Power*. It is said that God created the Drink, lest the Irish own the whole world.

[11] One can play all kinds of games with income, occupation, and education figures, depending on what populations one considers. If one includes blacks in the Protestant category, the Catholic advantage goes up. If one makes the comparison between whites (as I do in this book) the Catholic advantage diminishes. Then if one excludes Hispanic Catholics on the same grounds that black Protestants have been excluded, the Catholic advantage returns. If one then takes into account the fact that Catholics live in big cities in the northeast and north central regions, the differences decline again, as they do also if you look at differences between Catholics and Episcopalians and Presbyterians (Catholic income is about the same as Methodist income, more than Lutheran, Baptist and fundamentalist, less than Episcopalian and Presbyterian). But then if you look at the Irish, the first of the Catholic immigrant groups (and the most hated until the Hispanics became the inkblot for nativism), they are even more successful than Episcopalians. I spare my readers these contortions because they are irrelevant to and distract from the key issue: the parity of American Catholics with the rest of the population, a parity that was once not thought possible—and still is not thought possible by many. For those who are interested in these details, they are discussed, perhaps ad nauseam, in my *Ethnicity, Denomination and Inequality* (Beverly Hills: Sage, 1976); "Ethnic Minorities in the United States: Demographic Perspectives," *International Journal of Group Tensions* 7:64–97; and *Religious Change in America* (Cambridge: Harvard University Press, 1989).

[12] The following figures are produced by pooling GSS data from 1982 to 1987.

the 1970s,[13] 27 percent of the Catholic population and 29 percent of Protestants had attended college. Thus the Catholic increase in little more than a decade was twelve percentage points, a 44 percent increase in the number of college-educated people within the Catholic population. Those clergy and hierarchs who think that somehow the BIG CHANGE in the social status of their people is over could not be more wrong. If anything, the pace of change will increase.

One way of mapping the social change of a population is to consider the educational and occupational decisions made by those who are young adults at different points in the population's history. The 20,000 cases in NORC's GSS provide enough data for us to be able to "walk back" the Catholic population to the decisions of those who were born before 1900 and made their career decisions during the First World War. Even at that stage, when immigrants were still pouring into the country, 13 percent of young American Catholics were deciding to attend college. During the 1920s the proportion remained steady at 13 percent. Despite the Great Depression, it rose to 18 percent in the 1930s. In the two decades after World War II it increased again, first to 25 percent and then to 31 percent. The biggest increase in the century was during the 1960s when 47 percent of the Catholics coming of age elected to attend college (precisely at the time my own research was documenting the Catholic economic and educational revolution). In the 1970s the proportion increased to 52 percent, and in the 1980s to 55 percent.

Catholic college attendance had doubled twice during the century. The proportion of young Catholics choosing professional schools has increased from 8 percent in the World War I era to 25 percent among young people reaching maturity today and the proportion of white-collar workers has risen from 44 percent to almost 70 percent.

These changes are impressive. They are also, given the history of American immigration, ordinary. The research of Barry Chiswick has shown that it takes the immigrant on the average twelve years to catch up in income with the native-born of the same educational achievement. The sons of immigrants earn more income (by about 5 percent) than the sons of the native-born. America is indeed the land of opportunity, unless you happen to be Hispanic or native-born black.

[13] GSS data pooled from 1972 to 1977.

The mistake all along has been to assume that the children and grandchildren and great-grandchildren of Catholic (non-Hispanic) immigrants would somehow be excluded from this process of economic achievement because of handicaps imposed on them by their religion. It is safe to say that the assumption, however strongly some may still hold it (if only preconsciously), has been proven wrong. The Catholic story is merely the immigrant story writ for a different religious group than the Protestant groups.

There are two different dynamisms of upward mobility at work—that which affects the whole of society and that which affects those who at one time were disadvantaged in the society. The first is represented by the enormous increase in higher education in this century, the second by the even more rapid increase of certain groups which were catching up. We can picture both of these processes operating at the same time and for four Catholic ethnic groups by imagining first of all an ascending curved line on a page. This represents the log of the odds on college attendance to nonattendance (the best way to measure proportions over time) from 1910 to the present for all white Americans. It is a slowly ascending curve.

(One could draw similar upward-swinging curves on other sheets of paper to represent proportions choosing white-collar and professional careers. The former is similar to the college-attendance curve; the latter also climbs but the slope is more shallow.)

Then we place on the same page lines for four Catholic ethnic groups—Irish, German, Italian, and Polish. The German line is more or less the same as the national average.

The Irish line begins in 1910 at a level already above the national average and continues to climb so that at the end of the series it is even more distant from the average. There is a sharp drop in the 1930s (during the Great Depression) but the Irish line is still above the national average even then. After the Depression it soars again.

The Polish and Italian lines are below the national line and move up at about the same rate as the national line (the slopes are a little less steep) until the 1940s; then they suddenly turn sharply upward, crossing the national line in the 1960s and at the present are above the national average, though not yet as high as the Irish.

In a brief scheme, this is the story of Catholic ethnic groups in the twentieth century, one of them on the average, another above the average even at the beginning of the century, the final two "catching up" at the time of the GI Bill after the war and moving ahead in the last couple of decades. It is, I emphasize, not an unusual story in itself. What is unusual is that this path up the American ladder of dreams happened to groups who were not supposed to prosper and whose prosperity is still an affront to many, including even some of their own (who perhaps like to think that they are ahead of their fellow ethnics).

This story of immigrant success is one of which Americans ought to be proud and indeed one of which most Americans are proud. It is also a story of which the Irish, Italian, Polish, and German artists, musicians, professors, architects, lawyers, psychiatrists, commodity traders, and corporation executives (for example) are very proud indeed. It is also a story whose truth is self-evident to these folks and their neighbors and friends. Yet it is a story that must be denied by some academic and media elite and by Catholic self-haters of the *Commonweal* variety, types whose emotional investment in the "blue-collar ethnic" stereotype resists all factual refutation.

The Catholics who are the target of this bigotry are hardly aware of it and are unharmed by it. Who cares what stereotypes NBC News and *The New York Times* believe about American Catholics? The ones who are hurt are the ones who cannot give up their own unconscious bigotry. They deceive themselves about the shape of American society and they lose elections because of their self-deception.

When I had finished my dissertation[14] I began to tell every cleric and bishop who would listen that the Catholic population was in the midst of an educational and social class revolution. They listened, though for the most part they only pretended to listen. Sure, Catholics were going to college now and moving to the suburbs, but as one of my pastors remarked, the backbone of the Church was still the "cap and sweater people"; there were none left in his parish, but he had not noticed.

Later pastors are aware that their people are well-educated but they still cannot resist treating them like little children—remonstrating with them publicly when they are late for Mass or leave early or when their children make too much noise. That's not the way you deal with adults, but all too few clergy have had role models who taught them how to deal with adults—especially in an era when the laity can get in their car, hop on the expressway, and drive off to another church where no one complains about such trivia.

[14] *Religion and Career* (New York: Sheed and Ward, 1963).

"Don't go after those guys," one of the latter breed of pastors advises me. "Their people keep my place going."

Some parishes in the United States but almost no dioceses adjusted to the change. New offices were established, new organizational structures were introduced, but the same old game was played: the bishops and the priests ran the Church as they always did, and the laity were expected to contribute their money and do what they were told. There was no revolution in the style of church governance to match the socioeconomic revolution that was occurring among the Catholic laity. If it had not been for the changes introduced by the Vatican Council, conflicts with the well-educated laity and often badly educated clergy would have been even worse. The Council came not a moment too soon to protect church leadership from some of its own folly.

The basic, simple, and evident truth that you cannot treat college-educated and successful lay people like children or like illiterate immigrants has yet to make an effective impact on the clerical and hierarchical mind. The laity oppose the inept and authoritarian leadership that they must often suffer with the only weapon they have available—financial contributions.

I have insisted that Catholics stay in the Church because they like being Catholic and that they like being Catholic because of loyalty to an especially appealing religious poetry. It does not follow that their loyalty is docile. They don't leave; they stay and complain, often loudly, but apparently not loudly enough so that their leadership hears them.

Loyal and angry, I would call them. My friend Bishop Bill McManus says perhaps we might use the words "loyal and disappointed" or even "loyal and unhappy."

I won't quibble about the words. The implications of the revolution I felt at Christ the King and saw documented for the first time in Jim Davis's "Notre Dame beats SMU" line have yet to change notably the leadership style within the Catholic Church. Priests and bishops who are stil governing as if they presided over a nation of immigrants are for all practical purposes in the same condition of willful ignorance as academic and media and Catholic "liberal" elites who still believe in the "blue-collar ethnic" stereotype.

The second part of the sterotype is "conservative, hard-hat, chauvinist, racist" epithets that often precede the "blue-collar" adjective. The appropriate response to those epithets is that they are no more true than the "blue-collar" adjective. On almost any measure of political liberalism available in the surveys, Catholics are at the left end of the continuum, not far left perhaps but surely left of center. Thus in the middle 1980s, 60 percent of the Catholics, 50 percent of the white Protestants, and 67 percent of the Jews think too little money is being spent on the environment. Sixty-three percent of the Catholics, 62 percent of the Jews, and 54 percent of the white Protestants think that too little is being spent on government support for health care. Thirty-eight percent of the Catholics, 64 percent of the Jews, and 27 percent of the Protestants think that too much is being spent on arms. Eighteen percent of the Protestants, 19 percent of the Jews, and 22 percent of the Catholics oppose capital punishment. Forty-two percent of the Protestants and 52 percent of the Catholics and the Jews support open-housing ordinances. Twenty-four percent of the Catholics, 16 percent of the Protestants, and 12 percent of the Jews support school busing. Eighty-four percent of the Jews, 67 percent of the Catholics, and 59 percent of the white Protestants think that women are unqualified for politics.

Catholics also have higher scores than Protestants in opposition to gun control, in support for school integration (even in the North), in support for the legalization of marijuana, in support of disarmament, and in support of civil liberties.[15]

Despite the media stories about the "religious issue" (which usually these days means the abortion issue), according to political scientist Paul Lopatto, in only two Presidential elections since the Second World War has religion played an important role—elections in which religious groups departed from their historic voting patterns in greater proportion than the rest of the population. The first year was 1960, when Protestants defected from the Democratic Party (some of them never to return) and Catholics rallied to the Democratic Party over the issue of the first Catholic President. The net loss for Democrats in votes in the Kennedy election because of the candidate's religion was over 3 million votes (according to the study of the Survey Research Center at the University of Michigan).

The second year was 1972, when Catholics defected disproportionately from the Democratic Party to vote against George McGovern. According to Dr. Lopatto, this defection was especially puzzling because on the issues—peace and welfare—Catholics stood close to

---

[15] All these data are taken from the General Social Survey. The data sets are available from the Roper Center at the University of Connecticut if anyone wants to check my reporting.

McGovern. However, they objected to him personally. He sounded too much, in my judgment, like a self-righteous Protestant preacher.

Religion has not seriously affected any other Presidential elections—which does not mean that religious voting patterns are not important but that the patterns do not change at any greater rate than the overall national change in any given election. Catholics were less likely to vote for Carter, Mondale, and Dukakis than they were for Hubert Humphrey, but their lead over white Protestants in votes for these Democrats was the same as in the Humphrey/Nixon contest (in which 58 percent of Catholics voted for Humphrey).

It is difficult to find a single issue in American politics on which Catholics are not leaning in the liberal direction. They are not as far left as are Jews and/or blacks on some issues but they are surely left of center. In every county studied, Catholics are more likely to support government intervention in the economy and government welfare activities. They are conservative only in the sense that they are not at the very far left of the American political and social continuum, but that end is at the most 15 percent of the population. If the left-leaning moderates are to be rejected from your coalition then it has become a minority faction that is doomed to quadrennial defeat.[16]

They are conservative on abortion, screams the hard-line Harvard elitist. That isn't precisely true either. In fact the most conservative group in America on that issue are black Protestants.

And the most liberal ethnic group? Dare I say that it is the Irish who on virtually every issue are the most liberal Gentile group in the country—an assertion that is as counterintuitive to the academic and media elites as the assertion that they are also the most affluent and the best educated?

After Rich Daley won the Democratic mayoral primary, a TV reporter caught an elderly woman in Bridgeport (the Daley neighborhood) and asked her whether she was happy that Bridgeport was back in city politics. The answer was not what was expected.

---

[16] I have been beating this wild stallion for a long time. Among the pertinent articles which document my assertions in these paragraphs are "Attitudes Toward Racial Integration," with Paul Sheatsley, *Scientific American*, 225; "Political Attitudes Among American White Ethnics," *Public Opinion Quarterly*, 36:2; "Ethnicity and Racial Attitudes: The Case of the Jews and the Poles," *American Journal of Sociology*, 80:909–33; "How Conservative Are Catholic Americans?" *Political Science Quarterly*, 92:2; "Attitudes Toward Racial Integration," with D. Garth Taylor and Paul Sheatsley, *Scientific American*, 286:42–49; "School Desegregation and Ethnicity," in Walter G. Stephan and Joe R. Feagin (eds.), *School Desegregation* (New York: Plenunm, 1980).

"Yeah, well, he's probably won, but he's going to have to find a way to bring the colored into his coalition or he won't win again."

The instinct was both sound politics and sound ethics. The vocabulary left a little bit to be desired, but attitudes and insights are more important than the words with which they are expressed.

On the NORC feminism scale the highest scores are registered by Jewish women. Tied for second place are Jewish men, Irish women, and Irish men.[17]

As I draw toward the conclusion of this chapter, with the consolation that Rich Daley and Aurelia Puchinkski won even if Michael Dukakis lost, *The New York Times* exit poll tabulations appear. Forty percent of white Americans voted for Governor Dukakis, as did 47 percent of Catholics. (In 1980 the Democratic percentages were 36 percent and 42 percent, respectively, and in 1984, 35 percent and 45 percent: the Catholic defection was proportionate to the national average, in other words, and not excessive.)

If Governor Dukakis had received the votes of the sixteen percentage points of Catholics who voted for Democratic candidates for Congress but not for him, he and Vice President Bush would have run in a dead heat. This is a heavy price to pay for preconscious bigotry, for the "conservative blue-collar ethnic" stereotype.

The point here is that on the issues that are at the center of American political life, the Catholic Democrats who did not vote for him were Governor Dukakis's natural allies. He made no effort to reach out to them. What do I mean by effort? McGovern, Carter, Mondale, Dukakis—not one of them ever visited a Catholic school and praised the work that the priests and nuns and lay teachers do to provide quality education for the urban poor who are not even Cath-

---

[17] In *The New York Times* exit polls of the 1988 primaries, 9 percent of white Protestants, 12 percent of Jews, and 18 percent of Catholics were recorded as having voted for Jesse Jackson. This fact was reported in passing in a single sentence, with no further comment on what should have been an astonishing and exciting story. I wrote to *Times* editor Max Frankel suggesting that there might be an interesting story in further cross-tabulations to determine precisely who all those Catholics for Rev. Jackson were. I said that my guess, based on other research, would be that they were Irish-Catholic yuppies (also known as Yicups). Mr. Frankel, whom I had thought was a friend, did not deign to reply. If you observe that Catholics were twice as likely as Protestants and half again as likely as Jews to vote for Rev. Jackson and that those Catholics for Jesse might even be Irish, then clearly you're a crank whose mail can be tossed in a wastebasket.

I wondered whether Rev. Jackson's staff noticed the sentence in the *Times* story.

Is *The New York Times* newspaper, as Jimmy Breslin calls it, anti-Catholic? Or, in Breslin's explanation, is that merely the way things work out? On the basis of the information here, what do you think? Has unconscious bigotry blinded them to the facts and to a first-rate story?

olic. Candidates (and staffs) who do not think of that kind of painless and cost-free gesture don't deserve to win an election.

That they don't think of them is evidence to me that their pre-conscious or unconscious bigotry has blinded them to their natural allies. To some considerable extent the problem is imaginative. The Catholic political style is shaped by the analogical imagination or the Sacramental Imagination, as I will often call it for the rest of the book. American liberalism is a product of the dialectical imagination.

For the ideological ("knee-jerk," if you will) liberal, there are forces of light and forces of darkness in the political world. A stand with the forces of light on one liberally approved issue, such folk expect, ought to predict a similar stand on all issues. If you support open-occupancy ordinances you logically should support racial quo-tas and the Sandinistas. Society is evil and corrupt and only those with fervent belief can keep its wickedness at bay. The good liberal cannot compromise on any issue because that means one is compro-mising with sin.

The Sacramental Imagination tends to see the world in much grayer and problematic colors. Society is a sacrament, even if a flawed one. Opponents on one issue may well be allies on another. The relationships in a society require negotiation and compromise. No one has a monopoly on virtue and no one is totally a servant of vice. Decisions must be made pragmatically and empirically, issue by is-sue, and not as deductions from some overall program. Race riots to protect a changing neighborhood are wrong, but the people who live in such neighborhoods are confused and frightened—often with good reason.

To such an imagination—which affects many Catholics to some extent and some to a great extent—"self-righteous" ideologists like Mondale, McGovern, and Carter are abhorrent. They set the teeth of the Sacramental Imagination on edge. On the other hand, to the dedicated liberal who sees the whole of creation in left/right terms, the sacramental approach to social reality seems corrupt and evil. If you are not with us on everything, you are against us.

As I noted earlier, Catholic responses to political and value issues cannot be predicted on the basis of a left/right paradigm, but rather fit a model based on a different imagination of society. This "incon-sistency" is an affront to many liberals whose imagination is still dialectical even if their religion is no longer Protestant. The Catholic inconsistency from their viewpoint is immoral. Their rigid insistence on consistency, which does not seem to fit the complexity and the grayness of human society, appears to those who view the world from the perspective of the Sacramental Imagination as self-righteous and hypocritical (as in the case of suburban liberals who insist on the integration of neighborhood schools in the city but send their own children to almost all-white schools in the suburbs).

One would hope that there might be some effort from those with both political styles to try to understand one another, especially if they are part of the same political coalition. However, while the Sacramental Imagination forces you to listen to everyone, the dialectical forbids you to listen to sinners. If, as the knee-jerk liberal believes, blacks (and Hispanics and women and gays) are good, then white male ethnics are bad. Not only is there no need to try to understand the world from their perspective, it would be immoral to attempt to do so. In their division of humankind into the forces of light and the forces of darkness, Catholics fall in the latter category. The less you have to do with them the better. That way you remain pure, but you lose elections. You win moral victories, of course.

While there are lots of data to establish the fact that Catholics imagine political reality differently than do Protestants and differently than do liberals who are the heirs of the Protestant tradition of moral (or moralistic) politics, there is not much research on Catholic in administrative style, differences that may also cause conflict and misunderstanding across administrative lines.

Harvard Professor James Quinn Wilson, in his classic study of police officers, discovered that Irish cops, if they had a choice between formal and informal channels of communication, would invariably choose the latter. The reason, I submit, is that the Catholic imagination, respecting as it does the existing informal social networks as "natural," prefers them to the formal and usually artificial bureaucratic networks. The dialectical imagination, deeply suspicious of the sinful disorder in society, views formal bureaucratic process as a means to impose righteous order on sinful chaos.[18]

The Catholic social principle of subsidiarity—nothing should be done by a higher and larger social unit that can be done just as well by a smaller and lower unit—is but a philosophical formula that articulates a Catholic gut instinct based on the Sacramental Imagina-

---

[18] The Catholic Church is a bureaucracy, it will be said. Hence Catholics ought to like bureaucracies. But it is a very old-fashioned and inefficient bureaucracy in which informal communication links are much more important than formal links and in which the ultimate unit, the parish, has enormous freedom to do what it wants.

tion. It represents the way Catholic businessmen and administrators tend to work if they are given the opportunity.

Thus Cap Cities/ABC is administered by a small staff in a few offices on Fifty-first Street and Madison Avenue. I know of an integrated empire of companies worth billions of dollars, mostly picked up when they were about to expire and then turned around in a few months or a year or two by grass-roots administration, which is administered by four people. The secret of the cost-effectiveness of Catholic schools is that they dispense with the vast administrative staffs that are so heavy a burden to public education. The Catholic school systems, I submit, have small staffs not because they lack money but because Catholic administrators, in their gut and in their imagination, don't believe in them.

Despite their deviant imaginations, Catholics have become successful in America and the majority of them remain Democrats, even liberal Democrats, albeit pragmatic liberals and not ideological liberals. They have not turned conservative as they have moved to the suburbs. They are still concerned about neighborhood and family and still turned off by moralistic and self-righteous politics.

They are still an affront, it is much to be feared, to those who like neat left/right dichotomies and who don't believe that you can still be a Catholic and think for yourself.

Such bigotry doesn't hurt European Catholic ethnics much anymore (though parallel bigotry does hurt Hispanics). But it helps Democratic liberals to do what they now do better than anything else. Lose elections.

Just before I began to revise this chapter, I flew into Chicago from Tucson, where I teach at the University of Arizona the second semester of each year. It was only four days after the election and already a sign had appeared at O'Hare: WELCOME TO CHICAGO/RICHARD M. DALEY, MAYOR.

On my desk waiting for me was a book with a picture of a banner with the mayor's late father on it, a book about the end of Irish politics. Too bad about the Irish, wasn't it, especially since the mayor, the corporation counsel, the chairman of the Finance Committee, the chairman of the County Board, the assessor, the majority leader of the State Senate, the speaker of the State House, and the state attorney general were all Chicago Irish.

The book's argument was that with the end of patronage politics, the Irish "machine" (a metaphor the author never defined) had died.

It did not occur to him that Irish political culture was infinitely flexible when it came to adjusting to political change.

Oddly enough the same image of Catholics as on the fringes of American society is shared by many Catholic leaders and theologians. Cardinal Joseph Bernardin writes, "The Church of the future in this country will not be able to rely on general social support, the structures of popular culture or the kind of civic leverage formerly wielded by priests in Bing Crosby movies."[19]

And theologian Avery Dulles writes, "We have as yet very few eminent Catholic intellectuals on the national scene. Catholics, whether clerical or lay, are not prominent in science, literature, the fine arts or even, I think, in the performing arts and communications. We have all too few Catholic political leaders and statesmen with a clear apostolic vision and commitment."

The cardinal echoes this last point with his warning that in the future "the number of people who belong to the Church—really belong, not simply in a nominal or perfunctory way—will probably be fewer. . . ."

Note that I do not want to pick on either the cardinal or Father Avery. Both quotes are *obiter dicta* in otherwise excellent presentations. Nonetheless I think they represent a view of the state of the laity that is pervasive in the ecclesiastical institution.

William Kennedy, Walker Percy, Thomas Flanigan, Louise Erdrich, John Powers, J. F. Powers, John David Mooney, Mary Gordon, Thomas Clancy, Bruno Bartoletti, Kiri Te Kanawa, Rafael Kubelik, Sean Conlon, Charles Fanning, Peggy Noonan, Eugene McCarthy, Mario Cuomo, Dennis DeConcini, Thomas Foley, Richard M. Daley, Linda Ronstadt, David Tracy, Anna Quindlen, Seamus Heaney, Dan Rostenkowski, George Mitchell, Frank Patterson, Madonna, Elizabeth Shannon, Roland Murphy, Leo McCarthy, John Shea, Erma Bombeck, Edward Kennedy, Jordan Bonfonte, Kenneth Woodward, Daniel Patrick Moynihan, Raymond Brown, Kathleen Sullivan, Mary Cantwell, Thomas Doherty, Dan Herr, Michael Marsden, Bryant Gumbel, Thomas Murphy, James Burke, Maureen Howard, Roone Aldredge, Francis Ford Coppola, Brian Moore, Martin Scorsese, Martin Sheen, John Elston, Bruce Springsteen.

I could go on. So could lots of other people. It's not an exhaustive list. I probably have left off some Republicans.

You say some of those folk aren't Americans? Well, they live here

---

[19] This part of my analysis appeared originally in the magazine *America*.

and work here at least some of the time. If Mr. Heaney teaches at Harvard, I'm willing to count him as an American for the time he's there. If Maestro Bartoletti is musical director of the Lyric Opera in Chicago, why can't we count him as American for those months when the Lyric performs?

In the academic disciplines it is a little more difficult because one knows only one's own profession. In mine, Peter Rossi was president of the American Sociological Association, Reynolds Farley was president of the Population Association and chairman at Michigan, William D'Antonio is executive officer of the American Sociological Association, my coworker Michael Hout (still in his middle thirties) is chairman at Berkeley (come to think of it, I'm *his* coworker). Marta Tienda (Chicago) is sought by almost every department in the country. Terry Sullivan is deputy chair at Texas. Adrian Raftery (Washington) has developed a statistic (which he calls "bic," a nice manifestation of Irish wit) that has become enormously popular with those of us who use log-linear analysis.

Moreover, as I consult with colleagues at the University of Arizona in various departments, they all quickly spin off lists of names from their own professions in refutation of Father Dulles's argument, including his own Jesuit colleagues in the Vatican's Arizona unit (a unit led by Father George V. Coyne, sometime chairman of the Department of Astronomy and now director of the Specola Vaticana, and a student of Father Dulles a few years ago. The Vatican telescope will be the first one to be built at the new Mount Graham observatory—not bad!).

Since the Catholic move into the academy in large numbers began in the mid-1960s, most of the Catholic scholars are still young, under or around forty, and still not quite ready for the National Academy of Sciences or Nobel prizes. God willing, I'll live long enough to see Mike Hout and Ryn Farley (a graduate student when I was—and by the way an outstanding specialist on racial integration) become members of the National Academy of Sciences.

Some of these folks, it will be said, are not "good Catholics." At best they may be only "nominal or perfunctory," or even, perhaps by their own admission, "fallen away," as I am told Thomas Flanigan claims he is—as though you can ever exorcise the Catholic images from your creative imagination.[20] With all respect to the cardinal, I think that the state of their souls might better be left to God. They still identify as Catholic, no small matter given the behavior of the

---

[20] James Joyce did not; in fact, he didn't even try.

church leadership in recent years. Moreover, in many cases their work reflects Catholic vision.

Would the cardinal prefer Bing Crosby to William Kennedy or Louise Erdrich, *Going My Way* to *Ironweed* or *The Beet Queen?* I sure hope not.

Would Father Dulles deny that few if any Catholic leaders since Thomas More have understood the depths of Catholic social theory as well as Governor Cuomo—even if he does not take his orders from Cardinal O'Connor? I sure hope not.

Would Father Dulles say that absolutely first-rate social scientists like Professors Hout, Farley, Tienda, Sullivan, D'Antonio, and Raftery (to say nothing of distinguished astronomers like his Jesuit colleagues here in Arizona) are somehow not prominent in their professions? I trust not, because if he did he would be wrong.

All right, I've named names, but they're not typical. Catholics, the clerical mind argues, are still not adequately represented in any of the cultural and intellectual fields, are they?

In the NORC General Social Survey (almost 23,000 cases) a little less than 2 percent of Americans fall in the category of scholars, writers, performers, and artists. Catholics are no less likely than anyone else (save for Jews) to be in that 2 percent. Moreover, they are as likely to have Ph.D.s as anyone else. In addition they seem to be successful in these areas because they earn $5,000 more than the national average for this category. Finally, they may not have what Father Dulles defines as "clear apostolic vision," but they go to church far more often than do their colleagues who are not Catholic, *and also more often than typical Catholics.* About half of American Catholics go to Mass at least two or three times a month. Among those who fall in the artist-scholar-writer-performer category, 56 percent attend church regularly, a statistically significant difference (only 5 percent never attend Mass). Is this, *Eminenza,* merely "nominal or perfunctory" membership?

Not only are the Catholic cultural elites still Catholic, they tend to be devout Catholics.

If there are 40 million Catholic adults (a good rough estimate) there are almost a million Catholics who can make some claim to be part of the intellectual and cultural creative elites. More than half of them—perhaps half a million—regularly show up at Sunday (or Saturday evening) Mass.

Not bad. Has there ever been a larger or more devout elite? Why then are they literally invisible to the ecclesiastical institution?

First of all, the Catholic Church is still parish-oriented (to its enormous credit). While all the Catholics in the General Social Survey and in my lists are technically members of parishes and in many cases active members of parishes, they are viewed as parishioners and not as scholars or artists. When the National Federation of Priests Councils met in Tucson a number of years ago to discuss family relationships, Professor Hout was judged in the profession to be one of the most promising young demographers of his generation. Moreover, he and his wife (a painter) were active members of a progressive Paulist parish. But he was not perceived as someone who could make a critically important contribution to the study of the family.

John David Mooney lives in Chicago, a long stone's throw from Holy Name Cathedral. He is good enough to put sculpture on top of the Group W center in Beverly Hills and a wondrous aluminum and Waterford crystal sculpture (which he calls "Crystara"—and clearly she's an angel) in the atrium of the John Crerar Library at the University of Chicago. But the ecclesiastical institution in Chicago is not aware of his existence, and would surely never consider commissioning a work by him, not out of malice surely, but out of ignorance of his existence.

I suspect that these stories can be repeated a thousand, maybe ten thousand times, around the country: the parish is not (in its present configuration) capable of sensing its scholars and artists and their importance in the world.

Second, the kinds of laity with whom the clergy tend to be most comfortable are those who are still respectful and docile, those who do what we tell them to do, those who act as agents for the ecclesiastical institution.

Moreover, clergy seem to be threatened by scholars, artists, and writers. I cannot understand this phenomenon, but it seems to be a holdover from an era when the priest was the only educated person in the parish or at least the best-educated person. Somehow the brilliant lay person is perceived by some (many?) clergy as a threat to his position and authority. These bright, able, and successful people, in my experience, are especially likely to threaten bishops who still think that they are expected to know everything about everything.

"Intellectuals threaten me," a certain bishop remarked as I was driving him to a meeting. "I'm not as bright as they are."

"Don't worry," I told him. "*These* are nice intellectuals."

Later he admitted that they were indeed nice.

"The ones you met before must have been phonies," I assured him. "Real intellectuals don't have to threaten anyone."

Finally, one ought not to underestimate the importance of what Max Scheler called *ressentiment*—more bluntly, envy. There is a curious twist in clerical culture which leads us to resent and to demean those who are most successful. All too many priests have been willing to tell me bad things about some of the folk on my list, assertions that in certain cases I know to be totally false.

We're pretty good at dealing with head ushers, presidents of the Saint Vincent De Paul Society and the Altar Guild, and CCD teachers (all of whom I hasten to add are admirable and necessary people); but authors, political leaders, artists, scientists, performers—they scare the daylights out of us and make us envious.

In fact, everyone is important to the Church. The proper issue for the elites is not what the Church can do for them, but what they can do for the service of the Good News and how the Church can sustain and help them in that service.

Let me take as an example two books by authors who are in one way or another Catholic—*Ironweed* and *The Beet Queen*. Both books are profoundly Catholic in environment, people, rhetoric, and especially vision. They are Catholic classics in the making, books (and in the case of *Ironweed* a film, too) that have an enormous impact on those who read them and an impact that cannot help being Catholic. They are powerful instruments of "evangelization"—not because they win converts to the Catholic Church (and users of Sunday envelopes) but because they illumine, however implicitly, a deeply Catholic worldview. Meryl Streep's prayer to Saint Joseph (the Catholic patron of a happy death, if anyone still remembers) in the film version of *Ironweed* is a masterpiece of Catholic imagination (in case you are in any doubt about it, read William Kennedy's comment on the same scene in his novel—she was searching, in a way, for grace).

Yet are these books read in Catholic high schools and colleges? Are the authors studied in serious articles in Catholic journals of opinion? Are they treasured as persons who are making an enormous contribution to the work of passing on the Good News?

Of course not. Rather they are ignored.

In their own parishes?

I don't know. Maybe they're lucky.

In another era they would be valued. Their works would be commissioned by popes and religious orders. In ours their existence is denied. The reason for the pretense is that the ecclesiastical institution does not know what to do with this elite. Certainly it is not about to listen to them, much less to read them or learn from them. Father Dulles and Cardinal Bernardin are not all that different in their perceptions of American Catholics from Professor Galbraith.

I reflect again on the parties in Rich Daley's suite on the three election nights of the last twelve months. Not a conservative blue-collar ethnic in the room. A lot of Democrats, most of them pragmatic liberals, all, I think, with some version of the Sacramental Imagination or they wouldn't have been there. Most of them would have been utterly unwelcome at a real liberal Democratic gathering. They're the kind of folk that Professor Galbraith left off his list. Until the national party puts them and those like them back on the list, the Democrats will keep right on losing.

5

SEX AND FAMILY

N THE SUMMER OF 1976, Joseph Bernardin, archbishop of Cincinnati and president of the National Conference of Catholic Bishops, and I were sitting over drinks (nonalcoholic on both sides of the table) in the Seven Continents bar at O'Hare International Airport. The archbishop, whom I would then have described as a friend, had phoned me at my summer hideout in Grand Beach, Michigan, and invited me to join him for a conversation. It was a two-hour ride from Grand Beach to O'Hare and the temperature was in the middle nineties. The cardinal and I had been featured in opposite corners on a page in *Time* as part of a cover story on our research about the impact of the birth-control encyclical.[1] He had issued a statement as president of the hierarchy which questioned the report and said that in any event the Catholic Church did not make moral decisions on the basis of surveys (implying that my colleagues and I had suggested that it should, a notion we had explicitly excluded).

The conversation was pleasant enough, much of it, as I recall, devoted to the bizarre behavior of the then-archbishop of Chicago, John Cardinal Cody, a subject on which both of us could have talked for days.[2]

Surely, I thought, Joe has not summoned me here merely to talk about Cody. Finally, when the conversation lagged, he began, somewhat uneasily, to talk about our research and his statement.

---

[1] *Catholic Schools in a Declining Church*, with William McCready and Kathleen McCourt (Andrews and McMeel, 1976).

[2] For example, one of his wishes was a Dick Tracy–like wrist TV so that he could supervise and talk to every priest in the archdiocese whenever he wished.

"I had to say those things," he said, "because I'm president of the Conference and the Holy See expects me to issue statements like that. But I want you to know that you're right. I have a hard time sleeping at night because of the terrible harm that goddamn encyclical is causing in my archdiocese."

The cardinal now denies ever having said that. The language he insists is not the sort he normally uses. I quite agree, which is one of the reasons I was so astonished by his comment.

In fact, most American bishops are very well aware that their laity do not observe the birth-control encyclical and that their clergy make no attempt to enforce it. Nonetheless, they must pretend for the public record to keep the Vatican happy that the encyclical is accepted and that Pope John Paul II's attempts to reinforce it during the last decade have been successful.

The encyclical *Humanae Vitae*, issued in the summer of 1968, is the most important event of the last twenty-five years of Catholic history for two reasons. Unlike the changes of the Vatican Council, which had only marginal impact on the lives of the Catholic laity, the encyclical endeavored to reach into the bedroom of every Catholic married couple in the world. Moreover, in their response to it, many of the most devout Catholic laity (especially of Irish and Polish backgrounds) for the first time deliberately disobeyed the pope. The fact that they did so and were not greatly troubled afterwards prepared them for a future in which increasingly they would make their own decisions on moral and religious matters and yet continue to participate as active Catholics. At the present time Catholics are even more likely than Protestants to insist on conscience as the ultimate norm of moral action (a position that, by the way, the old Catholic moral theology books also taught, though they would have expected obedience to authority to be a decisive part of the formulation of conscience). The birth-control encyclical occasioned an experience of emancipation for the most devout of American Catholics—exactly the opposite of Pope Paul VI's intention.

A number of observations must be made to clarify what happened and what did not happen. Catholics did not start practicing birth control in the late 1960s. Quite the contrary: the various national fertility studies done at the University of Michigan and Princeton had reported that even in the 1950s and early 1960s almost all Catholic women eventually practiced some kind of fertility control to which the Church would object—usually at that point at which they decided they had produced enough children. They did not think it wrong if after four or five or six or seven children they felt they had honored their Catholic ethics sufficiently. In the first NORC Catholic study in 1963, 50 percent of American Catholics did not think birth control was wrong (about the same proportion did not disapprove of divorce).

My colleague Ellen Skeritt has suggested that during the Great Depression, the relatively small size of Catholic families indicates that some sort of fertility control was taking place and that folklore from that era suggests that many married couples were practicing contraception and as a result not receiving Holy Communion.

The biological and demographic origins of the problem are that the human reproductive systems evolved to facilitate the continuation of the race, that is, the replacement of the man and woman by two adult children who would in turn begin their own reproductive cycle. For most of human history—to the early part of the last century in Western Europe and North America (on the average) and in Eastern and Southern Europe almost to the dawn of this century—the production of two children who would live to adulthood required 7.2 live births per married woman. Today 7.2 live births mean eight children, most of them teenagers at the same time and all of them candidates for college educations.

The second source of difficulty is that the human reproductive urges are extremely powerful and can be resisted over a long period of time only by those with extraordinary motivation and compensatory reward systems.

The third difficulty is that one stream of Catholic theology has traditionally thought that sexual pleasure (a dubious pleasure at best) is justified only by procreation. Sexual pleasure without procreation had been considered a sinful concession to the weakness of human flesh. This notion, inherited especially through the writings of Augustine, virtually denies any bonding function to sexual love. It is "natural" in this truncated natural law theory to engage in sexual intercourse to produce children. It is unnatural to engage in it for pleasure. That the pleasure might promote love and reinforce the bonding of the man and the woman so that they might stay together to raise the child (the obvious rationale behind the evolution of specifically human sexuality as compared with that of the other high primates) is not an idea that occurred to many theologians or church leaders.

More than anyone else, Augustine's dualism is responsible for the dialectical imagination. His pessimism and his torments over his own sexual failings have cast a pall over Western Christianity for fifteen hundred years. Even though other theologians (most notably Saint Thomas) and the Church's marriage liturgies took a very different view, Augustine's theories persisted. They were finally refuted (though not explicitly) by Pope John Paul II in his audience talks on human sexuality. Note that if humankind's urgent sexual needs are sinful in themselves and legitimated only by procreation, then women—who stir up such needs in men—are, to use the words of medieval spiritual writers, swamps of vice and traps Satan has designed to enslave the souls of men. Augustine was surely one of the great geniuses of Catholic history. But his sexual attitudes have done enormous harm. Moreover, his shabby treatment of his concubine when he decided to give up sexual pleasure shows him to be a chauvinist and a cad. It will not do to say, as Augustine's admirers argue, that his behavior must be judged in the context of his times. At no time and in no culture is it justified for a follower of Jesus to treat another human being that way. The "saint" before his name seems to me to be inappropriate.

The healing and bonding power of intercourse is, needless to say, one of its most obvious effects for every married couple. While church authorities came eventually to admit that the "fomenting of love" was a valid goal of marital relations, it insisted that it was a secondary goal and indeed that it could be enjoyed only when there was no impediment to conception.[3] The continued insistence that

[3] Classic natural law theory was empirical. Saint Thomas Aquinas contended that third-level natural law principles—the practical applications of such norms as "thou shalt not steal"—were to be learned from observation of the practices of the *Gentes*—the nations. The details of the nature of human nature, in other words, were to be determined by the study of human nature in action. Occasionally Catholic leaders and thinkers pay lip service to the importance of the human sciences in the study of human nature. But in fact, quite at variance with the Catholic tradition and the natural law tradition, the Church's natural law theories today are almost entirely deductive—a corruption indeed of the natural law tradition. When one tells church leaders that the human sciences have established beyond any reasonable doubt that what is specifically human about human sexuality (as compared with that of the other higher primates) is designed—was selected by the evolutionary process—for bonding and not for procreation, they are distinctly uninterested. Such an idea, one told me, will never fly in the Holy See.

Well, I guess that settles that. Truth from the human sciences is only valid and valuable when Vatican bureaucrats are prepared to accept it.

A higher primate can procreate with a good deal less fuss than sex involves for us humans. Once in a given period of time the female goes into heat and the male is aroused. At other times, there is no sexual preoccupation. The agonies and the joys of human eroticism—at practically any time—are not required for procreation, but they are required to sustain the link between the male and the female so that they might remain together and rear their offspring. In this context, the Church's praise for men and women who forsake the sexual pleasures of marriage almost sounds like a violation of the natural law.

procreation was the *primary* purpose of sex devalued all other purposes, as if procreation and bonding, which is essential to continue procreation in the rearing and education of the human child, can ever be separated save in the mind of a celibate Vatican bureaucrat.

If you have as many children as you want or can take care of or your health permits or you can support financially, you should either practice rhythm (which was then and continues to be unsatisfactory in many respects) or, as many confessors said, sleep in different bedrooms. If married couples gave up sex by mutual agreement, it was counted high virtue. No one seemed to hear the lay people saying that sexual love was essential to heal the frictions and the frustrations and renew married love.

There were ways around the problem for a lay person if s/he found a sympathetic confessor. The moral theology books said that a spouse could consent to contraceptive intercourse if the other partner insisted and the sex was essential to prevent the marriage from breaking up and the unwilling partner remained "passive."

Did that mean, our moral theology professor at the seminary asked, that the unwilling partner could not enjoy what was happening? Don't be ridiculous, he answered his own question. How can one not enjoy it?

I have the impression that rather few priests used this escape hatch until the mid-1960s. By that time, the clergy had changed their mind. Along with the devout laity (the half that was still inclined to think that maybe birth control was wrong) they began to ask the not-illegitimate question "What does the Vatican know about married love?"

Two factors caused the increase of this question—the increase in educational attainment and occupational success among Catholics and the development of the birth-control pill.

Those two factors would have led to a slow erosion of lay (and lower clerical) acceptance of the official birth-control teaching in any case. But the peculiar dynamics of the situation in the late 1960s made the turnaround almost instantaneous and virtually destroyed the credibility of the Church as a sexual teacher for its own people—exactly the opposite of the intent of Pope Paul VI.

Pope John XXIII had established a commission to investigate the problem, most likely with the intent to change the teaching. To keep birth control off the floor of the Vatican Council, Pope Paul VI expanded the commission and seemed, in his vacillating, Hamlet-like fashion, also to be leaning toward a change.

For the laity who had already switched from rhythm to the pill and for the clergy, caught up in the euphoria of the Council and the years immediately after it, the fact that a change could be considered meant that the doctrine was not unchangeable. Therefore, they concluded, it would be changed. Catholic conservatives ranted that this was not so, that the commission *had* to decide in favor of the continuation of the traditional teaching, but no one listened.

Why wait? the laity demanded. We want to love one another tonight, not in five years. Do you think it wrong, the clergy asked, hinting broadly that if the married couple said something like "no, not really," they would be given an implicit signal to go ahead. The priests and lay people who were making these decisions were strengthened in their choices when the report of the majority of the commission was leaked to the press. It provided powerful and persuasive arguments for change.

The pope hesitated and procrastinated, vacillated and fretted. The curial old guard preyed on his sensitive conscience and warned him that he was betraying Jesus Christ. Finally, after several years of waiting, the encyclical was issued, apparently because the pope was firmly persuaded that the laity would respond to his apostolic authority. It did not address itself to the reasons his own commission had offered for change. Rather he dismissed them and reaffirmed the traditional doctrine as "the teaching of Christ."

But it was too late. If the pope had intended no change, he should never have assembled the commission. However, the nature of his personality precluded such decisive action. He locked the farm door after the horse had escaped. The birth-control teaching had been honored for decades only in the English-speaking world. (Now even the devout Catholics in those countries [including eventually even Ireland] with the tentative support of their priests.) The encyclical's only practical effect was to confirm and indeed increase opposition to the birth-control teaching and, as noted before, it led to a sharp and sudden decline in Catholic practices.

The laity had already made up their minds that the pill and later all forms of birth control were morally acceptable. They were not going to change their minds because a celibate in Rome told them to do so. Some of them in anger diminished their church attendance and, as we shall see, their Sunday contribution. Hardly any left the Church.

There are no data to enable one to know for sure, but the decision to stay in, remain an active Catholic, and continue birth control did not seem to trouble too many lay people in 1968. The moral agony and the decision had already been made between 1965 and 1968.

The more serious impact of the encyclical was on the clergy and the religious. The encyclical was a shocking disappointment. The ruling would not affect our lives directly but it told us that the forces of reaction were back in power in Rome. The conciliar forces of reform had lost. Resignations from the priesthood, a trickle before 1968, suddenly surged. The hope stirred by the Vatican Council died that summer, never to be born again in the lifetimes of many of us. The permanent morale crisis of the clergy had begun.

In the mind of those who swayed the pope at the end, sex was not the issue. They feared rather the loss of power. A change on this issue, they warned, would weaken the prestige and the influence of the papacy. They could not have been more wrong. More than three decades earlier, a similar Vatican power ploy had persuaded Pius XI at the last minute to include an explicit condemnation of birth control in his encyclical on Christian marriage—to teach the Anglicans a lesson because they had reversed themselves at the Lambeth Conference several years before.[4] Not to have done so, the conspirators warned him, just as their successors had warned Paul VI, would weaken the influence and the prestige of the Church. As one of my theologian friends would remark, to mess around with the intimate lives of men and women to protect your own power is demonic.

The teaching of *Humanae Vitae* is the official, if not infallible, teaching of the Catholic Church and must be treated with respect. It is not the task of a sociologist to discuss the moral theology of such a document. His role is rather to report the results of the encyclical. The latter can be summed up quite simply: the laity and the junior clergy did not listen and the Vatican's credibility as a teacher of sexual ethics was badly weakened.

The so-called sexual revolution of the next decade swept America. The Catholic Church had deprived itself of any ability to respond. No one took it seriously on sexual matters anymore, not even its own members, not even the devout ones.

---

[4] In the nineteenth and early twentieth centuries the clergy were counseled repeatedly not to trouble the conscience of the laity on these matters. Birth control was not approved, but neither was it loudly condemned. No attempts were made by confessors to raise the subject with their penitents. Leo XIII wrote his encyclical on marriage at the time France was solving its population explosion with *coitus interruptus*—as he was informed repeatedly by the French hierarchy. He deliberately chose to ignore the issue. The later encyclicals of Pius XI and Paul VI are a reversal not of the teaching itself but of the policy on how vigorously to push the teaching on the laity and the lower clergy.

In 1986 only 22 percent of American Catholics thought that premarital sex was always wrong (34 percent for Protestants), down from 32 percent in the early seventies. Forty-five percent thought it was never wrong (as opposed to 36 percent of Protestants), an increase from 30 percent in the previous decade. Eighty-seven percent of American Catholics and 86 percent of American Protestants approved of birth-control information for teenagers. On the other hand, there had been no change in Catholic opposition to extramarital sex (71 percent saying it was always wrong), homosexuality (69 percent disapproving), and abortion. In all of these matters, however, there was little difference between Catholics and Protestants.

In 1963, 88 percent of the Catholics surveyed in the first NORC Catholic school study thought that premarital sex was always wrong. In the 1988 General Social Survey that number had fallen to 18 percent as opposed to 34 percent for Protestants. The difference between Catholics and Protestants in attitudes toward premarital sex is now statistically significant: Protestants are almost twice as likely to disapprove. That change is conclusive evidence, if any is needed, of the utter collapse of the Church's credibility as a teacher of sexual ethics.

By the 1980s, Catholics were more likely to approve of premarital and extramarital sex and homosexuality than Protestants and were not statistically different from Protestants in their attitudes toward various abortion situations. If, however, race is taken into account, white Protestants are significantly more likely than black Protestants to approve of abortion. Thus 91 percent of white Protestants and 84 percent of black Protestants approve of abortion when the woman's health is in danger; and 30 percent of black Protestants and 42 percent of white Protestants approve of abortion if the woman wants no more children. When this tabulation is used, white Protestants are significantly more likely to approve of abortion than Catholics, and black Protestants significantly less likely.

One almost never hears, incidentally, of black opposition to abortion. It is never said that such opposition excludes blacks from the liberal coalition. Opposition to abortion among blacks apparently means something less to good liberals than opposition among Catholics.

Nonetheless, two observations are in order. First, most Americans of whatever religion do not fit in either the pro-choice or the pro-life camp. Second, there are no striking differences between Catholics and other Americans in attitudes toward abortion. The statistics cited above also indicate that Pope John Paul II's efforts to "turn around" Catholics on issues of sexual morality have not been successful. As my colleague Tom W. Smith has argued, the extent of the sexual revolution and its impact—as well as the alleged turn-around in morality because of AIDS—has been exaggerated.

The birth-control pill has made divorce easier and premarital sex more acceptable. But both the divorce rates and approval of premarital sex have stabilized. There has been little change in attitudes toward extramarital or homosexual relations. Moveover, attitudes on abortion have remained stable, as have attitudes toward pornography.

While there have been increases in the last few years in opposition to extramarital sex and homosexual relations, these increases have been only of a few percentage points, suggesting that, save perhaps among target groups, the AIDS epidemic has had less impact than mass media reports would indicate.

Ninety-five percent of married Americans have had no more than one sexual partner during the last year. Eighty-eight percent of all Americans, 82 percent of all sexually active Americans, and 68 percent of all unmarried sexually active Americans have had no more than one partner. Promiscuity seems to be concentrated among the young (under twenty-five) and the never married, and especially among the young, never-married men. After twenty-five and after marriage, Americans become monogamous (at least for a year's duration). While the questions about sexual partners have been administered in only one General Social Survey and hence detailed analysis of the behavior of various Catholic age groups cannot be analyzed, there is little preliminary data to indicate that Catholic behavior is different from Protestant behavior: virginity is rare (though not non-existent) among those under twenty-five and promiscuity is rare among those over twenty-five.

The picture of American sexual behavior does not fit easily into the categories of revolution and reaction. Most Americans now accept premarital sex. Most reject extramarital sex and homosexuality. Most Americans are monogamous most of the time, especially after their twenty-fifth birthday. Most approve of the availability of abortion when the mother's health is in danger, after rape, and when there is a danger of a defective child. Most reject it when it is merely another form of birth control. Catholics are in these matters not greatly different from other Americans.

In sexual matters, the Church has lost its ability to demand effectively different attitudes and behavior from its members. They assume that the leadership does not know what it is talking about on this subject and do not listen. It accomplishes nothing for the Catholic right to insist, as they often do when I report that finding, that Catholics *must* listen. Perhaps they should but in fact they don't. All the bellowing of the right and all the insistence of the Vatican do not change the situation.

"What do they know about the way my husband and I reconcile after a quarrel?" an angry Catholic wife demanded of me. "If we couldn't go to bed together, we would have broken up long ago. And, damn it, we deeply love each other. Those celibates don't know what it's like to love a man and not be able to make love with him."

I don't think celibacy is the problem. Celibate parish priests understand her cry. Rather the problem is the arrogance of power that makes many church leaders insensitive to the problems of ordinary people and heedless of their needs—and of the Holy Spirit speaking through their experiences.

It is this perceived insensitivity, often parading as an exhortation about the "need to sacrifice," which has cost Catholic leadership its influence on the sexual attitudes of its people. Until the pope and the hierarchy are perceived as sensitive and open to the experience of the married laity, that influence will never be recaptured.

I'm not arguing that this is the way the laity *should* react. I am merely saying that it is the way they *do* react.

American Catholics also have been affected by the so-called divorce revolution, in large part the result of the greater control women have over their fertility because of the pill, giving them greater access to employment. In the early seventies 24 percent of Protestants, 16 percent of Catholics, and 10 percent of Jews had been divorced. In the mid-1980s the figures had risen to 34 percent for Protestants, 27 percent for Catholics, and 24 percent for Jews. Half of the divorced men, only a third of the divorced women, and only a fifth of divorced Catholic women have remarried.

Recent scholarship has demonstrated[5] that divorce is a much greater hardship for women than for men: the standard of living for divorced men increases, while for divorced women it decreases. Unmarried people are much less happy, the data show, than married people; and it is much easier for a divorced man to remarry than for a divorced woman. On the average, divorce is much better for men

[5] See, for example, *The Divorce Revolution*, by Lenore Weitzman (New York: Free Press, 1985).

than for women—which is precisely what the forgotten Catholic family ethic would have predicted.

Of the women born in the 1950s (hence from twenty-eight to thirty-eight years old at this time), 40 percent are not married: half have never married and the other half are divorced or separated. The Catholic total is the same, although 12 percent of the unmarried Catholic women in the 1950 cohort are divorced or separated and 29 percent have never married.

The morale of unmarried women is about half as high as that of married women (and men)—17 percent saying they are "very happy" as opposed to 36 percent of the married. Thus the radical feminist myth of the "woman of the eighties" who is happy "on her own" is so much nonsense. One can support feminism (as I do and as most Catholics do) and still say that some of the social changes in the name of "sexual revolution" and "feminism" have had the unintended (but perhaps easily anticipated) consequences of victimizing women. When men can obtain easy sex from a woman without having to marry her, there will be fewer marriages, with resultant unhappiness for women. Moreover, since a woman's years of prime opportunity in the marriage market are more limited than those of men, the postponement of marriage for women has a much higher cost than it does for men. Finally, can anyone seriously argue that the breakup of a sustained premarital relationship causes no more pain for the woman than it does for the man?

My colleague (and boss at NORC) Bob Michael has evidence that most cohabitation relationships (actually living in the same dwelling) are rather brief and are intended as a "trial run" at marriage, especially by those who because of divorce in their own family are wary of marriage. Obviously these relationships are less harmful potentially than those that go on for many years and then end in separation. Moreover, they are also a useful technique for punishing your parents. Nonetheless, can anyone seriously claim that, on the average, there is no difference in cost or in pain between the woman and the man when such relationships terminate short of marriage? The evidence that the "sexual revolution" victimizes women is increasingly irrefutable, although feminist ideologues are still reluctant to accept the facts.

The Catholic Church, which could have predicted this outcome and did in fact predict it (usually in traditional terms that meant nothing to anyone except bishops, if to them), lost all of its credibility because even its own membership (even its own clergy) felt that the celibates in the Vatican understood nothing about the relationship between men and women in marriage.

Professor Mary Ann Glendon of Harvard University has argued that if law is the story society tells about itself (a conclusion drawn by Clifford Geertz in a theory that law is a culture system), the divorce and abortion laws in America tell a story of a society in which self-fulfillment has tended to replace responsibility to and for others—with potentially horrendous social consequences.[6]

The picture is mixed—high divorce rates, high promiscuity rates among the young (700,000 young men, according to NORC estimates, have had more than ten sexual partners in the last year), high abortion rates. On the other hand, monogamy rates are high, too, and opposition to easy divorce and extramarital sex has increased.

Catholicism, whose family ethic anticipated some of the problems that might have followed from the ready availability of inexpensive and efficient fertility control and easy divorce, has not made any effective contribution to the discussion because it has lost its credibility, even with its own members. If the leadership of the Church does not understand how important sexual love is in marriage, the argument goes, then it has nothing meaningful to say about any kind of sexual behavior.

The argument may be a non sequitur (or it may not be), but it is the argument that has carried the day.

The development of a positive Catholic approach to sexuality based on the images of human love as a sacrament of divine love—an approach for which there are rich resources in the tradition—does not seem possible as long as the Vatican continues merely to repeat negative rules, the theologians sulk, and the laity and the lower clergy do not listen.[7]

It does not follow from this melancholy analysis of the decline of the Catholic Church's effectiveness as an ethical teacher that the pope should not have issued *Humanae Vitae*. It merely follows that Catholic leadership ought not to deceive itself.

My own position on birth control can be summarized as follows:

[6] *Abortion and Divorce in Western Law: American Failures, European Challenges* (Cambridge: Harvard University Press, 1987).

[7] My theologian sister Mary Jule Durkin and I have tried to propose such a theory in our *How to Save the Catholic Church*. She and Joan Anzia, M.D. (a psychiatrist), have constructed an effective paradigm for such a spirituality in *Marital Intimacy* (Chicago: Loyola University Press, 1982). Doctor Durkin has written the only commentary in English on the pope's audience talks on human sexuality: *Feast of Love* (Chicago: Loyola University Press, 1983).

Along with Archbishop John Raphael Quinn of San Francisco (speaking at a meeting of the Synod of Bishops in Rome), I believe the issue should be reconsidered. I also hold, with Pope John Paul II, that in such matters the married lay people, by virtue of the charism of the Sacrament of Matrimony, have a unique and indispensable contribution to make to the Church's understanding of sex and marriage.[8] Finally, I agree with the pope that while social surveys are a useful way of making determinations about the *sensus fidelium* they are not the only way of approaching that *sensus* (through which God, according to Catholic theology, speaks every bit as much as S/He does through the institutional Church—or, to use the Lutheran word that obsesses bishops these days, the Magisterium).

If, as many Americans seem to believe, Catholicism is little more than a code of sexual rules, then it would seem that there is little left to Catholicism in the United States that would distinguish it from other American religions—a somewhat lower divorce rate (three-quarters of American Catholics who are married are still married to their first spouse) but not much else.

How is Catholic marriage and family different from that of anyone else? Does the Sacramental Imagination make any difference in family life?

If Catholics are more likely to imagine God as present in society and social networks to be sacraments, however flawed, of God's presence, then one would expect Catholic family networks to be more intense. The family, after all, is the most intimate social network, the one that is most likely to disclose the intimate presence of God.

Indeed it was precisely the intensity of Catholic family networks that Emile Durkheim argued had created the constraints that prevented suicide and that Max Weber saw as inhibiting social and educational achievement.

The prediction is sustained by reports of frequency of visiting and phoning family members. Catholics are more likely than white Protestants to visit with and phone their fathers, their mothers, their brothers, their sisters, their sons, and their daughters than are white Protestants, and by substantial margins. Nor is this phenomenon merely a function of the fact that Catholics tend to live closer to relatives than Protestants. Quite the contrary: the differences persist

---

[8] Perhaps, unlike the pope, I don't believe that such a contribution has in fact been made.

between Catholics and Protestants even among those who live close to their relatives. Nor do the differences decline in the slightest when we consider only Catholics under forty. Catholic family networks are more intense than Protestant family networks for young as well as old.

While child-rearing values (according to an analysis by Duane Alwin of GSS data) have converged, expectations of family relationships have not. Both groups sustain fairly high levels of family communication. But the Catholic levels are significantly higher than Protestant levels and do not seem to be affected by the passage of time.

Twenty-four percent of those who go to Mass at least two or three times a month call their mother every day and 17 percent call their father every day. The percentages for those who go less regularly are 15 percent and 8 percent, respectively. Fifty-seven percent of the regular church attenders call their sister at least once a week, while forty-one percent of those who do not attend Mass regularly make a similar call. Thirty-seven percent of the regular Mass attenders call their brothers every week as opposed to 29 percent of those who are not so regular in their churchgoing.

The family networks based on a Catholic imagination of society are thus intensified by frequent participation in Catholic liturgy (or perhaps vice versa).

Weber and Durkheim were right about stronger ties within Catholic families. They were both wrong, however, in thinking that such times were a necessary obstacle to either social and economic success or personal freedom.

Catholic sexual behavior, with the exception of somewhat lower divorce rates (although a quarter of the Catholics in the country have been divorced), is not distinguishable from that of other Americans. But Catholic family networks are sharply different. Propositional religion may have diminished—at least in its manifestation as sexual ethics—but the imaginative underpinnings do not seem to have changed at all. Catholics not only imagine God and society and the political order differently. They also appear to imagine family life differently and to imagine it in a fashion that makes for more frequent and presumably warmer relationships.

The repressive attitude toward married sex that affects the Vatican is a perversion of the genius of the Sacramental Imagination, a perversion that probably can be blamed on Augustine. There are two possible interpretations of the powerful sexual drives in human nature. The first is that they are sinful, and tolerable only because they produce children. The second is that God is present in human passion as S/He is in all of creation and hence it is sacramental.[9] The second is the one that Catholicism now accepts in theory and that it accepted in its liturgical practices for most of its history. The first assumes that God made human nature evil—a classic posture for the dialectical imagination. Catholicism rejects this theory in principle but has followed it for centuries in its moral practice. The Vatican, following Augustine, still thinks that what a man and woman feel when they lie side by side in bed at night is somehow perverse and cannot be enjoyed unless they intend to make the act in which they are engaging procreative. While this position is propounded as the "teaching of Jesus" it is difficult to find any basis in Scripture for such an assertion.[10]

The instincts of married people, in this case better informed by the Sacramental Imagination, tell them that what they feel toward each other at that moment is essential for healing and bonding their love and cannot be sinful. To them and their insights, alas, the Vatican is not listening, despite the pope's remark that their contribution is unique and indispensable.

If one had to choose, which would be better—a Catholic population that honored the sexual teaching or a Catholic population that maintained its more active family networks? In the short run church leaders would surely vote for the former—the alternative that would keep the Vatican happy. But in the long run the more active, more intense, and more appealing style of Catholic family life may hold men and women in the Church in time of crisis or lead them back in after a period of drift. Moreover, it may also sustain those most fundamental Catholic instincts that God is present, not absent; that human relationships are sacramental, not oppressive; and that intense human intimacy reflects God's intimacy with us. Are these insights more or less important than the birth-control teaching?

I fear many of the leadership would say "less" in answer to that question, some because they really believe it, others because that's

---

[9] I will return to the "sacramentality" of human eroticism later in this book.

[10] Jesus was much less interested in problems of sex than contemporary religious leaders. His major intervention in the matter was to declare the equality of men and women. Before his time men did not "commit adultery" against their wives when they were unfaithful. Their offense, such as it may have been, was against the husband of the other woman. Jesus abolished that casuistry when he said that men and women who are unfaithful to each other both commit adultery.

what Rome wants to hear. They don't seem to comprehend that if you still have the appeal of warm and intense community you may eventually be able to recapture your credibility when you try to teach sexual ethics. However, if you are an ethical teacher without a community that listens, are you still really Catholic?

6

HOW MANY?
WHO LEAVES?
WHO STAYS?

Y CLASSMATES told me long ago in the seminary that I was obsessed with numbers.

"What good are all those statistics?" they would demand.

"You win arguments with them," I would reply.

"What good does that do?"

"If the arguments are about the condition of Catholicism, they mean a lot to our work after we're ordained."

"We'll be curates all our lives. We'll do what the pastor tells us to do."

Thus is the importance of accurate information dismissed as an obsession with numbers. In fact, my mathematical skills are severely limited. I don't like math much either. Statistics are important to me not as an end in themselves, as I would try to explain in subsequent years and decades, but as a means to knowledge, and action-oriented knowledge at that.

When one is told for forty years that there is a continued drift away from the Catholic Church, is it not important to ask what proportion of Americans are Catholics and whether that proportion has changed?

No one really knows for sure and no one seems to care. In one of my less successful ventures I tried with the help of the *Official Catholic Directory* to calculate the population by collecting age-specific death information. The technique is simple: if you know the age- and gender-specific deaths of a population, you merely multiply those numbers by the inverse of the age- and gender-specific death rates and you have a reliable estimate of the population by age and gender. You then know, if you're working on a religious population, how large the group is that at least wants burial in your churches.

You can also do the same thing with births if you find out the mother's age at birth. You multiply that number by the age-specific birth rates and you have an estimate of the population in child-bearing years or baptism-seeking years. The latter numbers are more difficult to collect from Catholic parishes because there is no requirement as part of the baptismal ceremony to record parental age. But the former numbers are readily available. All the pastor has to do when he is filling in his form for the *Official Catholic Directory* is consult his death register, which provides the name and age of every person buried from the parish. It would require no more than five minutes to fill out the form and possibly less than that.

When the staff of the *OCD* mailed out the form with the request for age- and gender-specific deaths, it provided a careful explanation of what the numbers would be used for and why it is important to estimate the number of Catholics in a state or a region. When this was done, my name was not used, lest it offend clerics who don't like me.

Only a quarter of the pastors in the country returned the form. I suppose the task was harder than we had anticipated: they might have been forced to buzz the secretary or even, heaven help us, go down-stairs to the parish office to check the book. One certainly does not want a pastor to do too much work.

"You're obsessed with numbers," someone who knew of my interest in the project said to me. "What difference does it make how many Catholics there are?"

I think my activities are sufficiently well known so as to establish that I have other interests besides numbers. Moreover, how can any organization plan for its future or deal with its present problems unless it knows its own size?

What difference does it make if you have 60 million people instead of 52 million? I don't think you're obsessive about numbers if you believe that it is an important question. To put the matter differently, only a fool thinks that a difference of 8 million in membership is unimportant. A careful monitoring of population size can prove or disprove the fear that there is serious erosion from your membership.

Or so it seems to me. I think I may be the only person in the country who gives a damn about this issue. It is possible, however, that bishops and pastors don't want to know the numbers for fear that they will reveal more bad news. "Your studies always report bad news," a bishop said to me.

"Only if you read nothing more than the newspaper accounts," I replied, with perhaps an acerbic tone. "Is it bad news that most Catholics have elected to stay in the Church or that Catholic schools work?"

"Sure it is," he replied. "That would mean we'd have to build more Catholic schools."

The bad news is usually about sexuality. In the world of the hierarchy at any rate—with their eyes and ears always on Rome—that is the worst of bad news. No amount of good news can possibly cancel it out.

Before one can estimate the number of Catholics, one must dispose of the question of what is a Catholic. The surveys score you as a Catholic if in response to their question about denomination affiliation you reply "Catholic." Pastors in their annual reports count the number of people in their parish who seem to be Catholic (by various methods of counting, from accurate census counts of their parish to guessing). Conservative Catholics say that only "good Catholics" should be counted—that is, Catholics who accept all the official teachings of the Church; if you adopt that norm then no Catholic will ever dissent from anything because by definition dissent excludes you. Some clergy say that you shouldn't really count as Catholic those who rarely if ever attend Mass and do not contribute to the support of their parishes.

In fact, Canon Law adheres to a position not unlike that of the survey takers. You are a Catholic if you have been baptized a Catholic and have not formally apostatized by joining another denomination or publicly renouncing your faith. Note that informal apostasy won't do it. You don't exclude yourself from the purview of the Code of Canon Law by staying away from Mass and ignoring most of the Church's teachings.

The Code reflects the best of the Catholic heritage's propensity to define the boundaries out as far as possible so as to embrace everyone it can—an attitude that is catholic as well as Catholic.

Sectaries define other people as out. Catholics define them as in. There are, of course, Catholic sectaries, those who wish to exclude from the Church all those who do not accept their own rigid definition of what it is to be Catholic. Alas, just now the tiny group of right-wing sectaries in American Catholicism has enormous influence in Rome because the Curia wishes to believe that they speak for a vast "silent majority" of American Catholics—a fiction that the sectaries eagerly exploit.

In or out, it would seem that no one wants to know how many Catholics there are beyond the annual estimate from the *OCD*, which is based on counts provided by each pastor in the country, some of which are doubtless very precise and others of which are wild guesses picked out of the blue, or deliberate falsifications to prevent an increase in diocesan tax on the parish.

Depending on your sources, estimates of the proportion of Americans who are Catholic can range from 21 percent to 28 percent. The differences are not unimportant: each percentage point represents almost 2.5 million people. There may be more than 16 million Catholics for which the low estimate does not account.

There are six different estimates that one must consider. The first is drawn from the largest single study of American religious affiliation ever attempted—the Current Population Survey of the Census Bureau (as it was then called) in 1957. If the Catholic proportion was the same then as it is today there are approximately 59 million Catholics in the United States, 7 million more than reported in the *OCD* in 1986.

Recent surveys of the Gallup organization (reported especially in a book written by Jim Castelli and George Gallup, Jr.) estimate that 28 percent of Americans are Catholic, which would mean a Catholic population of 65 million.

The surveys of religion done at NORC since the early 1960s consistently report 25 percent of the population Catholic. The Gallup data, on the other hand, indicate an increase from 23 percent to 28 percent between the early 1960s and the present, a 20 percent increase in the proportion of Americans who are Catholic. In which estimate should more confidence be placed?

The *Official Catholic Directory* figures are helpful but not conclusive because the quality of information available to a pastor when he fills out his annual form is so varied, as is the care with which the form is filled out. While Gallup portrays an increase in the last quarter century and NORC no change, the *Directory* estimates indicate a decline (from 24 percent to 22 percent) in the Catholic proportion—which is compatible, of course, with an increase in numbers because the American population is also growing, at a faster rate than is the proportion affiliated with the Church, if the *Directory* is to be believed. (Why would pastoral estimates decline? In part perhaps because of the impression that the number of their parishioners is declining and perhaps in part because they know they will be taxed on the numbers reported.)

Baptism and burial records are likely to be more reliable than pastoral estimates of parish size, if only because of canonical regulations about keeping records and because the books are ready at hand, usually with numbers, when it is required of a pastor to tally the numbers (which doesn't necessarily mean that he looks at the books).

Thus at the present time, if the reports are accurate, a quarter of American births are Catholic and 21 percent of deaths are Catholic. These figures suggest that the Gallup numbers are too high—such a gross underreporting by the country's pastors seems most improbable.

Moreover, the proportion of burials (Catholic burials as a fraction of death statistics) that are Catholic has been consistently 21 percent since the early sixties while the proportion of births (baptisms divided by birth statistics) has fallen from 31 percent in 1962 to 25 percent at the present—a finding that is supported by the various fertility studies done at the University of Michigan and Princeton University. These studies show that from the mid-1960s on, the Catholic birth rate rapidly declined until it matched the national rate (despite the birth-control encyclical).

Why the difference in birth rates and death rates? The higher birth rate causes the lower death rate because it produces a younger population. In NORC's General Social Survey adult (over eighteen) Catholics are three years younger on the average than adult Protestants (forty-three years old versus forty-six). The younger population is the result of higher birth rates in the past. It will take many years for the present lower birth rates to begin to age the Catholic population so that it becomes as old (on the average) as the Protestant population.

If Gallup's figures are too high and pastoral estimates too low, why then are the middle-range figures (which show about a quarter of the country to be Catholic) so stable in the last twenty-five years despite the demographic changes that are going on?

The answer is that the figures mask a process by which Catholics leave the Church and are replaced. In the General Social Survey 28 percent of the respondents said they were raised Catholic. The 25 percent currently Catholic is the result of an equation in which the number of converts[1] and the natural increase from higher birth rates and immigration has been subtracted from the number of defectors. As a result of the decline of the Catholic birth rate and the decline of the number of converts, there will be a slow erosion in years to come. This decline from the 25 percent figure will not result in a decline of actual numbers of Catholics as long as the American population continues to grow, which it is projected to do into the middle of the next century. (Immigration may diminish or even cancel out this expected erosion in the Catholic proportion.)

In 1960 some 15 percent of those who were raised Catholics were no longer Catholic. Taking into account the shifting age of the American population (and the propensity of some to return to their denominations as they grow older), that figure has not changed in the last quarter century. Thus if the Catholic proportion erodes in decades to come, it will be the result of changing birth and convert rates (and perhaps changing immigration rates) and not of changing defection rates.

About half of the defectors have left to join other religions, usually in conjunction with marriages to those of other religions. The other half leave to no religious affiliation. The Catholic defection rate is (and has been) more than half again as high as the Protestant defection rate. Many of these are troubled by the authority and sexuality teachings of the Church. About half of them drift back to the Church as they grow older.

Perhaps the most useful statistic for estimating how many Catholics there are in a given area is a fraction in which the numerator is the number of baptisms the previous year and the denominator is the number of live births in the same area. Thus, by way of example (using the *Official Directory* for 1986 and the current *Statistical Ab-*

---

[1] The number of converts to Catholicism has declined because there is less Catholic pressure now in interreligious marriages for the spouse to become a Catholic, though many still do for the sake of family religious harmony. In my judgment such pressures are and always were intolerable. Moreover, if someone wishes to become a Catholic at the time of marriage, often because the person has no particular religious affiliation, I always tell them that they are not leaving their own heritage behind but merely bringing it to us. Catholicism embraces enthusiastically (in its best moments anyway) all that is good and beautiful in every religious heritage. You do not stop, I say, being a Methodist; rather you become a Catholic as well as being a Methodist. I note here (and to the potential convert) that such may not be the strict canonical view but it is psychologically and symbolically and imaginatively true. As David Tracy has always insisted, the Sacramental Imagination does not exclude the dialectical imagination but subsumes and embraces it. Catholicism really does mean "Here comes everyone"!

stract, both of which present data for 1985), I calculate that in 1985, 37 percent of the live births in the state of Illinois were baptized Catholic so that the Catholic population of the Prairie State is approximately 4.3 million.[2]

A diocesan official who thinks it useful to know how many Catholics there are in his territory (and many would, I suspect, hardly think it mattered) can learn from the relevant vital statistics offices the number of live births the previous year and use that as the denominator of a fraction in which the numerator is the number of infant baptisms that year. Then he could multiply the total population of the diocesan area by the fraction (proportion) and obtain a serviceable estimate of the Catholic population in his diocese.

To save overworked Chicago chancery officials the trouble of calculating an estimate, I have done so for them with 1987 data: I estimate 2.57 million Catholics, almost 10 percent more than the report in the *Directory,* which is approximately the same as the national rate of underestimates.

CATHOLIC POPULATION BY STATE

	Percent Total	Catholic (in thousands)
NEW ENGLAND		
Maine	27	314
New Hampshire	34	339
Vermont	31	166
Massachusetts	57	3,319
Rhode Island	53	523
Connecticut	55	1,746
MID-ATLANTIC		
New York	42	7,469
New Jersey	46	3,479
Pennsylvania	34	4,030

[2] In the 1989 *Statistical Abstract,* the live births for each state are on page 63 and the population of each state on page 22.

	Percent Total	Catholic (in thousands)
SOUTH ATLANTIC		
Delaware	27	167
Maryland and D.C.	19	953
Virginia	9	523
West Virginia	6	116
North Carolina	3	187
South Carolina	3	100
Georgia	4	239
Florida*	18	2,045
EAST NORTH CENTRAL		
Ohio	22	2,364
Indiana	16	879
Illinois	33	3,806
Michigan	24	2,818
Wisconsin	37	1,776
EAST SOUTH CENTRAL		
Kentucky	13	484
Tennessee	4	190
Alabama	3	120
Mississippi	5	130
WEST NORTH CENTRAL		
Minnesota	34	1,426
Iowa	26	750
Missouri	19	956
North Dakota	31	212
South Dakota	31	219
Nebraska	26	449
Kansas	21	514

CATHOLIC POPULATION BY STATE
(Continued)

	Percent Total	Catholic (in thousands)
WEST SOUTH CENTRAL		
Arkansas	4	94
Louisiana	33	1,478
Oklahoma	6	198
Texas*	24	3,929
MOUNTAIN		
Montana	13	119
Idaho	23	121
Wyoming	15	76
Colorado	22	719
New Mexico*	42	690
Arizona	22	701
Utah	5	77
Nevada	17	159
PACIFIC		
Washington	12	529
Oregon	11	296
California*	32	8,437
Alaska	10	52
Hawaii	22	231

* Estimates in Florida, Texas, New Mexico, and California are problematic because of a large Hispanic population, younger than the national average and with a higher birth rate.

This technique must be used with special caution in any area in which there is reason to suppose that the age and ethnic group distribution of Catholics is radically different from the rest of the country, as in the states of Florida, Texas, New Mexico, and California with their large Hispanic populations that are younger and more fertile. (The Hispanic birth rate is 20 per thousand as opposed to the 15.5-per-thousand national rate.)

In many if not most cases, however, an estimate using this technique is likely to provide the best possible numbers until the Church attempts a census as careful and as comprehensive as the government does.

The table presents the Catholic proportion and the estimated Catholic population for each of the states. In any state in which there have been many baptisms of the children of migratory workers from Mexico, one should discount somewhat the estimates in this table, especially as noted previously in such states as Florida, New Mexico, Texas, and California where there are large Mexican-American populations.

It is reasonable to conclude that Catholics are about a quarter of the American people, a little less than 60 million in number. Until the American population reaches stability (births replace deaths but do not add to population), the Catholic numbers will continue to increase, although the Catholic proportion may decline slightly because of the decline in the Catholic birth rate (if that decline is not canceled by immigration).

There are four possible ways to prevent this slow erosion—more births, more converts, more immigrants, fewer defections. The last might seem the most promising; but it must be noted that whatever the cause of defections, the present rate is not a result of the Vatican Council or the postconciliar changes in the Church or of changes in American society, since it has not changed in the last quarter century. Whatever the nature of the defection problem, its causes are deeper than the current controversies in the Church.

Attempts at "evangelization" which do not ask questions about the high Catholic defection rate seem to be misplaced—if not foolish. My research suggests that the most serious cause of defection—over and above the "average"—is the way authority is exercised, especially at the parish level.

The so-called evangelization movement is a farce if not an outright fraud. It means that offices are established in dioceses; journals, newsletters, and books are published; national conferences are convened; national organizations are formed; mandates are given by the bishops; an enormous amount of rhetoric (not to use scatological language) is generated; a great feeling of achievement and self-righteousness is exuded—without any notable change in either convert rates or the return of alienated Catholics.

In the present era, when the Catholic Church is faced with a problem, it establishes offices that in turn federate into national organizations. The effective functioning of these offices and the organizations that result is taken to be a sign of the Church's success in response to the problem. No attempt is ever made to measure empirically what if any impact all the organization activity might be having.

Not only is the Church not interested in how many members it has; it is not interested in whether any of its activities work, including those activities that are supposed to increase its members. Moreover, nothing is done to remove the most obvious barriers to either return or conversion—the vast array of extra canonical rules (called "guidelines" but usually enforced with grim legalism) that dioceses and clergy have imposed on those who wish to receive the Sacraments, or to have their children receive them, and the dreadful, dull, and *a prior*istic Rite of Christian Initiation for Adults (RCIA) through which converts and many returning Catholics must endure if they wish admission to the Church. Instead of the return or the entry being a celebration it becomes a somber administrative test that must be passed. And they call it "evangelization," the preaching of the Good News!

For all the happy talk about "evangelizing" and the enthusiastic national meetings, little is done to reach out to those in a parish whose religious imagination makes them Catholic, even if their church attendance is irregular—divorced men and women, particularly the latter, of whom it will be remembered that only 20 percent have remarried; those who have drifted away from the Church and who would like to return but don't know how; those whose practice is irregular because they have been hurt by priests or nuns in the past; those who are loyal to Catholicism after their own fashion, but have (or more likely think they have) theological problems; those who hesitate on the fringes but are troubled by what they see as the aloofness (alternating with "hard sell") of Catholic parishes; those sometime and would-be Catholics who think that "marriage problems" ban them from the Sacraments—problems of marriage and divorce that may no longer exist with the new annulment processes or the greater willingness of priests to use the "pastoral solution" for divorced and remarried Catholics.

A priest I know insists that he cannot believe that God wants to exclude anyone from the Sacraments; so, whenever he encounters a problem of a divorced and remarried Catholic, he says, "Don't let anything keep you away from God, especially man-made rules."

Perhaps he should say that, as church leaders insist, the rules are made by God and only interpreted and enforced by them (though there have been many other approaches to divorce in Catholic history). Nevertheless the priest is typical of many, perhaps most, priests today. The leadership has lost credibility and thus control not only with the laity but with most of the lower clergy, too.

The new annulment norms make use of the notion of "psychic incapacity"; it means in effect that the two partners may have been validly married civilly but that they lacked sufficient emotional maturity to contract a permanent bond that is sacramental, that is to say a reflection of the binding passion between Jesus and his Church, God and Her people. Under such circumstances and with sufficient proof, ecclesiastical tribunals will usually declare the persons involved free to contract a new marriage. There is considerable skepticism on all sides about this approach. Rome believes, not unreasonably, that there are few if any marriages which American tribunals will not annul. Liberal Catholics think, perhaps not unreasonably, that such rigmarole is just a dodge so that the Church can change its doctrine without doing so. Yet, as a social scientist (who is inclined to believe that the Church should get out of the ecclesiastical tribunal business which it did not need for the first thousand years of its history), I find the theory plausible enough. Most young people, it seems to me, are indeed innocent of the maturity required to enter a union that can be said to be so powerful and so durable that it reflects the union between God and His people. It takes years, I should think, for a husband and a wife to grow into a union that is so passionate and so strong that it really reveals to themselves and to others how God loves us. Maybe some people never achieve such a level of commitment to each other. Once they do, it is most unlikely that they will ever end up in a divorce court.

The so-called pastoral solution (about which we were taught in the seminary but with all kinds of warnings about using it almost never) consists of a priest listening to a person who has been divorced and for whom the annulment process is not possible—for one reason or another. If the priest concludes that the person believes in good faith that s/he is free to marry, then he notes that while the Church cannot grant "permission" and can't publicly validate the marriage, the person nonetheless has the right to receive the Sacraments. The person may or may not understand the complicated reasoning in the conversation but concludes, not unreasonably, that the priest has in fact given permission. On the occasion of such a marriage which can't take place in church, some priests will even provide a blessing in the church afterwards.

The two pertinent issues according to the books are (a) "scandal" and (b) the difficulty of obtaining an annulment. Many priests assume that no one can be shocked by anything that happens in the Catholic Church anymore and that no one will much mind if a divorced person begins to receive the Sacraments again. They also assume that an annulment becomes "morally" impossible when a person rejects the annulment process. Some priests even recommend the annulment process only when the person involved insists on it, either for reassurance of conscience or for a church wedding. These priests argue that a Catholic has the right under "natural law" to receive the Sacraments if her/his conscience is clear and that in "cases of necessity" (what isn't necessary these days?) ecclesiastical rules cannot and should not stand in the way of the exercise of the right to the Sacraments.

Such reasoning, it may be imagined, drives the Vatican and many bishops crazy. But the only way to stop it is to bug every rectory office in the country. This disregard for the law is what is likely to happen when those who are supposed to administer the law (parish priests) have become contemptuous of the lawgivers. Need it be said that this kind of contempt is not eliminated by increasingly angry reiteration of the rules.

"I don't care how often the pope tells me that I can't sleep with my own husband," the angry Catholic wife I quoted before raged at me. "He can't stop me."

The pope never said that she couldn't sleep with her husband. However, alas, the public image created by thirty-second TV clips and 750-word press association stories has persuaded many Catholics that he is saying something very much like that.

That image doesn't drive them out of the Church, but it does deprive the pope of credibility as a teacher.

For centuries, future priests were taught in effect that the Sacraments were more important than humans—the sanctity of the marriage bond (long after a marriage had dissolved) was more important than the spiritual and human welfare of the people in the marriage. "Let them sleep in separate bedrooms" was the standard advice proposed for the divorced and remarried. Now priests take seriously the ancient dictum *"Sacramenta propter homines."* They believe that sacraments exist for humans instead of vice versa. I don't see how the orders from the curias, local and Roman, can change that attitude—especially when many if not most canon lawyers agree.

Some parishes do indeed reach out to such people. My friend Monsignor Thomas Cahalane in Tucson, for example, has a series of sessions each year after Christmas and Easter for ACA—Alienated Catholics Anonymous—in which with gentle invitations and enthusiastic support from his parishioners he welcomes back those who would like to come and talk about their problems with the Church. Most of the problems, by the way, are the result of clerical cruelty in years gone by. Every year a hundred people, most of them almost pathetically eager to return, are welcomed back with great celebrations. It is an ingenious idea from a very ingenious priest. Yet it is so clever that no one else has thought of it; and rather few priests even try something like it. It is much easier to impose the new rules than to seek out those who desperately want to come back and then make their return a festival rather than a test.

Note the craziness of the Catholic Church's current attitude toward membership: It is uninterested in how many members it has. It pours vast sums of money into an "evangelization" campaign whose only success seems to be an increase in bureaucracy. It erects legalistic barriers to those who might want to join or return,[3] and it exerts little effort to win back or welcome home its own marginal members (though it may rail at their failure to contribute to Sunday collections). Many priests, needless to say, ignore this nonsense and do all that they can—but against the institution instead of with its help.

It is unfortunate that the possibilities for data collection offered by the *OCD* are not taken more seriously. The staff is intelligent and helpful, but they need direction from church leadership on what statistics are important and cooperation from parish clergy.

For example, for the last forty years most priests have believed that the rate of religiously mixed marriages has been increasing. Surveys, however, indicate no such increase. Moreover, the stable rate of Catholic exogamy is especially surprising since exogamy correlates normally with higher income, education, and social status—all of which have increased for Catholics in the last quarter century. (About three-quarters of Catholics are married to other Catholics and don't

---

[3] Dr. Durkin and I have written a book for Thomas More Press, *A Church to Come Home To,* which makes suggestions about how the returns might be celebrated—and why they should be celebrated.

believe any claims of something different.)[4] Mixed marriage data, collected by the *OCD* but not tabulated, would be extremely useful.

Moreover, a list of the parishes of the country, weighted by number of parishioners (in order of size), would make an excellent sample frame from which data could be collected without the necessity of obtaining cooperation from every parish.

Such useful and rather easily accomplished techniques will be used, however, only when Catholic leaders want to know more about their situation than can be learned by wetting one's finger and holding it up to the wind or listening to the voice of the Spirit as they imagine She talks to them in the middle of the night. Or talking to their friends over a drink after a session of the National Conference of Catholic Bishops.

One problem the leaders certainly don't want to hear about is the defection of Hispanics, a catastrophe going on in their midst about which they either know nothing or prefer not to be reminded.

Catholics of Hispanic origin are defecting to Protestant denominations at the rate of approximately 60,000 people a year. Over the past fifteen years this departure from Catholicism has amounted to almost a million men and women, almost one of ten (8 percent) of the Spanish Catholic population.

This conclusion is based on an analysis of respondents of "Spanish Origin" (the Census term) in NORC's annual General Social Survey. It confirms the impression of Hispanic conversion to Protestantism, but suggests that the rate is much higher than previously estimated.

There are, according to the Census, some 17 million Americans of Spanish origin. It is routinely assumed that most if not all of these are Catholics. In fact, according to the General Social Survey (a national probability sample), only 70 percent of those of Spanish origin (Mexican, Puerto Rican, and "Other Spanish") are in fact Catholic and 22 percent are Protestants. Thus at the most only 12 million of the population reported by the Census are Catholic.

If one pools all the annual GSS surveys since 1972, one has a Spanish-origin sample of 790, a sufficient number for analysis of the

---

[4] Assume a population of a hundred Catholics. Seventy-six of them marry one another; that means there are thirty-eight Catholic marriages. The other twenty-four marry spouses who are not Catholic. That means there are twenty-four mixed marriages, or that 46 percent of marriages are mixed. It is a small step for those who are either ignorant of elementary mathematics or who have an agenda of their own to assert not that almost half of marriages are mixed (which is true) but that half the Catholics in the country marry outside their religious faith (which is certainly not true).

change in the last decade and the difference between Protestant and Catholic Hispanics. There are weaknesses in the GSS sample: it has been assembled over sixteen years, it is not based on a Hispanic sampling frame[5] (which does not exist), and it probably misses the poorest of Hispanic respondents (as do all surveys). However, it is, as far as I know, the only data set, based on a national probability sample, which provides detailed information on the religion in which a respondent was raised and the religion with which the respondent currently identifies. (The excellent Gonzalez-LaVelle study—*The Hispanic Catholic in the United States*—omitted respondents who were not Catholic and therefore, despite all its merits, provides no data on the defection issue.)

In the first five years of the GSS (1972–77), 16 percent of Spanish origin respondents were Protestant (and 7 percent some other religion or no religion). In the five most recent years (1982–87), 23 percent were Protestant (and 7 percent other or no religion). Thus in the early seventies 77 percent of the Hispanics were Catholic. In the mid-1980s that had declined to 71 percent. The difference between the two time periods is statistically significant (at the .02 level). The Protestant segment of Americans of Hispanic origin is not only large, it is growing rapidly (71 percent/77 percent = 92 percent; 100 percent − 92 percent = 8 percent—the loss of Spanish Catholics).

The defection rates are higher among Puerto Ricans (24 percent) and "Others" (26 percent) than among Mexican Americans (15 percent). They are lower in the West (17 percent) than in the East (23 percent). Thirty-six percent of those who are currently Protestant were raised Protestant, making them second-generation converts (at least). A little more than three-fifths of both Catholic and Protestant Hispanics are native-born. About a third of each group are the children of native-born parents (so immigration does not seem to correlate with religious affiliation).

More than three-fourths of the Spanish-origin Protestants are either Baptists or fundamentalists. (One of the vice presidents of the Southern Baptists is Puerto Rican.) Moreover, they are more likely to believe in life after death than their Catholic counterparts (80 percent as opposed to 64 percent), more likely to reject abortion on demand (79 percent as opposed to 69 percent), more likely to think that premarital sex is always wrong (37 percent versus 26 percent), and

[5] A sampling frame is a pool from which respondents are drawn. A Hispanic sampling frame is one that takes into account the fact that Hispanics are not evenly distributed throughout the country but are concentrated in certain areas of the country.

much more likely to attend church regularly: 23 percent of the Catholics go to church every week as opposed to 49 percent of the Protestants (29 percent more than once a week). Thus it would seem that the Protestant Hispanics have joined fervent Protestant groups in which their religion provides them with intense activity and community support.

By some norms of religious behavior they are better Catholics than those who have stayed. Generally one hears two explanations for the defection of Catholics to Protestant denominations, especially to the sects to which most of them seem to be going:

1. Because the Catholic Church fails to reach the poorest of its Spanish members, a vacuum has been created into which the sects can rush with their enthusiasm, their grass-roots ministry, their concern about the religious problems of ordinary people, and their "native" (and married) clergy.

2. The sects have a special appeal to the new middle class because they provide a means of breaking with the old traditions and becoming responsible and respectable members of the American middle class (much as Catholicism provides a middle-class niche for some upwardly mobile blacks). The Catholic Church's failure in this perspective is to provide community and respectability for the upwardly mobile Hispanic American.

The latter explanation is supported by analysis done (most notably by Anne Parsons) of Italian-American Pentecostals during the 1930s and 1940s, an analysis that saw the Protestant sects as a means of "Americanization" for some Italians.

The second model seems to fit the data better than the first. Protestant Hispanics are better educated, make more money, are more likely to be married, and notably more likely to be managers and white-collar workers. Moreover, they come from backgrounds in which there was more paternal education.

They do indeed look like an upwardly mobile middle class for whom the Protestant denomination provides both a way of becoming acceptably American and a support community in which they are comfortable as they break with their old religious heritage. It is not only their old religion that is left behind: 59 percent of Hispanic Catholics are Democrats, while only 44 percent of Spanish Protestants are Democrats. (For which God forgive them, say I!)

The success of the sects, then, seems to be the result of the failure of the Catholic Church to be responsive to the emotional, communal, and religious needs of some of the new Hispanic middle class. The loss of so many Catholics is a catastrophe comparable to the loss of the Irish-speaking rural proletariat who migrated to the southern parts of the Colonies, mostly before 1800. But that loss took place because the Church in Ireland and the United States was devoid of resources and priests. The loss of the Hispanics is occurring in the richest and most resourceful manifestation of the Catholic Church that the world has ever known.

Becoming Protestant seems to have an economic and social payoff for Hispanics. The second-generation Protestants (those who say they were raised Protestants) have on the average 11.3 years of education and earn on the average $27,000 a year. Fifty-two percent of them are white-collar workers and 28 percent are managers. They remain fervent Protestants—26 percent of them attend church more than once a week.

Thus the president pro tem of the Chicago City Council and most powerful Hispanic political figure in Chicago, a Puerto Rican educated in Catholic grammar schools and high school, is now a devout Protestant. I don't know why he left the Church; I do know that he is proud of his new religion. I cite him as an illustration and not as an example.

I do not purport to be an expert on the Hispanic ministry. Rather I present this statistical analysis because I suspected that no one else would attempt it and because there certainly is not going to be a Church-sponsored study of the rapid defection of Hispanic Catholics to Protestant sects.

The loss of almost one out of ten members of its largest ethnic group is an ecclesiastical failure of unprecedented proportions. The statistics reported in this section of the chapter will be denied by church leaders—as are almost all sociological data that contain bad news. Church leaders seem to believe that if they deny truth to one another and to their Roman overlords then it stops being truth. All that such denials do in fact mean is that they are hiding from the truth.

When my first report on these findings appeared in the Jesuit magazine *America*, the reaction was underwhelming—one or two letters. I later learned, however, that it created quite a stir within the Hispanic church leadership, activists asserting that it was true, bishops and bureaucrats vigorously denying it. All right, fellas, then collect your own data!

What should the Church do? I am not qualified to say anything more than that the "National Pastoral Plan for Hispanic Ministry," approved by the bishops on November 18, 1987, seems to be an impressive document. I have been told by priests more familiar with the work than I am that it is indeed an excellent blueprint and there is no chance whatever of its being implemented.

I suppose that the most effective technique would be to turn the ministry in the Hispanic communities over to hundreds of married Hispanic deacons who could deal with their own people in their own language.[6] Surely such a plan would be opposed by bishops and priests and by the Vatican, which would sooner lose Catholics to Protestant denominations than give a hint that a married clergy might be possible. I would add that I think there ought to be ordained Hispanic deaconesses, too.[7]

In my experience with Mexican Americans in Tucson I have become convinced that theirs is a religion of festival and celebration—as one of my students remarked, "We believe that we are all a family and that God is part of our family and that when we celebrate God comes to our family and celebrates with us." This is the Sacramental Imagination with a vengeance.

Then she added, "Of course, we don't know much about the rules; that's why we send our children to Saints Peter and Paul, so that they will learn the rules like you Irish learn them."

I assured her that there was a time when the Irish celebrated, too, and that we might have more to learn from her than she from us. Hispanic Catholics would have a hard time finding much trace of festival in American Catholicism just now, although the Sacramental Imagination should incline us to festival.

Festival isn't high on anyone's agenda these days. The leadership of the Church in recent years reminds me of an overage, overweight, slightly punch-drunk linebacker. It lives on its past reputation; and despite its size and its strength it lacks the quickness and the creativity to respond to challenges—finances, vocations, Spanish defection.

[6] I am asked occasionally what changes I would institute if I were pope. I reply that I would ordain women, welcome married people into the process of illuminating sexual teachings, insist that bishops be elected by priests and people (as they were for the first thousand years and as several popes, quite correctly it seems to me, said was the only moral way to select them), and demand that bishops improve the quality of preaching in their parishes within the year or be replaced. Then I'd resign.

[7] Almost all serious historical research on the subject of the deaconesses in the early Church reports that they were considered to be in Sacred Orders. Roman theologians reject these data on the grounds that they simply could *not* have been in Orders; if the ancients thought so, they were wrong, that's all. Such obscurantist opposition to the ordaining of women deacons persuades me that the opposition to women clergy is in fact based on power concerns and not theology.

So it tries to pretend that the challenges are not there and occupies itself with lectures to the civil government on economic and military problems, as the linebacker tells everyone else on the team what they are doing wrong and ignores his own weaknesses. It is a game plan that guarantees that a bad situation will become worse.

7

MONEY:
ISOTOPE FOR ANGER

O CATHOLICS *have* enough money to pay for our schools?"
Bishop Bill McManus asked as he stretched out leisurely
(for him) on the couch in my house in Tucson.

"Sure they do," I said promptly."They earn more
than ever before."

"But inflation . . . ?"

"That's in inflation-free dollars. Look, Bill, when your brother
John and I were of high school age you could send two kids to high
school for four years, one to Trinity, the other to Fenwick, for what
it would cost to buy a top-of-the-line Chevy. You can do the same
today. Is a Catholic high school education worth a new Chevy?"

"A lot of priests don't think our people can afford Catholic education."

"That's because they don't want to work at building schools."

"Can you get together data for me? I have to give a talk at the
NCEA meeting at Easter."

Such are the strange tricks that reality plays on a scientist. Bill's
request sensitized me to one of the best indicators of the current state
of religion—the willingness of denomination members to put their
money where their affiliation is. That brief exchange produced a new
and important quest in my career as a sociologist of religion and a
student of American Catholicism. Financial contributions are a ra-
dioactive isotope running through the body ecclesiastic which provide insight and meaning that no other variable can offer.

It is a fascinating subject, though one, alas, not likely to increase my popularity with my fellow priests. For it adds a third component to my description of the current state of American Catholicism—Catholics imagine differently, Catholics are loyal, and now, Catholics are angry.[1]

After Bill left, I remembered that we had asked financial-contribution questions in both our 1963 and 1974 parochial school studies and had written a chapter about the decline in contributions in *Catholic Schools in a Declining Church*. Then somehow I had forgotten about the variable. If only we had comparable data on Protestants and recent data on Catholics.

A week later I noted in the *Tucson Citizen* that an organization called the Private Sector had done a survey of American charitable contributions with Ford Foundation money. I called the unflappable Sean Durkin.

"Sean? Uncle. Hunt down this Private Sector data. It's a Yankelovich study. And find me some Protestant data from the early 1960s."

And so he did. When we were finished we had six data sets, all of them with Catholic responses and four with Protestant responses, two from the early 1960s, two from the mid-1970s, and two from the mid-1980s. Here, in raw form, was the story of the religious contributions of the American people for a quarter century. The data had been lying around unanalyzed because no one had thought the question worth exploring or realized that it could be explored. Nor would I have except for Bill McManus's query.[2]

The data for my analysis, involving more than 10,000 cases in different surveys with different sampling frames, are the best that one can normally expect in social science. Agreement among different surveys about the responses to the question of contributions to the churches indicates that people are reporting their contributions consistently.

But are their estimates accurate? Did American Catholics really give $5 billion to the Church in 1987?

There is no way of being absolutely certain about that unless there were some central accounting office that tallied the accounts of all the Catholic institutions in the country. We can be sure that our respon-

---

[1] Bill McManus would rather that we use the words "disappointed" or "unhappy." Fine, just so long as it is established that the "disappointment" or "unhappiness" is costing us $7 billion in Sunday contributions.

[2] We published our research and policy recommendations in a book called *Catholic Contributions* (Thomas More Press, 1987).

dents are reporting variations over time in answers. But how certain can we be that our respondents are being careful, honest, and accurate in their estimates of contributions (even if they itemized them in their income tax returns)?

We had one reality check in the 1974 study which was enormously encouraging. We asked how much school tuition Catholics had paid that year. Multiplying by an estimate of the number of families and unrelated individuals in the country (one-quarter), we arrived at a sum of $805 million. The same year the NCEA collected data from all the Catholic schools on income from tuition. Their estimate was $790 million. I'd give their estimate more credit than ours, but the margin of error is much less than we could have expected in our wildest moments. Survey estimates of contributions, I conclude, are pretty accurate.

Although American Catholics earn, on the average, several thousand dollars a year more than their Protestant counterparts, Catholics' financial contributions to their churches are much less than those of Protestants: on the average, $320 a year as opposed to $580 a year for American Protestants. Catholics contribute 1.1 percent of their income to the Church while Protestants give 2.2 percent of their income to the Church.

This difference cannot be attributed to any failings of charity or generosity among Catholics, who on measures of attitude and behavior are at least as generous as Protestants. Nor can it be explained as a result of "inflation," because inflation affects all Americans. Nor is it caused by Catholic schools or by larger Catholic families. Those who send their children to Catholic schools contribute more rather than less to the Church than do other Catholics; and the greatest differences between Protestants and Catholics occur among those who have two children or less.

Nor can the difference be accounted for by changing levels of Catholic church attendance. The reason for the decline in contributions, according to the rector of Holy Name Cathedral in Chicago when *Catholic Contributions* was released, is that Catholics go to Mass less than they used to. Even though this man is a bishop and my coauthor is a bishop, the former felt no obligation to read our book before he explained it away. He was wrong, and not for the first time either.

If all Catholics went to Mass every week and contributed as much to the Church as those who now go every week, their contributions would still be less than those of their Protestant counterparts. Nor is the lower level of Catholic contributions the result of better-organized Protestant fund-raising in which fixed pledges are fulfilled every year. This difference between Protestants and Catholics in financial support of their churches persists in every demographic, social, and economic group—young and old, affluent and less affluent, white-collar and blue-collar, college-educated and not college-educated, and between Catholics and all Protestant denominational groupings. It also is independent of their perceptions of their disposable income. In fact, weekly church-attending Protestants who earn more than $40,000 a year give 4.4 percent of their income to their Church while their Catholic counterparts give 1.1 percent.

Moreover, the present situation is the result of a dramatic change in patterns of contribution to one's Church over the last twenty-five years. In the early 1960s, Catholics gave the same proportion of their income to their Church as did Protestants. In the last quarter century, the Protestant contribution rate has remained stable at approximately 2 percent of annual income while the Catholic rate has fallen from more than 2 percent to about 1 percent.

This decline cannot be explained by the decline in Sunday church attendance (which stopped in 1975 while the decline in financial contributions has continued), or by the costs of Catholic education or by inflation or by opposition to the Second Vatican Council. Some of the change (about a fifth) is the result of the influx of a younger generation of Catholics who contribute less to the Church than do their youthful Protestant counterparts. More of the change (about a half) can be attributed to changing Catholic attitudes on sex and authority in their Church.

The decline in Catholic contributions over the last quarter century is the result of a failure in leadership and an alienation of membership, not from the Catholic community or from sacramental participation—and certainly not from their Sacramental Imaginations—but from support of the ecclesiastical institution.

In my preliminary work on the question of Catholic contributions, I was inclined to think that the curtailment of Catholic contributions was a mostly unconscious protest and that the laity were not deliberately and consciously protesting against their leadership.

Now I am not so sure, both because of statistical reasons to be advanced in subsequent paragraphs and because of the comments of many laity after the publication of our book.

The typical comment was "What would make you think we didn't know what we were doing? When they listen to us and when they preach decent sermons, we'll increase our contributions."

Probably a mix of conscious and preconscious and unconscious motivations is at work in the decline of Catholic contributions.

Thus any of the reforms in Catholic fund-raising currently proposed are likely to have only small success, at best, if there is not some fundamental restructuring of the relationship between leaders and members. In the present situation, attempts to impose "tithing"—whatever that might mean—are likely to be counterproductive.

The financial losses to the Catholic Church of this decline in contributions are dramatic. If Catholics contributed not a tenth, not even a fifth of their income to the Church, but only the same 2.2 percent of their income that Protestants do, American Catholicism would have available almost twice the annual funds that it currently has—$6 billion more to maintain Catholic schools, to pay employees more than poverty wages, to continue to maintain its inner-city ministry, to found new parishes, and to do something more than talk about an "option for the poor."

The average American Catholic's contribution to the Church—as a proportion of income—has declined because Catholic contributions have not kept pace with inflation and with the rise in Catholic income.

Thus American Catholics contributed an average of $164 to the Church in 1963 out of an annual income of $7,645. In 1984 their contributions had doubled to $320 but their income had almost quadrupled to $27,500. Much of this change in income was, of course, the result of the inflation of the late 1960s and the 1970s, although, on the average, real income (net of inflation) improved during the last two decades for Catholics.

The Producer Price Index shows a 3.2 increase in the cost of living in the twenty-five-year period. That which cost a dollar in 1960 now costs $3.20. (The GNP deflator, another measure of inflation, has also increased 3.2 since 1960.) Protestant contributions not only have kept pace with inflation but have increased more rapidly with inflation while Catholic contributions have lagged behind the inflation rate.

The cost of living has approximately tripled between 1963 and 1984. To have kept pace with this change, Catholic income in 1984 would have had to rise to $22,935. Therefore, $4,565 in income above that number to $27,500 represents a "real," inflation-free improvement in "standard of living," a 20 percent increase in real income. Catholic contributions have not kept pace with inflation. Protestant contributions have accelerated more rapidly than inflation and have kept pace with the increase in real income.

Catholics today, on the average, have more money available to give to the Church (and to Catholic schools) than they did in 1963. That is not, be it noted, a personal opinion; it is a statistical fact.

Many Catholic leaders will refer briskly to "inflation as the cause of the decline in Catholic contributions" (in inflation-free dollars and in proportion of income). But that leaves them, in the face of the data adduced in this report, with the question of why Protestant contributions kept pace with the changes caused by inflation and the increase in real income and Catholic contributions did not.

When our report on contributions was published, a young priest remarked to a Catholic journal, "I don't see what the problem is. Those that gave ten dollars a Sunday twenty years ago are still giving ten dollars a Sunday." No one bothered to tell the poor young man that it takes thirty-two dollars to buy what ten dollars bought twenty years ago.

"Our people cannot afford to contribute more," one often hears it said, "because of inflation." In fact, they can afford to contribute more because their incomes have increased faster than inflation.

A typical clerical response to the discovery that contributions have fallen is to "guilt" (in the teenage sense of that word) their people—the only motivation that many priests seem to understand—and to demand "greater sacrifices"—an implication that the laity are selfish and ungrateful.

That sort of appeal still works with some Catholics, but returns from it will rapidly diminish. It does not address the problem of lay anger and probably aggravates it.

The image of the hard-pressed parishioner, struggling valiantly to keep up with rising prices while his/her income is not rising, tells more about the attitudes and needs of the priests and bishops who use it as an excuse than it does about the reality of the life of the average Catholic (which is not, of course, to deny that some Catholics are caught in such a bind, but merely to say that it is not typical). Something must have happened in the Catholic community during the last quarter century which did not happen in the Protestant community.

The simplest explanation is that Protestants, since they are more deeply involved in the finances of their congregations, are more likely to be aware of the increased costs of administering a full-service local church than are Catholics and hence more realistic in making decisions about contributions. If Protestants have quadrupled their dollar contributions in the last quarter century, the reason, it can be argued, is that they are more aware than Catholics that costs have quadrupled and that the apparently swollen parish budgets are not, in terms of any inflation-free dollars, any higher than they were in the early 1960s.

One rarely hears in funding appeals from Catholic clergy much reference with precise details to the effect of inflation on parish or diocesan budgets. Rather than being a specific multiplier, "inflation" seems in the Catholic financial approach to be a vague demon (like the Southwest Wind in Babylonian mythology) and indeed one not matched by the good angel of corresponding increase in dollar income (and some increase also in real income).

Therefore, not inflation as such but the inability of church leadership to respond to inflation may be a partial explanation for the decline in Catholic contributions. It is not likely, however, to account for more than some of the dramatic decline.

There are four other explanations that are offered, either singly or in combination:

—The rise in educational attainment of Catholics and the resultant independence of the Catholic laity
—The changes created in Catholic life by the Second Vatican Council
—The decline in Catholic church attendance
—The effects of the birth-control encyclical

To test any of these hypotheses in a strict social science fashion, one needs measures of both contribution and the other variable at two points in time. One must show that the two variables are correlated at both points in time and that the change of one is linked to the change of the other. Two variables, correlations, simultaneous change—all three are therefore required. It is also possible that the strength of the correlation between the two variables increases between point one and point two.

Thus Catholic educational attainment has increased, education and financial contributions are correlated, and the two have changed in the last twenty-five years. But financial contributions correlated positively with educational attainment, so one would have expected an increase rather than a decline in Catholic financial contributions.

The decline in contributions, then, runs against the trend of increased Catholic education. Moreover, the decline is equally distributed among all Catholic population groups as distinguished by educational attainments.

In 1963 the college-educated gave 2.43 percent of their income to the Church; in 1974 they gave 1.92 percent, and in 1984 they gave 1.3 percent. The comparable rates of those who attended only grammar school are 1.97 percent, 1.58 percent, and 1.0 percent.

Thus while Catholics act much more independently of church leadership today than they did in years past, educational achievement does not seem to explain their failure to sustain previous levels of financial contributions.

Only one question was asked in 1963, before the end of the Vatican Council, about church reform—English in the liturgy. In 1963, seven-eighths of the respondents supported the English liturgy. In 1974, almost a decade after the end of the Council, the proportion was exactly the same. Hence, this reform of the Vatican Council, not having changed in the eleven-year period, cannot be the reason for the decline in contributions. There are no measures in the 1984 study on such matters of Catholic attitude and behavior, but it is unlikely that liturgical change, unconnected with the first half of the collapse of Catholic contributions, could be an important dynamic in the second half.

Moreover, in 1974 support for Vatican Council reforms correlated positively with financial contributions. Those who approved of the English liturgy and the other changes were likely to give more to the Church than those who did not. Since the majority of the Catholic population endorsed the changes (only about a fifth were opposed), the Council should have had, if anything, a positive instead of a negative effect on church finances.

Undoubtedly, the erosion of Mass attendance has had an effect on Catholic contributions, particularly since the Sunday-envelope form of contribution is tightly linked to Sunday (or Saturday afternoon) presence in church. But the decline in Mass attendance stopped in 1975 and the decline in financial contributions has not stopped. Furthermore, the most striking decline has been among those who go to church every week—from 2.69 percent in 1963 to 2.15 percent in 1974 to 1.69 percent in 1984. On the other hand, among those who seldom go to church, the decline has been from 0.87 percent in 1963 to 0.74 percent in 1974 to 0.70 percent in 1984. If all Catholics went to church every week and contributed as much as those who now go every week, their rate of contribution would still be only three-quarters that of Protestants.

Thus one is forced to consider the impact on Catholics' financial contributions of their changing attitudes on sex and authority. Both sets of variables are correlated, both declined from the early sixties to the mid-1970s, and these declines were apparently correlated in the first decade of our research interest. Moreover, the correlation beween birth-control attitudes and contributions increased during the decade.

There was no question about Catholic sexual attitudes in the 1984 study, but erosion of support for the traditional teaching has continued since 1974, as has the decline in contributions.

Analyzing the 1963-to-1974 change with a complex mathematical model in *Catholic Schools in a Declining Church,* I concluded that 14 percent of the decline could be attributed to the erosion of Mass attendance, 15 percent to the influx into the population of a younger and less generous age group, 12 percent to changing attitudes on papal authority, and 38 percent to a decline in acceptance of sexual ethics. A final 21 percent of the change was unaccounted for.

Another way of explaining the phenomenon is to ask how much of the decline in contributions can be accounted for by the increase in the strength of the negative correlation between financial contributions and rejection of the Church's birth-control teaching. What if the decline in giving among Catholics who reject the birth-control teaching was no greater than the decline among those who accepted the teaching? What if, in other words, the correlation between the two was the same in 1974 as in 1963?

If this were true, the decrease, projected into the 1980s, would have been less than half of what it actually has been. More than half of the decline in Catholic donations is associated with the increase in the proportion of Catholics who reject the birth-control teaching and the increase in the negative correlation between rejection of the teaching and financial contribution. Not only did more Catholics reject the teaching, but their rejection had a greater effect on their contributions than did a similar rejection in 1963. The intervening event was the birth-control encyclical.

Thus of the various explanations for decline in Catholic contributions which have been offered, only the birth-control encyclical explanation seems to fit the data, at least from 1963 to 1974. About half of the decline in Catholic contributions during that period can be accounted for by a parallel decline in the acceptance of church teaching on authority and sex.

Partly because the models I was using in the mid-1970s were, for the time, relatively complex, they were challenged in many Catholic circles—though mostly for their interpretation of the decline in Catholic religious behaviors other than those of financial contributions—on the grounds that they represented personal opinion or that they left out other forces at work in the Church.

In fact, then as now, the models are not personal opinions or value judgments. They are mathematical equations: the changes in sexual attitudes account mathematically for the changes in Catholic attitudes and behaviors, including half of the decline in financial contributions from 1963 to 1974. There are two pertinent issues and only two: whether the equations are properly calculated and which way the causality flows.

In principle, the causal flow could occur in four ways: the decline in contributions could be the result of the decline in acceptance of teaching on authority and sex; the decline in acceptance of teaching could be caused by the decline in financial contributions; both could affect each other; and both might be the result of some antecedent variable that causes them both to decrease and to which both are related, a variable we might call "alienation." The second and third explanations are improbable: declining contributions are not likely to change sexual attitudes. Therefore, either the first or the fourth explanation seems to be the proper one. Either changes in sexual attitudes, in direct defiance of church teaching, have led to a decline in financial contributions or both are related to some prior influence. For the purposes of this report, which of these two explanations is chosen does not matter. If one chooses the "alienation" explanation, you must note that it is an explanation that nonetheless links contributions on the one hand with sex and authority on the other.

Note that this "alienation" has not affected either the reception of Holy Communion, which increased from 1963 to 1974, or the frequency of prayer, which increased from 1974 to 1984 (as measured in two other NORC surveys), or, since 1975, frequency of Mass attendance. It is an "alienation" from some teachings and from some institutional practices but not from church affiliation or ritual behavior, including in more recent years attendance at Mass.

Because of the absence of a question on Catholic sexual attitudes in the 1984 data, I could not assert in *Catholic Contributions* with complete confidence that the principal engine driving down Catholic contributions in the first half of the period under discussion is still at work in the second half of the period. Data collected later, on which I will report shortly, strongly suggests that lay Catholic anger is alive and well.

Obviously, respect for official teaching continues to erode (now more on the subject of premarital sex than on birth control or divorce, where almost nine-tenths of the laity no longer accept the official teaching). Obviously, too, financial contributions continue to decline at the same rate as in the first half of the period. If the two decreases are no longer linked to each other, then another and unknown engine has intervened to continue the two erosions. Such a phenomenon is not impossible, but it is highly unlikely; it requires a new engine to account for half of the continuing decline in contributions.

The point here is that the best explanation we have available from the empirical evidence for the slump in Catholic contributions is not to be found in inflation or greater education or the Vatican Council or a decline in Mass attendance or the costs of Catholic schools. The most useful explanation we have, accounting for half the slump, is a selective alienation, related to a decline in acceptance of the Church's authority, especially its authority on sexual matters.

It would appear that Catholics have chosen a certain partial alienation from the institutional Church, an alienation that can coexist with weekly church attendance and other forms of ritual and community loyalty but that at the same time tunes out certain church teachings and contributes much less to the financial operation of the institution.

For the scholarly sociologist of religion, this blend of alienation and loyalty is an extremely interesting and unexpected phenomenon, one that thus far seems to be limited to North America and the British Isles. You can be loyal to Catholicism and still be angry at the institutional Church. Why not?

The power of the Sacramental Imagination is precisely what enables you to combine these two emotions. In the absence of awareness of a deep-seated emotion that makes one like being Catholic, there is no explanation of why Catholics don't depart. But because they like being Catholic they stay and complain about the quality of preaching and protest about what they don't like in the parish and in the Church. Financial contributions become a way of expressing protest and anger—in fact the only way.

In the "picking and choosing" of this selective alienation, Catholics are choosing, perhaps semiconsciously, to give to the Church about half of what they gave in 1963 and about half of what their Protestant fellow Americans give today.

(An observation from Michael Hout—"A Dublin phenomenon: Middle-class parishioners drop 20p in the basket just as the Christian Brothers taught them to do. They forget the fact that they now drive to the church in a Mercedes or Ford Grenada. When 20p was established as the normal contribution, the *Irish Independent* cost 5p. Now it costs 45p.")

It would be a mistake for those who lead the American Church to mislead and deceive themselves on the subject of lay anger.

After the publication of *Catholic Contributions*, I added an annual question in the General Social Survey on financial contributions so that the variable could be monitored year by year. The results of such monitoring strengthen my thesis that the contributions are the isotope that traces lay reaction to church leaders. After stabilizing in 1987, the financial contributions of American Catholics to their Church declined sharply again in 1988. This decline is apparently the result of events that happened during the time from the early spring of 1987 to the early spring of 1988.

Data collected in the spring of 1987 revealed that the typical American Catholic contributed $310 to the Church. This number was not statistically different from the $320 reported in the 1985 Yankelovich survey that had provided the *terminus ad quem* for our twenty-five-year analysis.

It appeared, therefore, that the decline in financial contributions had stopped. Perhaps, like the decline in church attendance in the previous quarter century, it was the result of a sharp drop in the late 1960s and the early 1970s. Perhaps financial contributions had leveled off and would remain at 1.1 percent of income.

However, the 1988 General Social Survey collected in the spring of 1988 revealed another drastic decline—from $310 to $260 a year, a fall from 1.1 percent to 0.9 percent of annual income. In 1987, 36 percent of American Catholics had given more than $250 to the Church. In 1988 the proportion giving more than $250 had declined to 29 percent, a statistically significant difference. There had been, however, no significant decline in the proportion of Protestants giving more than $250. (There were 760 Catholics surveyed over two years.)

Catholic Contributions estimated the annual contribution of

American Catholics in 1985 as $6 billion. This new decline therefore cost the Church a billion dollars.[3] I confess that I was shocked by the abrupt decline. Was it the result of a new falloff in church attendance? Church attendance, however, had not declined between 1987 and 1988. In both years about half of the Catholic population reported that it had attended Mass at least two or three times a month.

Might it be the result of a sudden and drastic falling off of confidence in church leadership? The General Social Survey asks a series of questions about how much confidence a respondent has in those occupying various leadership positions in American society, including the leaders of organized religion (not necessarily the leaders of your own denomination).

There had indeed been such a decline—from 31 percent of American Catholics saying they had "a lot" of confidence in church leaders in 1987 to 19 percent in 1988. Moreover, the difference between financial contributions became insignificant when this factor was taken into account. The sudden decline in confidence in church leaders accounted for the decline in contributions.

But what had happened? What event or series of events during the previous year angered Catholic laity so that they were curtailing their contributions? I wondered if it had been the unfavorable publicity about the cost of Pope John Paul II's trip to America in the late summer of 1987. Might the constant drumbeat of unfavorable publicity in press and television about how much the trip was costing explain the decline in contributions?

If this were the case, I reasoned, it would very likely be manifested in the areas the pope had traveled where the barrage of attacks on the high price of the pope's journey was a daily mass-media staple. The North might be exempt from the decline in contributions while the decline would be concentrated in the South and the West.[4]

In fact, the decline in the proportion of those saying they had a "lot" of confidence in church leaders was much more precipitous among Catholics in the South and West than in the North. In the latter it was nine percentage points—from 31 percent to 22 percent.

[3] According to the Census there are approximately 85 million families and unrelated individuals in the United States. A quarter of the population is Catholic. Thus there are about 20 million Catholic families and unrelated individuals. Twenty million times $50 equals $1 billion.

[4] The North was defined as the census regions called North East, Middle Atlantic, East North Central, and West North Central. The South and West (or non-North) was defined as the South Atlantic, East South Central, West South Central, Mountain, and Pacific.

In the former the decline was more than twice as large, nineteen percentage points, from 32 percent to 13 percent. In 1987 there had been no difference in confidence between Catholics who lived in the North and those who lived in the West and South. A year later there was a nine-percentage-point difference.

Moreover, the decline in contributions of more than $250 in the North was only three percentage points—from 36 percent to 33 percent; the decline in the South and West, however, was thirteen percentage points—from 34 percent to 21 percent. The former difference was not statistically significant, but the latter was.[5]

It might be suggested that there were other factors in the South that would account for the decline in Catholic contributions—the Swaggart and Bakker scandals, for example. But surely these phenomena would affect Protestants as well as Catholics, perhaps more than Catholics. In fact, however, there was no decline in the proportion of Protestants giving more than $250 a year to their churches.

The reaction to *Catholic Contributions* was underwhelming. It was occasionally derided (by *Our Sunday Visitor*), sometimes dismissed, mostly ignored. It would be naïve to think that the fate of this analysis will be different. Those who cannot admit on the record the decline in contributions are certainly not going to admit to themselves that there might be further decline because of a media-induced backlash to the papal visit. A billion-dollar backlash to the papal trip would seem to such folk almost an obscene thought, an idea that threatens the whole structure of reality.

Nevertheless, until another explanation is established and proven against the data, the following observations seem appropriate:

The media have a set of paradigms, of explanatory pictures, with which they organize reality so that they might report on it. The religion/money picture is part of this repertory. (Most journalists are religiously insensitive; many sincerely believe that all religion is a financial scam.) Anytime the Church engages in a major public venture, the cost of the venture will become a target. The Church must be prepared to respond to such attacks with something more effective than the assertion that we do what we want with our money.

In the absence of effective participation in the financial decision-making, the Catholic laity are quite capable of using their checkbooks as a means of protest, while their religious devotion remains unchanged. It may be that the protest recorded in this analysis is only

---

[5] There were 263 Catholic respondents in the South and the West, 454 in the North.

temporary and that contributions will rise again next year. Time will tell.

Ignoring or dismissing research findings may be an emotionally satisfying response. But such a response does not change reality. The Church's financial problems are serious. Apparently they are getting worse. Bishops and priests cannot afford to hide their heads in the sand much longer. They must recognize that the laity are angry and that the collection basket is the only way they have of communicating their anger upward.

The stroke-of-a-pen elimination of forty-three parishes in the archdiocese of Detroit at the end of 1988 illustrated the atrocious financial condition of the Catholic Church in the United States. Although American Catholics are the most wealthy in the world, their Church has become a monetary disaster area. Cardinal Szoka's authoritarian action is one more proof of the law that when you're in trouble you do not do good things; rather, you do the things you do well. Closing parishes, especially in poor neighborhoods, is more reassuring behavior than asking where all the money has gone. And why.

Hardly a parish is closed anywhere in the country without outraged protest from parishioners who have not been consulted about the end of their community. "They claim they don't have any money," an elderly woman said to me, tears in her eyes. "We gave them a lot of money in our day. Now we won't give them anymore. When they're through closing all the churches, they're going to have even less money than they do now."

Since the publication of the Greeley and McManus book there is at least some willingness on the part of church leadership to admit that there is a financial crisis. (I don't deceive myself that our work is responsible for this admission.) The most frequently heard explanation is that the problem is a decline in lay generosity which should be corrected by such heightened motivational efforts as "tithing" or "stewardship" or "sacrificial giving."

It's your fault, guys, not ours. Get it?

In such an explanation there is no room for acknowledgment of either clerical or hierarchical failure or lay anger. The anger theme, which I stressed in my section of our report, has been dismissed by virtually every priest with whom I've discussed the book. Their laity, they tell me, are simply not angry at them or at the Church.

Even on *a priori* grounds that reaction should be suspect. The laity have rarely been consulted by church leadership in the quarter century since the Council. The only vote they have is with their fountain pen. Can one be asked to believe seriously that Catholic laity are so passive that they would not express their opinions with the only method available to them? Are they as charmingly docile as most of their priests seem to think they are?

A Gallup poll before the pope's 1987 visit, commissioned by the *National Catholic Reporter*, provides an opportunity to search for a link between negative lay reaction and financial contributions. In the first question respondents were told, "I will read eight items and after each, please tell me if it has strengthened your commitment to the Catholic Church, weakened it, or had no effect one way or another." In the first of the accompanying tables we observe that substantial proportions of the population reported that their commitment was weakened by the events of the last several decades, with the birth-control issue, the revelations about gay priests, the ordination of women, and the punishment of dissenting theologians being the most serious causes of weakened commitment. However, the more "liberal" actions of the Church—stands on poverty, nuclear arms, the economy, and changes in the Mass—have also taken their toll on commitment.

The complacent conventional wisdom that stories about Vatican or hierarchical stands in the papers and on the tube have little effect on the laity does not stand up in the face of the data—as they could not be expected to unless we were dealing with an illiterate population.

A factor analysis produced two clusters. Those high on the first cluster were more likely to say their commitment was weakened by the decisions of the Church about birth control and similar issues, those low on that cluster were more likely to say that their commitment was strengthened by such decisions. On the second cluster those who scored high were more likely to say that their faith had been weakened by the changes in the liturgy and the liberal stands of the bishops. Those who were low on it were more likely to say their faith was strengthened by the language change and liberal episcopal stands.

By dichotomizing the two clusters and cross-tabulating them, I produced a four-cell typology of American Catholics. The first group, whom I call the Pragmatists, are those who are not likely to have had their commitment weakened by either the "conservative" or the "liberal" decisions of the Church. Neither birth-control teaching nor option-for-the-poor teaching, for example, has affected their commitments.

The second group, whom I call the Leftists, are likely to report their commitment weakened by the "conservative" teachings and strengthened by the "liberal" teachings. Just as this group is consistently "liberal," so the Rightists are consistently "conservative"— their commitment, they tell us, has been strengthened by teachings on abortion and birth control and the punishment of theologians and weakened by the changes in the liturgy and the liberal stands of church leaders.

The final group, the Negativists, are those who are more likely than the rest of the sample to be turned off by everything—both the birth-control teaching and the option-for-the-poor teaching, for example.

The Leftists are younger than the other two groups; the Rightists are older; and the Leftists have greater educational achievements. The Leftists and the Negativists have the highest income. Those with two or more levels of Catholic education are the most likely to be Negativists, as are women. The Irish are more likely to be Leftists than other ethnics.

If there is no relationship between financial contributions and negative reactions (for which a useful summary name might be "anger") to what has happened in the Church during the last two decades, it would follow that the proportion of annual income given to the Church should be the same for all four groups in the typology. If, on the other hand, the anger phenomenon is at work, one would expect the highest contribution to be among the Pragmatists and the lowest among the Negativists, with consistent ideologists somewhere in between.

Simply put, the issue is whether events in the Church influence financial contributions. If they don't, the numbers in the cells of proportion of income contributed should be the same. If the lay people are affected by what is happening in the Church when they write their checks, then the largest numbers should be in the first cell and the smallest in the fourth cell.

Right?

The Pragmatists give three times as much of their income to the Church as the Negativists. The Leftist ideologists are slightly more generous than the Rightist ideologists.

Moreover, the same effect exists even among those who go to

Mass every week or almost every week. Even those who are devout are influenced by events in the Church when they reach for pen and checkbook.

A similar phenomenon can be observed among the Irish, the most generous of contributors. Irish Pragmatists contribute four times as much of their income to the Church as do the Negativists and the Rightists. Irish Leftists give twice as much as do Irish Rightists and Negativists. If you inherit a parish of Irish Pragmatists and Leftists, your worries are over.

Let's put the matter concretely: If you're a pastor and you try to lay on your people such notions as "tithing" or "stewardship" or "sacrificial giving" and you ignore the relationships described in this chapter, you're courting disaster. You may get away with it if they like you, but you'd better be very sure about your popularity before you try it. If you try it in the archdiocese of Detroit, you might be lynched.

What can you, as a pastor, do about the angers that seem to be smoldering out there and that are affecting Sunday collections even among those who are at the Eucharist every week, even among the Irish who are there every week? You can't reverse the decisions of popes and bishops for which you are apparently being held responsible, can you? If the folk are taking out their grudge against church leadership by curtailing the flow of money to you, what is left for you to do?

In my response I go beyond the data, though perhaps not beyond common sense: you can give them a share in the decision-making about how the money is raised and for what it is spent—in other words, treat them the way virtually every non-Catholic cleric in America deals with his laity on the subject of money.

Some of the enthusiasts of "sacrificial giving" insist that the "sacrifice" is lost if you want to know how the money is spent. Fine. Maybe even that will work if your people like you and you preach good homilies. Indeed, if you are one of the 20 percent of priests whose preaching the laity rate as "excellent," you can do anything you want to raise money—even stand in back of church with a hat in your hand. There may be other realistic ways of responding to the financial crisis in the American Church besides the sharing of fiscal power. I don't know what they are, however, and I don't think anyone else does either.

Will it happen? Come on! Will the Cubs play in the World Series next year?

8

THE PARISH:
WHERE IT'S AT

HO IS the papal secretary of state? Who is the president of the National Conference of Catholic Bishops? The vice president of the NCCB? Who are the auxiliary bishops in your diocese? Who is the vicar general? The moderator of the Curia? The chancellor? Who are the American cardinals?

Who knows? And who cares?

But who is your parish priest? Almost everyone knows that. Religion is where you live, not in the upper levels of the bureaucracy about which, for example, *Time* is usually concerned.

What is the strongest predictor of regular religious devotion among Roman Catholics? The second strongest? Sexual attitudes? Acceptance of papal authority? Attitudes toward social justice? Satisfaction or dissatisfaction with changes in the Church?

The argument proposed thus far in this book might make the reader skeptical about some of those answers. The mass-media issues, as I have already demonstrated, have no effect on whether a Catholic is thinking of leaving the Church. Yet they do have an impact on financial contributions. Furthermore, reaction to the birth-control encyclical led to a decline in Mass attendance between 1968 and 1975 until the decline was short-circuited by the residual loyalty of American Catholics.

And did I not say that the birth-control encyclical was the most decisive event in the last quarter century of Catholic history? Sexual love is so important to married people that the Church's attempt to inhibit it should have a crucial impact on their devotional behavior even today, should it not?

The weakness of the assumption behind all these questions is that it fails to realize that ordinary human life is much more likely to be shaped by local issues than by national and global issues. Once Catholics resolved the birth-control issue and decided that they would vote against what they didn't like about the institutional Church by curtailing their contributions, the global issues became unimportant. The most important religious influences are local—the religious behavior of your spouse and the quality of preaching by your priest.

So the spouse and the priest are the critical religious influences in the life of the ordinary lay person. The influence of the spouse ought not to be surprising, but the quality of preaching?

If one puts all the mass-media variables into a regression equation designed to explain the variance in Mass attendance and then adds the quality of Sunday preaching (as judged by the respondent), the other variables shrink to statistical insignificance. If religious devotion of the spouse is added, however, the quality of the sermon (or homily, if one wants to be modern) continues to make a significant contribution to the explanation, though not as powerful as the devotion of the spouse.

There are four important religious socialization experiences, four sets of influences that shape your religious life—your parents, your spouse, your parish priest, and your children.[1] Parents are most important of all, but your spouse (whom you may well have chosen because s/he shares religious values with you) will powerfully reinforce or even reverse parental influence. The parish priest is not as important as either parent or spouse, but he's still important.

As for the pope, the Vatican, the National Conference of Catholic Bishops, your own bishop and his chancery, they simply don't matter in your ordinary religious life. I intend no disrespect to the Vatican or the NCCB or the diocesan curia or the officials in power in these institutions. I merely wish to assert that the parish and the home are where the religious action is.

If all the higher institutions can facilitate the work of parish, neighborhood, and family, then the Catholic tradition will be passed on more effectively. If the higher institutions ignore (save in empty words) the importance of the local institutions, they are depriving themselves of power. If through malice or ineptitude or jealousy over

---

[1] Children socializing parents—so-called reverse socialization—certainly takes place; but there are no data to establish conclusively that it happens in religion. In the old days what was a parent to do in the face of authority in a child's assertion, "BUT, S'ter says . . . "?

their own power they try to intervene and control what happens in the low-level institutions, then the high-level institutions are wasting their time.

A pope, a cardinal, a bishop should display great humility and great respect for home and parish when trying to teach. Without the cooperation of the home and the parish, the religious leader is without effective power, no matter how great his splendor, how important his title, how grandiose his claims, and how impressive his theoretical authority. Without the family and the parish priest, institutional leadership can do very little. Nor will orders and rules win the consent of family and parish priest—not in these days and, in truth, probably not ever.

Church leadership should be modest about the real impact of its theoretical power. When less than a fifth of Catholic laity have even heard of the National Conference's much touted pastoral letters on nuclear weapons and poverty, the bishops clearly have much to be modest about.

It is hard for those invested with sacred power to believe that they are dependent on what goes on out in the neighborhood, even if they protest that they are only the servants of the servants. How can all the dignity, the fine robes, the exalted titles be irrelevant to the actual religious lives of their people? In fact, the designation "servant of the servants" is literally true. Church leaders are effective only if they help the spouse and the parish priest do their work. Otherwise, forget it!

It is the parish where the people do their living and dying, their loving and their quarreling and their reconciling, their doubting and their believing, their mourning and their rejoicing, their worrying and their praying. Even without the empirical data I have cited, how can anyone seriously think that other institutions can make much difference in these activities besides the spouse you sleep with, the neighbors you live with, and the priest who is, in practice, the Church for you?

In the parish where ordinary religion occurs, there is no sign of "loss of faith." Ninety-eight percent of Catholics believe in God, 85 percent in the divinity of Jesus, 75 percent in life after death (and 17 percent more say that they are "not sure"), 70 percent believe in heaven. Forty-three percent say they are "strong Catholics."[2] A third

[2] Up from 41 percent in the early 1970s.

are members of some kind of religious organization. Twenty-five percent pray more than once a day, 50 percent pray at least once a day, more than 90 percent pray at least several times a week. None of the percentages for these items have declined in the slightest over all the years for which empirical data are available, except for the frequency of prayer, which seems to have *increased* somewhat over the last twenty years.

Contributions are down drastically, papal infallibility is accepted by only a little more than 25 percent, the birth-control teaching is dismissed. But people still pray often and believe in life after death.

"I can do without the pope," a middle-aged layman told me. "I'm a historian and I know that at most times in history Catholics had only the vaguest notion of who was bishop of Rome. But I can't do without God or the Church or the Blessed Mother."

Thus speaks the self-conscious Catholic imagination.

One must ask church leadership what is more important, belief in God and Jesus and life after death or belief in infallibility? What is more important, frequent prayer and its implication of awareness of the presence of God or not practicing birth control?

I fear that many leaders would say that infallibility is more important than life after death and birth control more important than prayer. Such a response shows how important the good opinion of the Vatican is to them and/or how out of touch they are with the religious life of their people and indeed with religion itself.

The priest is the heart of the parish (though sometimes I think the basketball courts are almost as important!). Despite the low morale of the Catholic clergy (about which more later) today, often tinged with self-pity, it would be difficult to overestimate the significance of the priest's role. In our research on Catholic young people we discovered that the drift of young people back to the Church during the religious "downtime" in their life cycle is often helped by contact with a sympathetic priest. Similarly, Catholic feminist women, angry at the way the Church treats women, still remain regular in their church practice if they have contact with a priest whom they trust. If a young married woman has a confidant relationship with a priest, both she and her husband are more likely than those couples in which there is no confidant relationship to report that their sexual fulfillment is "excellent." These couples with high scores on the confidant scale are also more likely than other couples to support both the ordination of women and the continuation of celibacy. It almost seems that they are voting for similar confidant relationships between men and celibate women priests.[3]

The study of young Catholics my colleagues and I did for the Knights of Columbus[4] is the best source of information on parish and parishioners[5] currently available. The data from that project are especially powerful because they are based on interviews with people who are at the bottom of the religious life-cycle curve.

Four-fifths of the young people approve of their pastor's performance, one-half say that their religious development has been positively affected by sermons, more than two-fifths say that they have been positively affected by a conversation with a priest or a nun, two-fifths also describe their parish as an "active" one, and more than a third say they have been greatly affected by their parish. That's the good news.

The bad news is that only a third say that their priests are very understanding, only a third say that the laity have a lot of influence in the parish, and only a little more than a tenth say that the sermons are "excellent." Moreover, the quality of the sermons has a strong impact on the development of the religious imagination of the young people (as measured by the GRACE scale discussed previously). There is a .54 correlation (very, very high for social research) between evaluation of sermons and warm images of God for those who have attended Catholic schools. The mix of Catholic education and good sermons has a

[3] I think this is one of the most powerful arguments for the continuation of celibacy; in fact, I once suggested that I ought to be made a monsignor at least for uncovering such a finding. Church leadership, however, has made nothing of it (and patently has not made me a monsignor!), I suspect because they are profoundly suspicious of all relationships between priests and women.

[4] The Knights were very supportive and helpful in this project, which was the last (and best) study my colleagues and I did of American Catholics. Unfortunately for the project, the Knights quietly disowned it after publication because the two reports appeared at the same time as *The Cardinal Sins*, my first novel. If the novel had not been such an extraordinary success, I don't think the Knights would have been embarrassed by the reports of which they enthusiastically approved, save for one exception to be noted in the next chapter. The books were Andrew Greeley, *The Religious Imagination* (New York: Sadlier, 1981) and Joan Fee, Andrew Greeley, William McCready, and Teresa Sullivan, *Young Catholics* (New York: Sadlier, 1981). In addition, I did a special report, *The Young Catholic Family*, for Thomas More Press in 1981. I have the feeling that the reports slipped between the cracks because of the controversy over my novel. However, I doubt that Catholic leadership or elites would have taken them seriously anyway. The mood in the American Catholic Church at that time and since has been sullen about sociological studies, especially when they report a mixture of good and bad news likely to offend almost everyone.

[5] I do not discuss the much-publicized "parish" study done at the University of Notre Dame because it did not work with probability samples—for which good public relations are no substitute.

powerful impact indeed on the religious imaginations of young people.

The Sacramental Imagination, which is in part responsible for the importance of the parish in Catholic life (the parish, like all communities, tends to be perceived preconsciously as a revelation of the God who is Present), also is shaped by the activities of the parish, especially by that which the parish does not seem to do all that well—its preaching.

There are almost no other data on the interaction between priests and people besides the confidant phenomenon which was teased out of recalcitrant data, partly because there has never been any funding for such research and partly because the research design is tricky. The three findings reported here were serendipitous. While they do hint about the direction future research on priests and people might take, they also suggest how complex that research would have to be. One would have to find interaction networks of priests and people in a parish and race the ebb and flow of action in these networks. A research design is possible (with many pretest experiments), but no one is likely to fund it.

Such a study might be called "Successful Ministry" or the "Successful Parish Priest." Don't hold your breath.[6]

But despite the absence of detailed research (which would be of enormous utility in the training of future priests), it is clear from the relationship between quality of preaching and religious devotion that the role of the priest is important. However, most Catholics give their clergy mixed grades on the quality of their professional performance. On the one hand, more than three-fifths say that their pastor is

[6] My sister, John Shea, David Tracy, and I wrote a book in 1981 about the relationship between priest and people, *Parish, Priest and People* (Thomas More Press). Some years ago I proposed a study of preaching in which a random sample of laity would designate "excellent" preachers and then we would study the priests to see what qualities, characteristics, techniques, and preparations were conducive to effective preaching. The implications of such a project for the training of seminarians and priests would have been enormous. At the suggestion of Archbishop Hurley I submitted the proposal to the American Board of Catholic Missions, of which he was at the time vice-chairman and under whose rubric it clearly fell. Archbishop Bernardin wrote a strong letter endorsing the project. But Archbishop Sanchez, the chairman, did not even submit the proposal to the board and "directed" his secretary to write me and thank me for my interest—an exercise in arrogance that bishops use to put you in your place. I was assured by those who knew that the problem wasn't my proposal but the novels. I considered trying to fund the project with royalty income but was told that the fact that I had funded it would discredit the results even before the project was launched.

Those who judge the work of a sociologist, need I say, by the kind of novels he writes (or more precisely the kind of novels they think he writes or the kind of novels they judge by a page someone has given them to read) are guilty of ignorance and bigotry.

doing a good job. On the other, they do not rate the critical skills of their clergy very high. Only a fifth of the adult population and only a tenth of those under thirty say that the quality of preaching and the sensitivity to human problems of their priests are "excellent." Like Willy Loman the parish priest seems to be liked but not "well-liked." Surely, on the average, they are not respected for their skills at that which is such a powerful predictor of religious devotion.

Note the ironic paradox: the parish is the Church for most people and the priest is the parish and the homily is the priest (the most important contact the priest has with his people), yet the people rate the quality of the homily very low.

One wonders how much more powerful the impact of the parish on the life of lay people would be if priests were more skillful preachers. In the 1950s, 40 percent of Catholics rated the quality of preaching as excellent. It is generally said, by those familiar with our findings, that the decline from 40 percent to 20 percent is the result of changing tastes and standards. The change in the proportion giving "excellent" scores does not represent, it is argued, an actual deterioration in the quality of preaching.

Maybe and then again maybe not. Maybe the lay people do expect more. Or maybe they expect what they always expected and are getting less. The assumption that they expect more and hence are less satisfied may be a dangerous self-deception.

I have received more hostile letters from priests (and had my column dropped from more Catholic papers) because of my writing on the quality of preaching than because of anything else I've done—including my novels. Nothing makes the typical priest more angry than the suggestion that the laity are dissatisfied with the preaching they hear on Saturday afternoon or Sunday morning. I'm not sure whether they really think they're doing a good job in the pulpit or whether they subconsciously fear that they're not.[7]

There is a curious conspiracy of noncommunication between clergy and laity on the subject of preaching. All one has to do at a dinner party or a lecture is to mention the subject and there is an outburst of lay rage that will dominate the rest of the evening. Yet this rage is never directed at one's parish priest. It's all right, you see,

[7] "Who the hell are you to criticize?" is the frequent comment. "You never preach on Sundays!" But I do preach on Sunday, every Sunday, and whether I preach or not is irrelevant to the sociological data. I thought we had learned at the seminary about the invalidity of *ad hominem* arguments.

to complain vehemently to the itinerant scholar or storyteller, but you say nothing at all to your parish priest.

A woman summed it up: "Every time a new priest shows up at the parish, I say to myself that maybe this is the one who can preach a good homily. So far I've been wrong, but hope springs eternal."

"Do you tell that to your priests?"

"No, of course not."

"Why not?"

"I don't want to hurt their feelings."

I believe my next remark may have been scatological.

There is an obligation in strict justice (commutative justice, we used to call it) to preach the Gospel effectively to the lay people. Those priests who don't are not entitled to their salaries and are bound to restitution.

I note that the various national and local "peace and justice" staffs around the country rant about the obligation of "middle-class" Catholics to help the "poor." None of them, however, talk about the obligation of priests in justice to preach the Gospel to middle-class Catholics. I guess some obligations in justice are more important than others. At the bottom of the list is the obligation to pay the employees of the Church a living wage and to preach the Gospel effectively.

That's old moral theology and highly moralistic. But if doctors and lawyers and accountants can be sued for malpractice and be held to restore that which they have taken without adequate care and indeed be forced to pay punitive damages for failing to meet professional standards, by what ethical norms are priests excused from similar responsibility?

I am convinced, given the correlation between preaching and devotion, that large numbers of those who drifted away from regular practice because of the birth-control encyclical would drift back. Those who prate piously about evangelization and persuade the bishops to issue "mandates" on the subject might be better advised to put their energies into enhancing the weekend homilies. If the "excellent" rating could be pushed from 20 to 40 percent, perhaps regular church attendance might jump back to where it was before the birth-control encyclical.

The conclusion from the data seems to me to be inescapable: given the importance of the parish, the priest, and the homily, the most critical single step the Church could take to improve its effectiveness in the United States is to upgrade the quality of its preaching. It is much easier to issue pastoral letters on nuclear weapons and poverty (all the while paying your employees poverty wages) than to improve homilies, easier to tell other people how to do their business than to do your own.

How can it be that something so important is so badly done? Some priests will argue with me that the homily is not that important. They do many other things during the course of the week which are much more important—teaching, instruction, counseling.

Yet it should be obvious that the only contact the priest has with most of his parishioners from one end of the year to the other is the weekend homily. If he is the Church for them, they know the Church from what he says in the ten or fifteen minutes after the Gospel.

The Catholic people have not been driven out of the Church by the turbulence of the last quarter century, not by the birth-control encyclical, not by the Church's terrible discrimination against women. They haven't even been driven out by the inexcusable quality of clerical preaching.

Nothing will drive them out.

Why is preaching so bad that only 20 percent of the laity (10 percent of the young laity) give their clergy "excellent" ratings? I can think of four reasons, three of which are less important than the fourth. Like the woman in the conversation I mentioned earlier, the laity are still too respectful of their priests to tell them that they're rotten preachers. For decades priests could argue that the administration of the Sacraments was what counted and that, unlike Protestant ministers who had to rely entirely on their preaching, priests had more to offer. There is no link between professional performance and promotion or reward for a Catholic priest. Quite the contrary: if you are too good at anything, you might stir up envy from your fellows which would impede your career.

The most important reason, however, is that priests are badly educated. The homiletics programs in most seminaries in years gone by were the worst courses the seminary imposed on its students. Even today the good programs seem to be few and far between.

Preaching is not merely a craft that is taught in a homiletics class. It is a creative art that requires imagination, discipline, practice, sensitivity, reflection, willingness to listen to others, openness to feedback. Crafting a homily is as much an act of creativity as writing a poem, telling a story, painting a picture, sculpting a statue, cooking a gourmet meal. To do it well one must read, think, imagine, experiment, play. There is very little in seminary training that is designed to facilitate such activities or to promote the development of the creativity which everyone has and which is essential for preaching. Psychology (usually of the pop variety) has replaced manual theology, when in fact if one wishes to train preachers one should supplement theology (not replace it) with literature. A priest who does not read is not likely to preach well. A priest who has not had sustained contact with great works of literature is not likely to preach well. A priest who has not been challenged to develop his own creativity is not likely to preach well.

Our competitors are no longer the storytellers in the saloons or in the workplace. They are Dan Rather, Kathleen Sullivan, Chris Wallace, Peter Jennings, Bryant Gumbel, Jane Pauley. They are good at what they do and we are not.

I have often argued that no one should be ordained who has not displayed a serious effort at improving his creative imagination—producing a cycle of sonnets, a collection of short stories, a novel, a one-act play, a photo exhibit. The usual response to such a suggestion from an audience of priests is derisive laughter. They think I'm joking, but I'm not.[8] If one does not value one's own creative imagination and seek to develop it for the rest of one's life, then one is not likely to be an effective preacher.

The Catholic Church in the United States is in pretty good shape at the grass roots. How much better its condition would be if the professionalism of the clergy could be improved. Parish priests are the most influential people in the Church. Think of how much more influential they would be if they did well that which is their most important function.

As Blessed Julian of Norwich would put it, "Then all manner of things will be well!"

Why do parishes flourish often in spite of the poor performance of their clergy? A layman put it to me succinctly after he had complained about his pastor (a neurotic ninny, not to put too fine an edge on matters): "It's my community as much as it is his and I'll be damned if I let him drive me out. I was here before he came and I'll be here after he leaves."

Just as the Church is their Church—and they like being part of it even when the leadership is inept and insensitive—they like their

---

[8] I think the same requirements should be imposed on everyone as a prerequisite for college graduation, lay and clerical.

parishes even when the leadership is boorish and incompetent—which it often, perhaps even usually, is.

The Sacramental Imagination sees the need of hierarchy to maintain a pattern of ordered relationships in human society. But when hierarchy (or authority) bungles badly, it does not follow that the community is corrupt or sinful, but only that the sacrament (the revelation of God) which the community is has become even more flawed. Those who believe that human communities are God-forsaken will tolerate much less than those who believe that they are sacramental. One puts up with the idiot over in the rectory because, while he is the visible Church for you, it's still your parish.

If there is any doubt about how important the parish is to those who live in it, one must merely consider the outrage that inevitably erupts whenever the chancery tries to close a parish or a school or tear down a church. Diocesan bureaucrats are baffled ("dumbfounded"[9] was the word used by the auxiliary bishop of Detroit in reaction to the protests of the laity when the ineffable Cardinal Szoka eliminated with a stroke of his pen forty-three parishes).

Why do people cling so desperately to a community that rational economics indicate is no longer viable?

Why do laity value their parish more than church leadership does?

Or to put the matter differently, why do church bureaucrats fail to understand the symbolic importance of the parish to the people who live in it? The Sacramental Imagination is at work: the parish is a sacrament of God's presence—which is what we've told them, but which they believe, however inarticulately, more than we do.

An answer in terms of rational-choice economics may come to the same thing. The parish represents both investment capital and consumption capital. You put your time and money and work into it, so it's yours. No one else, so the argument runs, has the right to take it away from you, and certainly not without asking you. Moreover, you are familiar with it, skilled in its procedures and protocols, identified with its rituals and routines. How dare some dummy from downtown drag you out of that which has become commonplace in your life!

The American neighborhood parish is one of the most ingenious communities that human skill has ever created. Its overlapping network of religious, educational, familial, social, and political relationships has created what my colleague James S. Coleman (who is not

---

[9] He had the first half of the word right.

Catholic) calls "social capital," a social resource in the strict sense of the word because it comes not from individual investments but from relational patterns. To call the overlapping networks of human relationships "capital" is to say that, as with any capital, more can be accomplished because the relationship networks exist (just as more can be done if you build a new steel mill than if you don't). Coleman contends (as we shall see in greater detail in the next chapter) that it is precisely the social capital in Catholic schools which enables them to be more effective educational institutions than public schools.

Social capital is the extra energy generated by overlapping networks of relationships. It is the economic result of a community shaped by the Sacramental Imagination. Coleman's insight reinforces what Catholic theory used to believe about the parish. Oddly enough, just at the time when one of America's most distinguished sociologists discovers the importance of the neighborhood parish, Catholic theorists seem to have abandoned their faith in it.

Greeley's First Law: *When others discover the value of something Catholic, Catholic theorists lose confidence in it.*

And Greeley's Second Law is like unto it: *When others lose confidence in something of theirs, Catholics discover it for the first time.*[10]

Every time a parish is closed (however necessary the closing may be) some social capital is destroyed—a rich and valuable resource is lost. The capital equivalent of a steel mill is torn down. Less important than the buildings of a parish "plant" are the relationship networks of the neighborhood parish, of which the "plant" has been both the physical center and the symbol.

In the various journals and books from which clergy and religious and lay Catholic educators draw their (usually shallow) ideas, every experiment in community formation that has been tried everywhere else in the world for the last forty years has been applauded with demands that American Catholics must do something like it—from the worker-priest communities in Paris after World War II to the base communities in Latin America today (both of which have had minuscule impact on religion in their societies). But the neighborhood parish is ignored if not condemned, although it has already established the community formation for which these new and experimental (and dubiously successful) institutions have been created.

[10] The Third Law is that the willingness of leaders of an institution to offer advice to leaders of other institutions is in inverse proportion to the internal well-being of their own institution: bishops meddle in foreign policy and offer advice on the economy precisely at the time they have lost control of their own internal affairs in the Church.

At a press conference in Rome during one of the synods, Cardinal Manning of Los Angeles (a good and gentle man who was much too smart to be made a cardinal today) was explaining to us what the Latin Americans meant by "base communities."

"Cardinal," I asked, with the infinite respect I always tender to pastors of the Holy Roman Church, "might our neighborhood parishes in America accomplish the same purpose?"

The cardinal was bemused. He frowned, thought about it for a moment, and then said in his soft brogue, "Oh, no, Father. I don't think they're anything like that."

I let it go. I didn't respond (such is my respect for Princes of the Church) that the neighborhood parish has two advantages over the base communities: it grew naturally out of the human condition and was not imposed on reality by *a prioristic* theorists; and it works and has worked for a century.

There is a third advantage: it's ours. It's not something which in a burst of self-hatred we have borrowed from another culture and attempted to graft on to the life of our people (who with good sense and good taste ignore it).

If the Sacramental Imagination values neighborhood community more than does the dialectical imagination, then in the cities of the country Catholics should be more reluctant to move out of their neighborhoods, even their homes, than are their Protestant neighbors. In fact such is the case. The average urban Catholic has lived in his/her neighborhood for 20.4 years, the average urban Protestant for 19.1 years. The Catholic has lived in the same home for 10.4 years, the Protestant for 9.7 years. There is built into the Catholic style of relating to the physical environment a greater propensity to stay in the same place.

The neighborhood parish happened by chance. Priests assigned to minister to the immigrants brought their experience from peasant villages in the old country. They discovered that their people had clustered together—for help and protection—in tight geographical communities. These clusters were often not only from the same country but also from the same towns and villages: cousin living next door to cousin the way they had in the old country. So the priest adjusted and adapted and continued with the old ministries, now Americanized. As soon as he could he built a school to protect his people from the public schools, which were viewed not as godless but as Protestant. His theory, almost always implicit, was that the faith of the people must be protected from Protestants, who would try to take it away from them, and that the people must become successful and thus demonstrate that they could be good Americans as well as good Catholics.

The fear of Protestant assault was legitimate enough during the times of the Know-Nothings, and the nativists, and the Ku Klux Klan, and the APA (American Protective Association). The fear that Catholics would leave turns out in retrospect to have been less valid. Few were about to join the "dirty APAs" as the saying went. The availability of priests, the ties of the parish, the support of their fellow immigrants made them often more devout and more loyal Catholics than they had been in their land of origin (loyalty only emerges as a virtue when other options become available).

Critics of the neighborhood parish often suggest that the clergy forced the immigrants into such communities. The opposite was more usually the case: the immigrants flocked to where the churches were.[11] When there were no clergy, groups of laymen (especially Eastern European) demanded that bishops furnish clergy. When there were no national parishes (parishes for members of one ethnic group), the laity insisted that such parishes be established. The neighborhood parish emerged from a chance convergence of religion and immigration, from the identification of religion with ethnic identity and from an ambivalent response to the new society—a desire to become part of it and at the same time remain true to one's own past (which is everyone's right in the "American Way" in its nonnativist moments).

By chance then, fortunate chance I would say, the old peasant village was salvaged and re-created in the modern world, a touch of the archaic revivified in the big cities of North America, a hint of *Gemeinschaft* in an increasingly *Gesellschaft* society. In later years, when the nation would become manic in its "quest for community," the Catholic Church already had communities of overlapping networks, religious, social, civil, fraternal, ethnic, political—a rich, rich resource of social capital.

I do not want to appear to argue that the neighborhood parish was perfect. Like all human institutions[12] it was and is flawed, sometimes

[11] Father Arnold Damen, S.J., built the vast Holy Family Church in the prairies on the West Side of Chicago (the largest church in North America at the time) because he knew the Irish were coming and he knew they would swarm around a church. The archdiocese of Chicago, with its usual sense of the importance of history, now wants to tear it down—as well as St. Mary of the Angels, a lovely and historically important Polish church.

[12] All human institutions have their own peculiar inherent flaws that, according to the perspective of the Sacramental Imagination, does not mean they are evil, only human. The proper response to an inherent flaw is not to destroy the institution but to take into account the flaw and do the best one can to minimize its harmful effects.

by human frailties, sometimes by weaknesses that are peculiar to it and inherent in its structures. Not surprisingly the neighborhood parish tends to be parochial; sometimes, perhaps often, it was and is obscurantist and oppressive; on occasion it has fallen into the hands of an insensitive (and affluent) elite; it has never attracted all of its potential members, and only on occasion do most of its members seem integrated with it. (It does not take away the free will of its members and hence does not constrain but at the most attracts active participation.)

However, to compare the neighborhood parish with all its existential frailties and imperfection with, let us say, the base community in its theoretical perfection, is unreasonable and *prima facie* evidence of elitist self-hatred.

That the American neighborhood parish, a survival of the archaic in urban industrial society, is a Catholic phenomenon is not accidental. With their proclivity to imagine (preconsciously) community as sacrament, Catholics have a special tendency to set up intense communities wherever they can. The American neighborhood parish is the Sacramental Imagination (which itself is archaic) working its way in the set of circumstances in which it found itself in the big cities of North America.

One of the reasons that we don't respect it is that we take it for granted; it is as commonplace to us as the air we breathe and as unself-conscious and pragmatic as falling asleep at night. Our sister and brother Catholics in other nations develop an idea, perhaps test it once (though if they're Germans even one test isn't really necessary), and immediately proclaim it to the world as True, and indeed universally so. We tend to act on hunch and instinct and reflect, if we do so at all, only when the alienated within us say we should be doing what the foreigners say we should be doing.

A few days ago I heard a liturgist on a tape lament the individualism of American society and American Catholics. In the ghetto, he said, we had a communal overlay because of ethnic identifications. But those communal ties wane when we move into the suburbs and encounter full-scale American privatism.

I stopped my car in dismay and turned on the Bears game (which was just starting and which they won). I could hardly believe that so much fallacy and so much dialectical imagination could be crowded into three or four sentences.

First, American society is too big, too complex, too fluid, to be described as "individualist" and "privatist" or "consumerist" without qualification, nuance, and description of powerful countervailing trends. The liturgist in question (who is a prophet of the "Religious-Education/Liturgy/Rite-of-Christian-Initiation-of-Adults" clique that is struggling for power within the parishes and the whole American Church) settled the issue with a quote from sociologist Robert Bellah, whose book *Habits of the Heart* has become the new bible for the "Religious Education" elite and is now quoted with the same reverential fervor with which American Dominicans used to quote Saint Thomas Aquinas. In fact, despite Bellah's unsupported assertions, civil activities in America have surged dramatically in the last two decades. Granted, there are powerful strains of individualism, as Professor Mary Ann Glendon has argued, but there are also powerful strains of communalism, not all of them the "touchy/feely" variety left over from the 1960s. The community organizations and environmentalist groups that have sprung up all over the country are proof enough of that. Moreover, the research of my colleagues Norman Nie and Sidney Verba (whom Bellah footnotes but apparently does not understand) completely undercuts the "individualism" paradigm as the only valid description of contemporary America. (Bellah's book is a classic example of the "Golden Age Fallacy" in social science: things are bad today, but once they were better than they are now. Proof that they were ever better is almost always nonexistent.)

Second, to write off the immigrant neighborhood parish with the slur word "ghetto" is to do scant justice to its major achievements and to reveal a dialectical imagination hard at work.

Third, it will be news to many suburbanites that the world they live in is privatized. Quite the contrary: they might be more inclined to say that it is a madhouse of communal activities.

The persistence of a communal imagination among Catholics under forty, previously demonstrated in this book, shows that the Catholic propensity toward community does not wither among a new and younger generation.

Last of all, like most of those who want to convert the Catholic Church into a counterculture resisting everything in American society—instead of discerning what is to be embraced and what is not to be embraced[13]—the liturgist assumes that the suburban parish is not as intensely communal as the one in the old neighborhood. The

---

[13] Like others of his ilk the liturgist assumes that he and his followers have a monopoly on grace and that there is no grace to be found anywhere in American society or culture. The United States is graceless and God-forsaken. This is the dialectical imagination pushed to its ultimate cultist conclusion.

neighborhood parish, such folk say, was fine in its day, but its day is over. Such an assertion becomes almost a matter of faith, a reality in which they invest enormous emotional energy. Their faith in the decline of the parish community is in inverse proportion to the proof to support such faith.

They have made up their minds, in other words, and they're not interested in facts.

I wonder how many suburban parishes they know. The St. Angela parish in which I was raised was far less communal than the Christ the King in which I served happily or the Mother of Sorrows in Tucson where I work. The shape of the communal structure may have changed, but to describe the fringe parishes around the cities as "privatist" is to impose theory on reality with utter disregard for the nature of reality. Catholics, in the grip of the Sacramental Imagination, for the most part liked their neighborhood parishes in the old neighborhood and strive mightily, and on the whole successfully, to reproduce them in the new neighborhoods.

The liturgist saw America as an atomized society of isolated and alienated and "privatized" individuals. How many different ways does one have to say it: Catholics like their Church precisely because it values community as they do, too, precisely because they are Catholic. When one community erodes, given half a chance, and decent leadership, they will try to build another one just like it, only better— especially if the cultural environment reinforces community organizations, as American suburbia does.

I am tempted to call men like the liturgist, whose tape I listened to before I abandoned him for the Bears, pernicious; except that the laity and many of the clergy will listen politely to him and his disciples and then continue to be Catholics the way they always have.

The "elite" (which is not all that elite in terms of its ability and education, but which is the best the institutional Church can do just now) might be dangerous if it were not so irrelevant. That they do not value the neighborhood parish, past and present, is likely to have little effect on the propensity of the laity to flock to parishes and reconstitute them whenever possible.

Catholics, to repeat one of my key themes, imagine differently. That's why they tend to like parishes. Some may opt for the cultlike structures advocated by the pseudo-elite like my liturgist. Most will want neighborhood parishes like those in which they grew up. They are not likely to change their mind because the resident director of religious education says they should.

How can you be so reactionary? I am asked. You support the ordination of women, you criticize church leaders, you are a liberal in many ways. Yet you support conservative notions like the neighborhood parish and, God help us, the Catholic schools. What are you *really?*

As I have argued before in this book, the "left/right" paradigm does not cope readily with Catholic attitudes and behavior. But the religious imagination paradigm does. What I am really is a Catholic in the grip of a Sacramental Imagination, one that says, "Here comes everyone!"

So of course I like the neighborhood parish and the Catholic schools, as does almost everyone else—except those members of the Catholic pseudo-elite who get their kicks out of denouncing their own origins and their own people.

9

THE TOUCHSTONE:
CATHOLIC SCHOOLS

UMMER 1966: my first summer at Grand Beach (where I had escaped from my alcove in a rectory basement). Monsignor George A. Kelly, a fellow sociologist, was on the phone.[1]

"You're in terrible trouble!"

My stomach turned uneasily. Being in terrible trouble was a new experience for me.

"Did you see the piece about your report in the *Times?*"

"There was nothing in the *Sun-Times* about it."

I was still so naïve as not to know, except when you're in London or Dublin, that the *Times* is what Jimmy Breslin calls *The New York Times* newspaper.

"*The New York Times!* Spelly has read it and he's furious. You're attacking Catholic schools!"

"You read the manuscript, George. I don't attack the schools."

"It looks that way in the *Times* and Spelly is fit to be tied."

My stomach had stopped turning. I was a lot less worried about Cardinal Spellman than I was about the new archbishop of Chicago, John Cody. I had brought him the galleys of *The Education of Cath-*

---

[1] George was then a "liberal" and a close friend; indeed, he invited me once to talk to the clergy of New York. Since then he has turned sharply to the right and blames me and Hans Küng for all the bad things that have happened to the Church. While it is always an honor to be linked with such a scholar as Father Küng, I fear Monsignor Kelly gives me too much credit. Catholic married people did not and do not make their decisions about birth control because of what sociologists write, probably not even because of what theologians, even those as distinguished as Father Küng, write.

olic Americans and was greeted with questions about who gave me permission to work at the University of Chicago[2] and how much money I made and what I did with it. He was uninterested in the report. I departed, as I came, the galleys under my arm.

I did not realize that if something appeared in the *Times* it was officially true. If *The New York Times* newspaper reported that our research showed that Catholic schools had failed, then they had officially failed. George Kelly said he would mail me the front page of the second section special delivery and suggested I write a refutation and send it to the cardinal with a nice letter of explanation and a copy of the report.

I was astonished when the *Times* article arrived at Grand Beach. It was a thoroughly dishonest exercise in selective journalism, the worst I would ever see in all the years of daily reading of the *Times* since then. The writer had gone through the book and taken out of context everything that might sound unfavorable about Catholic schools and ignored everything favorable, sometimes even cutting out part of a sentence to reverse my meaning.

I wrote a letter of protest to the *Times* which was never published. I sent a copy with a letter and the book to Cardinal Spellman, who replied very graciously. Much later John Cogley, then the religion writer at the *Times,* phoned to apologize for the incident, noting that both he and Clifton Daniel, the editor of the *Times,* were on vacation when it happened. They never did print my reply, however.

The following week the *National Catholic Reporter* weighed in with an attack on *The Education of Catholic Americans*[3] that had little to do with what the book actually said. I wrote a letter to the editor asking him to document some of the assertions he had made. He replied that he had only glanced at the volume but was responding to what he knew to be my "general" opinions on the subject of Catholic schools. He didn't apologize, however.

What sociologists find in their research, you see, is dictated by their "general opinion" and not by their data!

Commonweal had already ridiculed a preliminary report as a "whitewash of Catholic schools."

A few years later at a wild meeting in the Marriott Hotel near Washington National Airport, a nun/sociologist attacked Catholic high schools on the grounds that students at such schools were racist

[2] His predecessor, Cardinal Albert Meyer.
[3] Andrew Greeley and Peter Rossi (Aldine Press, 1966).

bigots. It was an era in the late sixties when there was an open season on all things that the Church had ever done before the appearance of Dan and Phil Berrigan. The Greeley/Rossi report, Sister continued, proved that Catholic schools did not have any effect on the lives of the people who attended them.

I rose to a point of personal privilege: Sister was misquoting the findings of the report. Catholic schools did indeed have a positive impact on the attitudes and behavior of those who attended them, even on their racial attitudes. Afterwards a bevy of angry nuns swarmed around to castigate me. I knew what Sister meant, they insisted; why had I disagreed with her? I replied with more mildness than I felt or they deserved that all I knew was what Sister said and what she said was not true.

Years later I was eating breakfast in the historic Roosevelt Hotel in New Orleans before presenting findings from the Knights of Columbus study about the effect of Catholic education on young people growing up in a time of turbulence in both Church and nation. (The presentation would take place in the same Superdome where the Bears would triumph over the Foxboro Patriots.) Two of the other priests at the table were diocesan directors of the Confraternity of Christian Doctrine, which is responsible for the "religious education" of Catholics who do not attend Catholic schools. What was I going to say? they demanded nervously.

I should have known better by that stage in my life, but I told them the truth. I could find no correlation between attendance at CCD programs and adult attitudes and behavior. On the other hand, the measures of relationship between Catholic education and adult behavior, which had increased between 1963 and 1974, had increased again and were now quite strong indeed. Moreover, attending Catholic schools had an especially powerful effect on the return to the Church of young people who had drifted away during the bottom of the religious life cycle in their early and middle twenties.

My two companions pleaded with me to suppress the findings. CCD was a new movement, it lacked money and resources, it required time to "catch up" with the Catholic schools. My report would discourage bishops from increasing CCD funding.

I was unable to see then, and I still cannot see, how they expected to accomplish more in one hour a week (at the most) than the Catholic schools accomplished in twenty-five hours a week, especially since the secret of the religious success of the Catholic schools was their ability to integrate young people in the parish community.

And I don't suppress truth, not then, not ever. Nonetheless they and their colleagues conspired to persuade the Knights of Columbus to delete from our report the observation that the CCD had no observable effect.

Our research had started out shrouded with fears that we would destroy Catholic schools; it ended up in fears that we would sustain them. In the interim it made a rapid journey from inkblot to myth. In the process the reports went largely unread and the facts largely ignored. Serves me and my colleagues right for becoming involved in such an emotionally charged subject.

Most of our findings, in six projects and as many books, were in fact more favorable to Catholic schools than not. Nonetheless, in the years between the publication of *The Education of Catholic Americans* and *Minority Students in Catholic Schools*,[4] the construction of new Catholic schools ground to a halt. In Chicago not a single new one has been opened since 1966. Shows what research findings are really worth.

Even though the books have gone unread, it is now pretty clear to almost everyone that they report findings which indicate that Catholic schools are quite successful. So I find myself both praised and damned as a great "friend" of Catholic education. That is not, however, true. I am rather a friend of empirical evidence. I began my research a dispassionate skeptic, rather impressed by my own Catholic education and by my experience in teaching at Christ the King school as a newly ordained priest, but I was not at all convinced that the schools were worth the cost.

If I now think they are worth the cost (that indeed they pay for themselves), the reason is not that I have a bias in favor of them but rather that I have been convinced by the evidence.

I call the Catholic schools the "touchstone" because opposition to them is so irrational and in such defiance of overwhelming evidence that I take it to be *prima facie* proof of self-hatred and self-rejection, a turning against the community ethos of the Sacramental Imagination in favor of the individualist ethos of the dialectical imagination,[5]

---

[4] Brunswick, N.J.: Transaction Books, 1982.

[5] Dialectical in the strict sense of the word because opposition to Catholic schools rejects the network of relationships between past and present, between what we did then and what we do now. The Sacramental Imagination seeks to preserve every last bit of wisdom and sensitivity that the past has to offer; it rejects efforts to link the past with the present only when the evidence is incontrovertible that a given artifact or custom of the past can no longer be harmonized with the present. The dialectical imagination for its part rejects the past as sinful and corrupt in all its particularities and strives to build a new order *de novo* that is free from links with the past.

an elitist perfectionism, and an overreaction to the assimilationist pressures of Americanization.

There is no phenomenon more paradoxical in Catholicism since the Council than the Catholic schools. On the one hand, the evidence is overwhelming that the schools are remarkably successful both religiously and academically. On the other hand, enrollment in the schools is diminishing and Catholic leadership does not appear to be as committed to Catholic schools as it was before the Vatican Council.

At the time of the 1979 study of young adults, 88 percent of the respondents between eighteen and thirty had some kind of Catholic education; 64 percent of these had attended Catholic grade schools for a time, 36 percent had attended Catholic grade schools for all of their elementary education, and more than a third of those who did not spend all their years in Catholic schools had at least four years of religious instruction. On the other hand, 50 percent of the young adults surveyed received no religious instruction in high school. Of the other 50 percent, 25 percent attended the CCD religious instruction classes. Seventeen percent of the Catholics during their high school years had four years of Catholic high schools; only 8 percent had four years of CCD. Seventy-three percent of those who attended public schools at least some of the time said there were years when they did not receive religious instruction. The reasons given (they add up to more than a hundred because the respondent was permitted many different reasons): 26 percent said poor teaching, 45 percent had no interest in religion, 11 percent said friends weren't going, 13 percent said there were no classes offered, 14 percent said parents did not care, and 11 percent said they already knew enough religion.

So one can conclude that the Church gets some instruction to most of its young members, a lot to elementary school children, and much less to high school youth. However, poor teaching and the unavailability of religious education classes account for only about one-third of the nonattendance at high school religious education classes. Thus, despite the pleas of CCD supporters that more classes and better teaching would attract more "uneducated" young Catholics, the major reasons young people who do not attend Catholic schools also do not seek religious education are a lack of interest in religion and a lack of support from their parents or friends for religious education classes.

The study demonstrated that Catholic school attendance had a statistically significant impact on the religious behavior of young people: 43 percent of those who had more than eight years of Catholic school attended Mass every week as opposed to 32 percent who had less; 32 percent received Communion every week as opposed to 17 percent; 72 percent believed in life after death as opposed to 60 percent; 13 percent belonged to parish organizations as opposed to 5 percent; 12 percent had thought seriously of a religious vocation as opposed to 6 percent; 37 percent had read a Catholic periodical as opposed to 25 percent; 64 percent were opposed to abortion if no more children were wanted by the mother as opposed to 54 percent.

Moreover, these effects of Catholic school education were not merely surrogates for the influence of a religious family or a religious spouse. Rather, they were additional effects when family and spouse influence was held constant. The influence of Catholic school on the religious behavior of young Catholics is stronger than that of the family of origin. It is only slightly less strong than the family of procreation even when the influence of the other is taken into account. The old explanation of the success of Catholic schools, that they were merely duplicating the work of the Catholic family, is simply not valid.

Catholic schools seem to have their effect on those who attend them not so much through formal religious instruction class but rather through the closeness to the Catholic community that the experience of attending Catholic schools generates.

Attendance at CCD classes does not have anywhere near the same effect. Indeed, there are virtually no statistically significant correlations between attendance at CCD and later religious beliefs or behaviors, but there are strong and statistically significant correlations between attendance at Catholic schools and adult religious behavior.

Attendance at Catholic schools continued in the late 1970s to have the same moderate and statistically significant impact on the behavior of young Catholic adults as had been found in our earlier studies. More than eight years of Catholic schooling does not produce a statistically significant impact on attitudes toward birth control, living together, and frequency of prayer. Neither did Catholic education produce such an impact on the analysis reported on the education of Catholic Americans based on 1974 data. Nor is there a significant difference among those who had more than eight years of Catholic schooling. However, on all the other tested variables—Mass attendance, Communion reception, belief in life after death, activity in parish organizations, thought of religious vocation, Catholic periodical reading and TV watching, participation in home liturgy and study

groups, and opposition to abortion—Catholic schools do have a statistically significant effect.

How impressive is the magnitude of that effect? The question is
not easier to answer now than it was in either our 1966 or 1975
reports. Those who attended Catholic schools are twice as likely to
receive Communion almost every week, to belong to parish organizations, to think of religious vocations, and to attend home liturgies.
Indeed, only 12 percent of them have considered a vocation, but that
is twice as many as the 6 percent who have not had more than eight
years of Catholic schooling. Only 10 percent have attended a home
liturgy, but that is still twice as high as the 5 percent of those who
have not had more than eight years of Catholic schooling. Are these
differences large or small? A little more than a quarter of those who
have attended Catholic schools are uncertain about life after death
(less than 10 percent say they do not believe in life after death; the
others report they do not know for certain). If the goal is 100 percent
commitment to belief in human survival, then Catholic schools have
failed. If the goal is notably and significantly to improve the likelihood of believing in life after death, then Catholic schools have succeeded.

In the propaganda for Catholic schools many years ago, it often
seemed to be said that Catholic schools would turn out exemplary
Catholics almost without exception. The critics of Catholic schools,
taking that "argument" as a norm, have never ceased to point out
enthusiastically that the schools simply do not achieve such a goal.
The defenders of Catholic schools who accept such a statement of the
question have been embarrassed and defensive.

Any serious reading of the educational impact literature would
reveal that schools should not reasonably be expected to undo the
work of home, family, peer group, neighborhood, social class, and
ethnic culture. Though schools can make a difference under some
circumstances, the boundless American faith in the power of formal
education has never been sustained either by empirical evidence or by
everyday impression.

Where does this leave us on the subject of the effectiveness of
Catholic schools? They do not produce graduates who are universally
exemplary Catholics. They do have some effect. How much effect?
Far more effect in terms of statistical size than is used to justify racial
integration. Is the effect worth the cost? One would think, given the
difficulty of affecting human religious behavior at all, that the effect

is worth the cost until an alternate system, technique, or method can be devised that does as well.

This interpretation is basically the same one that was originally presented in *The Education of Catholic Americans* and appeared in *Catholic Schools in a Declining Church*. Catholic schools do have a limited effect, a not unimpressive effect as educational impact effects go. It does not seem reasonable to give up on them unless one has an alternative system that will produce the same effect at less cost.

In the three NORC Catholic school studies, 1963, 1974, and 1979 (of young adults), perhaps the most interesting phenomenon was that in each year the importance of Catholic schools to the religious behavior of Catholic adults increased. The correlation between attendance at Catholic schools and a wide range of measures of adult religious attitudes and behaviors—church attendance, reception of Communion, attitudes toward vocation, belief in life after death, activity in parish organizations, closeness to the Church—increased as the stability of the Church decreased. The question asked in the second Catholic school study, *Catholic Schools in a Declining Church*, whether Catholic schools were more important in a time of crisis in the Church than a time of stability, has been clearly answered and now twice: Catholic schools are much more important—as measured by the strength of correlation between Catholic school attendance and adult behavior—in a time of crisis in the Church than in a time of stability. Nevertheless, Catholic school enrollment declines and confidence in the worth of Catholic schools also seems to erode.

In the 1974 study it appeared that the decline in Catholic school attendance was the result of smaller numbers coming of school age and the failure to build new schools in the areas into which Catholics were moving. Thus the decline in support for Catholic schools at that time seemed to be the result of decisions on the part of school administrators not to build new schools and not the result of decisions by parents not to use the schools that were available. It also appeared on the basis of the 1974 study that while Catholic schools were a substantial extra cost to a parish, most if not all of this extra cost was absorbed by the larger contributions of parents with children in the Catholic schools and by the more substantial contributions to the Sunday collection of parishioners who had themselves attended Catholic schools. In fact, this sort of analysis indicated that Catholic schools actually not only paid for themselves but may even have been moneymakers for the parishes in that contributions from present and past users of the Catholic schools more than made up for the costs the schools incurred.

In a previous chapter I reported a life-cycle phase in which young people drift away from religious practice, a phase that begins after high school graduation and seems to come to an end when the young person approaches his or her thirtieth birthday. The correlation between Catholic school attendance and return to the Church in one's late twenties is .35, a very powerful correlation. There is no correlation at all between attendance at CCD classes and return to frequent religious practice in one's late twenties. Indeed, in some cases the correlation is negative: the more one has attended CCD classes, the less likely one is to return to active religious practice in the late twenties. In all the research we have done on the effects of Catholic schools we have not been able to find any persuasive evidence of *any* effect of participation in CCD courses on adult religious behavior. For all the enthusiasm, for all the energy, for all the financial commitment, it simply has to be said that as of 1979 the Confraternity of Christian Doctrine as a substitute for Catholic schools is simply a waste of time. CCD does not attract a substantial proportion of Catholics—at least half the Catholics of high school age receive no religious instruction at all, most of them because they don't want to receive religious instruction—and is not in any meaningful sense an adequate replacement for Catholic schools.

The Catholic schools are the most effective contribution the Church is making to the service of the poor. While Catholic school attendance has been declining, the enrollment of blacks and Hispanics (at least half of the former not Catholic) in Catholic schools has been increasing dramatically. Research done by James Coleman and myself on secondary school students indicates that the Catholic schools have an enormous impact on the sons and daughters of the disadvantaged. Holding constant twelve different parental background variables and academic scores in the sophomore year, the seniors in Catholic schools perform substantially higher on standardized achievement tests than do the seniors in public schools. Moreover, this finding applies not only to Hispanic and to black young men and women but also to white students. The Catholic schools are more effective as secondary educators than public schools for all three racial groups.

It is especially among the disadvantaged and even more among the multiply disadvantaged that the impact of Catholic secondary schools is likely to be greatest. Those young men and women who are disadvantaged by poverty, or by low levels of parental education, or by low personal self-esteem, or by disciplinary problems when they were sophomores, or by being on the fringes of the school community, or by low academic scores in their sophomore year are the ones most likely to benefit from the two years in between sophomore and senior year in Catholic schools. Most of the effectiveness of Catholic schools in dealing with disadvantaged young men and women can be attributed to the fact that the schools demand more homework from the students and more advanced course work, especially in mathematics and English.

Those public schools that demand several hours of homework a night and more advanced course work have the same effect as do the Catholic schools on disadvantaged young men and women. But many, indeed most, public schools are not either able or willing to demand more homework and more advanced course work than the Catholic schools, perhaps because the latter have fallen behind the educational fashion, are able to make such demands and thus able to have remarkable academic effect on their students, particularly on those students who come from one or another disadvantaged backgrounds.

On my desk as I revise this chapter are two newspaper clippings, one a bitter attack by a priest in the *National Catholic Reporter* on Catholic schools, the other a celebration of them by James S. Coleman in the *Wall Street Journal*. The former denounces them as a reactionary fraud on the Catholic people and a misuse of parish funds, the latter praises them as the most effective educational institutions in America.

As Pete Rossi would say, there are a lot of ironies in the fire.

Among the many curious paradoxes that affect the present condition of Catholic schools is that in the years since the Second Vatican Council, and especially in light of the conciliar document "Gaudium et Spes," the Church has insisted vigorously on its obligations to the poor and on the necessity to exercise the "preferential option for the poor," and at the same time has phased out as quickly as it could much of the most effective service it has ever done for the inner-city poor in the Catholic schools.

It is difficult to think of any other efforts of the Catholic Church in the largest urban centers of America which reach so many of the poor or reach them with such notable effectiveness. Nonetheless, Catholic schools in the inner city are slowly being closed and there seems to be little protest from those Catholics who are enthusiastically committed to the cause of "justice and peace" and to the "preferential option for the poor."

The evidence is now completely persuasive that Catholic schools do indeed render an important service to the poor. It is odd, to say the least, to see these schools being closed precisely at a time when the Church takes frequent public stands in favor of the "preferential option for the poor." Obviously there was nothing in the documents of the Second Vatican Council which suggested that the Catholic schools should be "phased out" and replaced by some form of "religious education" like the Confraternity of Christian Doctrine program. Nevertheless, in the intellectual and religious climate that developed in the American Church after the Second Vatican Council, the decision to proceed away from Catholic schools and in the direction of CCD was made without the benefit of consultation with the Catholic laity, serious consideration of the available empirical research, and public discussion of the reasons behind the decision. Suddenly the decision had been made: Catholic schools were out and CCD was in.

The Catholic schools have not been completely closed down, but new ones are rarely built and enrollment in the old ones is declining as the Catholic population shifts into the new areas of the suburban fringes of the large cities of the country. The religious- and community-building function of the Catholic school has been sustained by empirical research beyond any reasonable doubt. The service-to-the-poor function of the school is both self-evident and has also been sustained by empirical evidence.

Nonetheless, Catholic schools simply are no longer as important to the ecclesiastical institution as they were at the time of the Vatican Council. Just as there has been a loss of nerve and confidence in the priesthood, despite the fact that priests are more important rather than less important than they used to be, so there is a loss of nerve and of confidence in Catholic schools even though they are now more important both to Catholics and to disadvantaged non-Catholics than they used to be.

There is no research evidence to explain the reason for either of these losses of nerve. Still, the conclusion is inescapable: Catholic schools are a casualty of the era following the Second Vatican Council. They have not disappeared completely but they are in trouble— and they are in trouble despite the fact that the consumers of Catholic education are, for the most part, very happy with the product they purchase when they send their young people to parochial schools.

What is the secret of the "modest" or "moderate" or "important" effect of Catholic education on the behavior of young Catholic adults? (Readers may choose their own word, depending on their criteria for educational success—though we would remind them that in most educational research, relationships of the size reported in our research would be taken very seriously indeed.) How can the effectiveness of Catholic schools be explained? Is it the result of specific religious instruction, of different techniques used, or of the various courses taught? Is it the integration of religion with other parts of the curriculum, or perhaps the integration of the educational experience with the liturgical life of the parish or school?

I had begun to assume in the late 1970s that the primary effectiveness of Catholic schooling was based on cultural and social structural factors. Now I would add that these forces are supported by an imagination of God-as-present in the world and in the community. Those who attended Catholic schools, I suspected, would have a closer sense of affiliation to the Church, simply because they had spent more time on church property and would more likely have more experience with religious personnel, over and above the influences of their families, either of origin or procreation. I argued that it is precisely this sense of "closeness" to the Church which would be the primary intervening variable between Catholic schooling and religious behavior in adult life.

About a third of the difference between those who have had more Catholic education and those who have had less can be accounted for by familial factors, but all of the rest of the difference is accounted for by the fact that those who have gone to Catholic schools feel that they are closer to the Church. It must be remembered that this feeling of "closeness" is over and above whatever closeness to the Church might be accounted for by either spouse or family of origin. It is "pure" Catholic school effect.

The secret of the schools, if it may be called that, is that they integrate young people more closely into the Catholic institutional community. However, not all those who go to Catholic schools are close to the Church. But it is the greater "closeness" of some of those who go to Catholic schools which "explains" virtually all of the religious effectiveness of Catholic education. The point for Catholic policymakers is clear: if you can find another institution that can have the same effectiveness in integrating young people into the Catholic community and Catholic institutions, you do not need Catholic schools. Unless and until we find such a technique, then the continuing decline of the proportion of the Catholic population in Catholic schools will inevitably lead to a diminished level of Catholic commitment in the years ahead.

Finally, does Catholic school attendance incline a young person to choose not merely a spouse who is a Catholic but also one who is more likely to be a devout Catholic and, therefore, more likely to activate and reactivate a respondent to religious devotion? The question is hard to answer because it is difficult to separate spouses' influence on respondents from respondents' influence on spouses. Yet if one considers a three-variable model one can see that it is possible to make a tentative test. We know that Catholic education affects the Communion reception of our respondents. We also know there is a relationship among Catholic education, the respondents' own Communion reception, and the spouses' Communion reception. Logically, there ought not to be a direct correlation between the number of years a respondent went to Catholic schools and the Communion of her or his spouse. How, after all, could a husband's Catholic education affect a wife's Communion reception, except, say, through the example of the husband's Communion reception? Nonetheless the direct relationship between one's own Catholic school attendance and that of the spouse is also statistically significant. One must assume that the closeness to the Church community—resulting perhaps from joint Sacramental Imaginations—inclines the family community as such to link itself more intensely with the Church.

Twenty-five years ago Mary Perkins Ryan published her controversial book, *Are Catholic Schools the Answer?* It was the beginning of a powerful ideological assault on Catholic education. Mrs. Ryan's answer was a powerful "no." Religious instruction classes of the sort provided by the Confraternity of Christian Doctrine were the answer. From that time on CCD claimed the image of a "movement" in the "new" Church while Catholic schools were relegated to the status of an institution of the "old" Church.

Bishops denounced Mrs. Ryan's solution but before the decade was out, all the while protesting their dedication to Catholic schools, the hierarchy was in fact adopting her "answer." Somehow, by a process not yet clear to me, the decision was made by bishops and priests that no more new Catholic schools were to be built and that CCD was to become the *de facto* substitute for the schools. Apparently fears of financial pressures brought on by "inflation" were crucial in this decision (or decisions, since they may have been made independently in many places).

The decision to give up on them—I can think of no other description for what happened—was made in the teeth of research findings: Catholic schools had a religious impact over and above that of the Catholic family, while CCD had no measurable religious impact. The schools were more important in the transition after the Council than they were before the Council. They paid for themselves because of the extra Sunday contributions made by those with children in Catholic schools.[6] They provided better education than most public schools and as good as the best public schools. They integrated young men and women into parish communities of which they would be part for the rest of their lives. Their students were less prejudiced and more enlightened than Catholics who went to public schools. They were especially successful in educating the disadvantaged—the educationally, emotionally, economically, racially, academically impoverished. Much of their accomplishment, as James S. Coleman has demonstrated, came from their "social capital," the overlapping networks of school, church, and neighborhood.

The system that church leadership sent quietly into that good night was abandoned at the height of its success.

Brand-new data show how golden the twilight is. In a sense this conclusion represents the fifth NORC report on Catholic education.[7] In their twilight the Catholic schools have produced a substantial impact on the educational, political, moral, religious, sexual, and financial behavior of those adults who attended them during their school years, the kind of impact that no other institution can claim. Moreover, these effects are not of the sort that could be attributed to the family background of those who attended Catholic schools.

In the 1988 General Social Survey, NORC added a special "module" of questions about religion which it will repeat intermittently in years to come. One question asked about the number of years the respondent attended church-related schools. The Catholic population was dichotomized into two segments, the 265 who had less than eight years of Catholic schools (which included all those who had no Catholic schools) and the 109 respondents who attended Catholic

---

[6] Perhaps one of the reasons for the continuing decline in Catholic contributions is that parents no longer view their offerings as part of the support for the parish school because there no longer is a parish school.

[7] Previous reports were *The Education of Catholic Americans, Catholic Schools in a Declining Church, Young Catholics in the United States and Canada,* and *Minority Students in Catholic Schools.*

schools for more than eight years. With such small numbers only high correlations become statistically significant.

NORC routinely administers to its respondents a ten-word vocabulary test that is a rough measure of intellectual achievement and intelligence. The Catholic school group scored 6.6 on the scale, the other group scored 5.5. The difference, as all that will be reported in this article, was statistically significant.

Those who went to Catholic schools scored systematically higher on measures of support for the equality of women: 90 percent of them rejected the notion that women should limit themselves to taking care of the home (as opposed to 80 percent of the other group), 84 percent approved of women working (as opposed to 76 percent), 35 percent strongly rejected the notion that wives should support their husbands' careers (as opposed to 21 percent of the other group), 73 percent thought that working mothers did not harm their children (as opposed to 63 percent), and 70 percent disagreed that it was better for the man to work and the woman to take care of the home (as opposed to 58 percent).

Twenty-four percent of the Catholic school group described themselves as "conservative" (the rest were "moderate" or "liberal"), as did 36 percent of those who did not have at least eight years of Catholic schools.

The Catholic school group also consistently scored higher on measures of morale: 36 percent said they were "very happy" (as opposed to 28 percent), 69 percent said their marriage was "very happy" (as opposed to 56 percent). Forty-four percent said their health was "excellent" (as opposed to 27 percent), 47 percent said they received a "very great deal" of satisfaction from their family life (as opposed to 40 percent).

Furthermore, they are more likely to take a benign view of their fellow humans. Forty-seven percent say that other people can generally be "trusted" (versus 38 percent), 35 percent say that most people tend to be "fair" (versus 29 percent), and 63 percent say that others are "helpful" (versus 45 percent).

They are also more likely to have benign views of God: 35 percent say that they imagine God either as a "mother" or equally as a "mother" and "father" (versus 26 percent), and 37 percent picture God as a "spouse" instead of as a "master" (versus 27 percent).

They are much more generous to the Church. Those who have had eight or more years of Catholic education give $347 a year to the Church as opposed to $222. The additional contribution of those who went to Catholic schools above the average amounts to $750 million a year, not a bad return on investment.

They are more likely to stress the importance of their own conscience even above the orders of church authorities by a rate of 53 percent to 38 percent and to reject the notion that right and wrong are usually a simple matter of black and white without shades of gray. They are only half as likely to have drifted away from the Church (10 percent versus 20 percent). Finally, they are twice as likely (19 percent versus 9 percent) to say that intense sexual pleasure has strengthened their religious faith.

Virtually all the criticisms aimed at the Catholic schools are refuted by these data: they are not rigid or repressive or dull or restrictive. On the contrary, they seem to facilitate greater happiness, more support for the equality of women, more confidence in other people, more willingness to see sex as a sacrament, greater generosity to the Church, more benign images of God, greater awareness of the complexity of moral decision-making, and higher intellectual achievement.

Not bad.

Are these really Catholic school effects or are they the result of the fact that those who go to Catholic school are likely to achieve higher educational levels? Is the effect really a Catholic school function or merely an educational function?

When educational attainment is taken into account the Catholic school effect diminishes somewhat but remains statistically significant. Moreover, the correlations do not diminish for Catholics under thirty, those whose Catholic education began after 1964 as the Vatican Council was drawing to an end. Quite the contrary: for some variables the strength of the relationship increases for those under thirty. On political and feminist attitudes and for happiness, the gap between those who attended Catholic schools and those who did not has grown larger among the postconciliar generation.

I confess that I found these relationships exciting. I would not have expected most of them beforehand and I certainly would not have expected them to be so strong (as correlations go in social research). I doubt that even the small remnant of enthusiastic supporters of Catholic schools would have anticipated that those adults who attended Catholic schools for eight years or more would be happier, more feminist, smarter, more tolerant of other people, more benign in their images of God, more accepting of moral complexity, and more likely to see sex as sacramental. Catholic schools seemed to have been more successful than the teachers and administrators might have imagined in their wildest dreams. The news is almost too good to be true—and some, I think, will say that the findings simply cannot be accurate.

Let the latter do their own research. None of the standard demographic or social explanations account for the findings reported in this chapter. They appear to be the result of either classroom instruction or the ambience and atmosphere of the schools themselves.

I have no illusion that these data will reverse the decline of Catholic schools. Bishops will continue to think that they can't afford to build new ones. Suburban pastors will continue to believe that life is a lot simpler without a school to worry about. Those laity who imagine themselves to be independent-minded and sophisticated because they do not send their children to Catholic schools will continue to congratulate themselves on their own wisdom. The CCD "movement" will continue to claim superior virtue for itself although none of the effects discussed in this chapter can be found for their programs. Catholic educators will continue to feel apologetic and perhaps even sorry for themselves. The implacable critics of Catholic education will ignore these findings as they have ignored all previous findings.

James S. Coleman has shown how the effect of Catholic secondary schools can be attributed to the "social capital" created by the overlapping networks of school, parish, and family which enable the Catholic schools to demand more from their students—and get what they demand. My own research demonstrates that it is precisely the "community-forming" component of Catholic education which makes them effective—another manifestation of the work of "social capital."

It does not seem unreasonable to suggest that the Catholic schools were, and still are, an example par excellence of the Catholic communal ethos and the Sacramental Imagination at work. Not only are Catholics more likely to value community, they are also more predisposed to use it effectively and to be influenced by it. The past impulse to build the schools, the dedication to them, and their effectiveness are all proof that Catholics imagine social reality differently and are more likely to be affected by it.

The neighborhood parish, I argued in an earlier chapter, is a survival of the archaic in the modern world, a residue of the curious notion that God is especially present in the local community where people live. Similarly the parish school is also an archaic survival, a residue of the curious notion that young people can best be educated not by outsize educational bureaucracies that care nothing for local communities, but by an interaction network of church, neighborhood, and school.

However well they might work, the fact that they do work is offensive to those who reject the archaic and the local—and apparently to the educators themselves who have lost their nerve and their faith in what they have been doing.

Thus historians of the future can marvel at how foolish we were to give up, because of loss of nerve and loss of faith, what might have been our best resource.

Catholic schools, after all, were the answer.

A Note on Catholic Higher Education

As was noted earlier, the two Canadian scholars, R. L. Schnell and Patricia T. Rooke, examining the question of the relationship between Catholicism and the intellectual life in the United States, concluded that there was no conflict between Catholic faith and academic achievement, but the institutional Church had not caught up with the educational and academic advance of the Catholic population. Most especially, the two scholars noted that Catholic colleges and universities had not achieved a quality of intellectual excellence which seems to be justified by the advanced educational achievement of the Catholic population.

There is no reason to doubt that Catholic colleges are presentable undergraduate institutions. In research done in the late sixties, my colleagues and I documented the fact that the men and women who had attended Catholic colleges and universities were more loyal to them than graduates of other colleges, were more likely to want their children to attend such schools, and felt that they had received excellent undergraduate instruction at these institutions. While no new study[8] of Catholic colleges has been attempted in the last fifteen years, there is no reason to assume that the situation is any different

---

[8] My two books on the subject were *From Back Water to Main Stream* and *The Changing Catholic College*, the former published in 1969, the latter in 1971, both by McGraw-Hill.

now. Certainly the young men and women who attend Catholic colleges do very well in graduate school, in fact better on the average than Catholic students who attend public institutions, and are successful in their business and professional careers. However, as centers of learning, as institutions of research, the Catholic universities are considerably less successful. In a study done by the Conference Board of Associated Research Councils on the quality of academic departments at American universities, Catholic institutions ranked very poorly. Only three Catholic departments were above the mean on the rating scores—two departments at Notre Dame and one at St. Louis University, and all of them just slightly above the mean.

The average ranking of the Catholic graduate departments was substantially below the mean. Indeed, on the average, Catholic institutions rated only at the high end of "marginal" in comparison with other universities. None of them rated as "adequate" or "good" or "excellent" or "eminent." And some of the Catholic universities were in the bottom sixth of American institutions of higher learning. Despite the "secularization" of ownership and control in the late sixties and the early seventies, despite the serious attempt to enter the higher educational mainstream, and despite attempts to modernize and update in line with what was taken to be the spirit of the Second Vatican Council, the Catholic universities are thus far failures as research institutions (with some exceptions in some departments in a few universities) and have not on the average even begun to approach what would be considered presentable mediocrity in the American academic marketplace.

Why are the Catholic universities unable to take advantage of the increased economic and educational achievement of the American Catholic population to attain at least a little bit of excellence, a small number of quality graduate departments?

My guess is that academic excellence is a notion that is antithetical to the ethos of the religious orders as they now exist in this country. The serious scholar is often suspect within his/her own community of priests/nuns. Even if the orders no longer are the technical owners of many of the colleges and universities, their spirit still pervades them, a spirit steeped in envy and mediocrity.

There has been very little progress in updating the effectiveness of Catholic universities as research institutions. Moreover, in the late 1950s when the Catholic Commission on Intellectual and Cultural Affairs first sounded the tocsin against the inferiority of Catholic universities there was considerable concerned reaction in the Catholic higher educational institutions. At that time there was little inclination to deny the charges of Monsignor John Tracy Ellis, Father Gustave Weigel, and Professor John Donovan that the Catholic higher educational institutions were not centers of intellectual excellence. In the early 1980s, however, when the report cited here was presented, there was almost complete silence as though acceptance of and resignation to inferiority had become total.

It would appear that Catholic higher educational institutions at the present time are resigned to a permanent condition of inferiority. The director of the graduate program of the University of Notre Dame, responding to the findings of the project, said that graduate programs and research had not been and were not an important part of the Notre Dame mission and that Notre Dame had no desire to become a Catholic Harvard. As a statement of fact, his remarks were undoubtedly accurate. As a statement of policy and plans for the future, they seem to suggest that while Notre Dame will continue to call itself a university and continue to justify its existence as a university because of its graduate programs in the professions—law, business, and architecture—in fact, it does not aspire to excellence in arts and sciences graduate programs. This is a perfectly legitimate decision for a university to make, but it confirms the impression that the Catholic universities (of which Notre Dame has the highest average ranking in graduate programs, followed closely by Georgetown) do not aspire at the present time to become centers of high-quality professional research. That the Church might have need of such centers in the postconciliar era does not seem to be a factor that influences this decision.

Notre Dame is currently "number one" in football; that's fine. It is nowhere near "number one" in graduate university scholarship and apparently does not aspire to be. That's not only a shame. That's shameful.

10

THE TWO PASSIONS: LOVER AND GOD

HEN I AM HASSLED by bishops and priests about my allegedly steamy[1] novels I patiently try to explain that human love is a sacrament of divine love, that the two passions illumine each other—a strict Sacramental Imagination argument: God is present in human passion, not absent from it. Did not Saint Paul say that marriage was the "great sacrament"?

If I'm lucky enough to get by the blank stare or the response that Saint Paul was talking about marriage and not about sex or the companion response that it is inappropriate[2] for a priest to discuss such matters, I try to explain the material around which this chapter is structured and add that the data on the relationship between husband and wife from the Young Catholic study were one of the reasons I began to write fiction: the findings were too important, too fascinating, and too good a story to be limited to sociological reports.

If one takes seriously the theory of the religious imagination and the notion that Catholics "imagine differently," then one might expect that Catholics might deal with the relationship between religion and sex differently than Protestants do. However, the institutional Church clearly has a massive hang-up on sexual pleasure—suspicious of it if not downright opposed. Sex then becomes a classic test case of

---

[1] They are not even remotely steamy either by the standards of contemporary fiction or by the standards of the Bible; they only seem steamy to those who think that the oils of ordination remove sexual hormones from a man's body.

[2] "Inappropriate" is not a vague word at all; it means exactly what a bishop wants it to mean.

what happens when the formal teaching of the institution is at odds with the instincts and insights of the imaginative tradition that has been entrusted to the tradition.

The Sacramental Imagination must say (or picture) human passion as a hint of divine passion. If God is present in the world and if God is love, then surely S/He is present in sexual love. The ecclesiastical institution since the time of Augustine, however, has frowned on sexual love if it has not quite condemned it. Even in this day it still maintains a "separate bedroom" theory of family limitation.

What wins in a millennium and a half of confrontation between institution and imagination?

Do Catholic spouses approach their sexual pleasure with images and pictures that are different from those with which the institution tries to fill their heads? Can they sustain that different approach over a long period of time?

The question would seem absurd if it were not for the theory of the Sacramental Imagination. Even with such a theory as a justification for asking it, it will still seem absurd to many, not excluding Catholics, who are convinced that Catholics are raised with terrible sexual hang-ups. Nonetheless, if the Imagination triumphs over the Institution, we have come upon very important evidence that the Catholic tradition is broader than its institutional and propositional formularies.

In its special religion module the General Social Survey of 1988 provides material for answers to those two questions from the entire adult population—and hence background before I turn to the Young Catholic study that investigated only Catholic men and women under thirty.

The key question asks, "How often have these events strengthened your religious faith—often? sometimes? never?" The fourth item on the list is "intense sexual pleasure." Eleven percent responded "often," 22 percent "sometimes," and 67 percent "never."

There are no differences between Catholics and others either in the distribution of answers to this question or the question on how happy the marriage is. But the pertinent issue is not the distribution of responses but the relationship between seeing intense sexual experience as a source of faith and marital fulfillment. The theory of the Sacramental Imagination would predict that for Catholics the relationship would be stronger than for Protestants because Catholics would be more inclined to see passionate relationship with a spouse and passionate relationship with God as linked.

As improbable as such speculation might seem, it is in fact sustained by the data. Eighty percent of the Catholics who report that intense sexual experience has strengthened their faith say that their marriage is very happy as opposed to 57 percent of those who do not report intense sex as a source of faith. However, the differences between the two Protestant groups in marital fulfillment (71 percent and 62 percent) are not statistically significant.

Catholics are no more likely than Protestants to see intense sexual love as sacramental (a victory for the ecclesiastical institution), but when they do, the impact on their marriage is greater.

Moreover, that impact is especially high for those who describe themselves as "strong" Catholics. Ninety-two percent of the strong Catholics who say that intense sex has strengthened their faith also assert that their marital fulfillment is excellent as opposed to 70 percent of the "strong" Protestants.

It is precisely those who think of themselves as "strong" Catholics who are the most likely in the sample to report that intense sex has strengthened their faith. Almost half of them say that this has happened sometimes and a fifth say that it has happened often—twice as many as those who do not think of themselves as "strong" Catholics.

Paradoxically, therefore, the institution has succeeded in breaking the linkages among sex, religion, and marital fulfillment for those who do not identify strongly with the Church, but has been much less successful in breaking those links for those who do strongly identify.

If the Catholic imagination has not won the battle against the ecclesiastical institution over the sacramentality of sexual pleasure, it has at least not lost it completely. As was noted in the previous chapter, the impact of intense sexual experience on faith was especially strong for those who attended Catholic schools. The institution itself, therefore, seems to be caught in internal conflict between its suspicion and distrust of sexual pleasure and the instincts of its own imaginative heritage.

I now turn to a study of the marriage relationship itself as described by both spouses in the Young Catholic study. A relationship is considered to be "very satisfying" only if both spouses describe it as such and a "relationship rating" is considered to be "excellent" only if both spouses assert that it is "excellent." To the extent that such descriptions and ratings are an accurate reflection of the quality of married life, one could say with some measure of confidence that we are dealing with reasonably happy marriages.

By this standard, about one-half of the younger Catholics in the United States (56 percent) are in marriages in which both partners say the relationship is "very satisfactory." Sixty-five percent of the couples are "very satisfied" in the first two years of marriage. The proportion declines to 50 percent from the third to the eighth year and increases to 70 percent—higher even than in the first two years—in the last two years of the first decade of marriage. Obviously, something extremely important happens between the eighth and tenth years of a Catholic marriage.

Is this decline and resurgence of marital satisfaction a function of actual duration of the marriage, or is it part of an age cycle that happens to coincide with the marriage cycle? If we compare those marriages in which the primary respondent is between twenty-five and twenty-seven and those in which the primary respondent is between twenty-eight and thirty, we see that the marriage cycle seems to be a phenomenon of the duration of marriage itself and not to be a function of the age of the respondents.

Just as marriage satisfaction goes through a life cycle in the first decade of the marriage, so do sexual fulfillment, value consensus, and emotional satisfaction. Sexual fulfillment declines from 34 percent to 21 percent and then rebounds to 42 percent. Value consensus declines from 26 percent to 16 percent and rebounds to 33 percent. Emotional satisfaction varies from 22 percent to 13 percent, and back to 20 percent.

Traditional teachings on divorce, birth control, premarital sex, and living together do not relate either to a satisfying marriage or a sexually fulfilling one. On the other hand, more liberal attitudes on these issues do not promote either a more satisfying or sexually fulfilling relationship. Sexual values—insofar as they can be measured by attitudes on divorce, birth control, premarital sex, and living together—seem to have nothing to do with the quality of a relationship that develops between a man and woman once they are married (it ought to be noted that we are here speaking of attitudes, not of premarital behavior, since we know nothing of the premarital behavior of the respondents in this project). However, a couple's capacity to disagree and to love as these capacities are reflected in their sexual life plays a considerable part in shaping their marital satisfaction.

There is nothing particularly surprising about these preliminary observations from the Young Catholic study. The critical question is what role religion plays in the emerging relationship during the first ten years of a marriage.

Many of these scholars, Christian and non-Christian, who are convinced that the world has become "secularized," and that religion has little impact on daily human life, would not expect religious devotion to notably influence youthful marital satisfaction, especially not to influence sexual fulfillment.

In fact, just the opposite seems to be true: when husbands and wives both pray frequently (not necessarily together), when they both go to church frequently (again, not necessarily together), and when they both believe in the afterlife, these forms of religious devotion are likely to have a statistically significant impact on their marriage relationship. All three kinds of devotion affect the consensus between husband and wife that their sexual fulfillment is excellent.

Faith seems to contribute to good sex—or at least to sex about which one does not complain.

A young married couple, friends of mine in Tucson, reacted to my explanation of these results by reaching for each other's hands.

"Our best sex," the wife said, "is when we come home from our prayer group meetings."

"It's even better if we say some prayers together, quick ones," her husband added, laughing.

"Do you want me to leave now?"

"We'll give you another half hour."

Devout and conservative people, they would be exactly the ones that the Pontifical Commission on the Family had in mind when it announced that the married laity should be warned against the dangers of unbridled passion. However, an older and richer Catholic tradition—one that hasn't made the formal documents of the Church yet—had drowned out the voice of the official institution.

There are also statistically significant correlations between such matters as mixed marriage, a valid marriage, and a marriage after divorce, and various forms of marital contentment. Thus, whether or not a couple was married by a priest influences both their general satisfaction and their joint rating of their sexual relationship as "excellent" (perhaps it ought to be repeated here that a "joint" rating as "excellent" means that both spouses on their separate questionnaires have rated the marriage as "excellent," not that they have worked together to achieve this description of their relationship). The religiously mixed marriage has a negative effect on value consensus, and marriage after a divorce has a negative effect on whether both the husband and wife consider their marriage to be very satisfactory.

Sixty-four percent of those families in which both spouses go to church say that their marriage is "very satisfactory" as opposed to 51 percent in which either or both do not go to church. Similarly, 37 percent of the churchgoers say their sexual fulfillment is excellent as opposed to 25 percent of others, and 29 percent say their value consensus is "excellent" as opposed to 19 percent of the others. Virtually the same percentage distributions apply when one considers the influence of frequent prayer and belief in life after death. Those who go to church more often, pray more often, and believe in life after death have more satisfactory and more sexually fulfilling, more value-consensual marriages. Presumably, it is religion that affects marital happiness, and not vice versa. One can imagine, for example, that the hopefulness that comes with belief in life after death would account for believers being half again as likely to say jointly that their sexual fulfillment is "excellent," rather than the sexual fulfillment making them more likely to believe in life after death. Nonetheless, in the real world there is probably a reciprocal causality, with belief in life after death generating the hopefulness that is necessary for the risk-taking of sexual intimacy and the satisfactions of such intimacy strengthening the conviction that husband and wife live in a universe that is more benign than not.

Marriage by a priest and the absence of a previous marriage both relate statistically to satisfaction in marriage. If they were married by a priest, 58 percent of both the spouses say their marriage is very satisfactory as opposed to 49 percent of those who are not married by a priest. Fifty-seven percent of those who were not divorced say their marriage is very satisfactory as opposed to 41 percent of those cases in which one or the other spouse had been divorced.

In the early years of the first decade of married life, there is no difference in the satisfaction levels of both Catholic and mixed marriages. However, at the end of the decade, after a sharp decline in mixed marriages and a somewhat less sharp decline for Catholic marriages, the Catholic marriage is five percentage points higher in the proportion saying that they are "very satisfied" than was true at the beginning of the marriage, whereas in the mixed marriage the proportion in which both spouses say they are "very satisfied" is six points lower. The two marriages begin at the same level of satisfaction but the Catholic marriage, at the end of a decade, is eleven percentage points more likely to be described as "very satisfactory" by both respondents.

Both joint commitment to the Catholic Church and joint commitment to certain religious practices affect the first decade of the marriage life cycle, especially toward the end of the life cycle. In the middle of the marriage, both those who are high on the religion scale (made up of a combination of joint church attendance, joint belief in life after death, and joint prayer) are at an all-time low, with a smaller portion saying that they are both "very satisfied" with the marriage. However, the couple in which both spouses are devout seems to have a much better chance to work its way through the crisis point between the eighth and the tenth years of marriage. The rebound for the religious marriages is statistically significant, for the other marriages it is not.

Devout couples also have a much better chance of working through their problems of sexual fulfillment and value consensus. Shared religious commitment, then, seems to especially facilitate shared satisfaction and shared fulfillment at the turning point in the latter years of the first decade of marriage (and satisfaction and fulfillment may also in turn lead to great religious devotion).

Religion, then, does indeed have a varied and pervasive effect on the marriage relationship of young Catholics. It is still an important part of their married life together, even if they are not aware explicitly and consciously of its importance. Their rejection of the Church's teaching on birth control—the only important thing the ecclesiastical institution seems to think it has to say to young married people—does not mean a rejection of the Catholicism or the elimination of its importance to their lives.

The question remains, however, of whether this religious impact is a result of a specifically Catholic imagination that pervades their lives and their picture of human communities, including the marriage relationship that exists between them.

If one applies the theory of the Sacramental Imagination to marriage, one might argue as follows: husbands and wives "reveal" to each other whether the "real" is benign or malign, "warm" or "cold." When two people marry they merge their individual stories in "our" story. "Your" religious imagery influences "my" religious imagery, and vice versa. Therefore, in the course of the marriage, there will be a tendency for husband and wife to converge in their religious imagery. Convergence will in part be the result of their experiences of love, but will also have a profound influence on the further development of their marital satisfaction. Husband and wife are a "sacrament" for each other, "grace" for each other (in the sociological if not the theological sense). Therefore, a substantial amount of the ebb and flow, the rise and decline, and rise again of the quality of their relationship will be interpretable in terms of the changing patterns of their religious imagery.

Four items were selected as measures of "sacramental" religious imagery, a GRACE[3] scale—God as a lover, Jesus as warm, Mary as warm, and the afterlife as a "paradise of pleasure and delight." (Each of these images, incidentally, is a story because it implies an ongoing relationship.)

A five-point scale was constructed from these items for measuring the relationship between individual (as opposed to joint husband-wife) religious imagery and marital adjustment. Thirty-three percent of those who thought of none of the warm images as "extremely likely" reported excellent sexual fulfillment in marriage, as opposed to 69 percent of those who checked all four as "extremely likely." Similarly, 27 percent of those low on the scale described the value consensus in their marriage as excellent, as opposed to 63 percent of those who were high on the scale. Religious images, then, do indeed affect the quality of married life as that quality is perceived by an individual respondent. But the crucial issue is communal: does the combined imagery of husband and wife affect their combined view of the marital satisfaction?

A joint GRACE scale was composed to measure the religious imagery of the family unit. This scale correlates positively and significantly with marital satisfaction, sexual fulfillment, and value consensus. If there is an atmosphere in the marriage in which husband and wife tend to share warm religious imagery, then their marriage satisfaction, their sexual fulfillment, and their value consensus are likely to be higher than if they do not share such religious imagery. How you imagine Jesus, God, Mary, and the afterlife does indeed affect "your" marital satisfaction and "your" sexual fulfillment. Religious images do indeed have an impact on what goes on in the bedroom (though, of course, people need not be aware of this impact).

If husband and wife are on the high end of the GRACE scale, they are sixteen percentage points more likely to say that they are both very satisfied with the marriage, fourteen percentage points

---

[3] This is an earlier version of the scale which was discussed in Chapter 3.

more likely to both say that their sexual adjustment is "excellent," and twelve percentage points more likely to say that their value consensus is "excellent." All three differences are statistically significant. Religious warmth, as measured by the GRACE scale, is good for a marriage. Religious warmth and marital warmth correlate with each other.

Religious warmth declines in the middle years of the first decade of marriage, at the time spouses are experiencing an increase in problems in their married life and individual respondents are experiencing problems in their religious belief systems. However, in the last two years of the decade the warmth scale rebounds to where it was at the beginning of the marriage.

There is much greater convergence between husband and wife in their religious imagery as the story of their marriage develops. In the last two years of the first decade of marriage, there are strong and statistically significant correlations between husbands and wives in their view of God as a lover (.40) and their view of afterlife as a paradise of pleasure and delight (.23). Common religious imagery, then, does indeed tend to emerge out of the "story" of common life together.

In the first two years of marriage there is a very high probability that if your spouse says that God is a lover, you will think so. This proportion declines precipitously from 79 percent to 51 percent by the middle of the marriage. But then in the final two years of the first decade of marriage the convergence becomes quite dramatic. Your spouse's image of God has a far more powerful impact on you than it has had since the first years of the marriage. On the other hand, if your spouse is not likely to think of God as a lover (one must remember that respondent's imagery and spouse's imagery are collected from different questionnaires), the deterioration of your own image of God as a lover continues even into the ninth and the tenth years of the marriage. The greatest difference between those whose spouse says it is extremely likely that God is a lover and those whose spouse does not say it is in the final two years of the decade. Sixty-seven percent of those whose spouse says it is "extremely likely" that God is a lover themselves say that it is "extremely likely" whereas only 12 percent of those whose spouse says that it is not likely for them to think of God as a lover themselves say it is likely for them to think of God as a lover. In other words, by the end of the first decade of marriage, if "your" spouse thinks of God as a lover, it is highly probable that you will. If "your" spouse does not think that way, it is very unlikely that you will think of God as a lover.

Sexual fulfillment in marriage has a considerable impact on the image of God as a lover. Seventy-one percent of those who say that their sex life together is excellent say that God is a lover and their spouse says that God is a lover. Only 56 percent of those with less than excellent sexual adjustment reflect the spouse's conviction that God is a lover. Precisely then, in those marriages where the sexual fulfillment is high, there is the strongest relationship between a spouse's image of God as a lover and one's own image of God as a lover.

Nineteen percent of our respondents are either extremely likely or somewhat likely to say that they imagine God as a mother. There is a statistically significant difference between those whose spouses have such an image and those whose spouses do not. Twenty-eight percent of those who have spouses who think of God as a mother share this imagination, whereas only 17 percent of those whose spouses do not think of God as a mother have this imagination themselves.

The convergence of imagery of God as mother increases as the years of marriage increase. The size of the relationship between the spouse's image of God as mother and the respondent's image doubles between the third and the eighth years of marriage. Finally, the association between spouses on the subject of the maternity of God is much stronger in marriages in which the spouses are very satisfied sexually than it is in marriages where both spouses are not very satisfied. Thus both marital satisfaction and the passage of time lead to a convergence, even of the somewhat unusual image of the maternity of God.

"Sacramental" religious imagery raises marital satisfaction and sexual fulfillment, and husband-wife imagery converges after the mid-decade marital crisis, as a common marriage "story" evolves and a common repertoire of religious imagery tends to appear to resonate with the story, both influencing it and being influenced by it.

Having established, then, that religious imagery affects both sexual fulfillment and marital satisfaction, I turn to the question of whether family background experiences—a warm family life and childhood—also relate to present marital warmth. There are statistically significant, though moderate, relationships between a respondent's description of happiness as a child and joint satisfaction with a marriage and joint sexual fulfillment in a marriage and value consensus in a marriage. There are also statistically significant relationships between closeness to the mother and joint satisfaction and value consensus, and between closeness to the father and sexual fulfillment. Happy and intimate childhoods, therefore, relate positively though modestly with happy marriages. Furthermore, and finally, adult religious imagery is related to childhood experiences both of the respondent and the respondent's spouse.

Warm religious imagery acts as a funnel that gathers together childhood influences and passes them on to marital happiness. Marital satisfaction is influenced by sexual fulfillment, sexual fulfillment is influenced by warm religious imagery, and warm religious imagery is influenced by childhood experiences. The religious stories about a person's life (religious imagery) act as a link between childhood family experiences and adult family experiences. The links are modest because there are many other factors that impinge on the development of religious imagery, sexual fulfillment, and marital satisfaction. Nevertheless, religious images do precisely what our theory suggests they would do: they are the stories that link the beginning of the story of a person's life in his family of orientation with the middle of his story in the family of procreation and point toward the ending of the story—an ending, if the warm religious imagery is to be believed, which will involve a love affair in a garden of paradise and delight.

The path of decline and rebirth of marital happiness—the *Kramer vs. Kramer* story of the first ten years of marriage—is paralleled by a decline and rebirth in religious attitudes, images, and behaviors. Are the two "U" curves not only parallel but related?

Marital satisfaction declines from the first to the eighth years of marriage by some nineteen percentage points. Most of the decline can be explained by a decline in warm religious imagery and by the decline in the capacity to express love and affection. The decline in sexual fulfillment is not the cause of the decline in marital satisfaction; it is the conduit through which these prior causes work.

The same model explains 55 percent of the twenty-percentage-point increase in marital satisfaction from the eighth to the tenth year of marriage—a highly successful effort in most social analysis. Religious imagery, then, plays an extraordinarily important part in the decline and rebirth of marital happiness. It directly influences and channels childhood experiences toward decline and rebirth of sexual fulfillment in marriage, and it in turn operates through its impact on the ability to find sexual fulfillment on total marital satisfaction in the Catholic family. To summarize the model, warm families of origin produce warm religious imagery that in turn produces warm sexuality that in turn produces warm marriages. The decline of religious imagery and the decline of sexual fulfillment account for most of the decline in general marital satisfaction, and also the rebirth of religious warmth, sexual warmth, and love warmth leads at the end of the first decade of marriage to a rebirth of marital satisfaction.

"How else do I know what God is like?" a young Catholic man demands of me. "If he's not like my wife, I'm going to feel cheated."

His is a profoundly Catholic instinct, one that, alas, the leadership of the Church does not always recognize.

Minimally, the reader who may have been skeptical about the impact of religious imagery on sexuality and marital satisfaction can see that a reevaluation of the impact of the religious imagery on human life, especially human marital life, is in order.

In summary, the chances of marital happiness are much better for young Catholics when they both possess the "Catholic Imagination." The ebb and flow of their joint Sacramental Imaginations—their views of God as present—accounts for the decline and rebirth of married love during the first ten years of their marriage.

Christian religious theory has always maintained that there is a link between human love and divine love. As husband and wife love each other, so do God and the Church. Similarly, husband and wife ought in their relationship to try to imitate the love of God for the Church. The imagery is a two-way street: marriage revealing the passion of God's love for His people, and the generosity of God's love providing an ideal for the married life. Saint Paul himself frequently gets his syntax confused as he tries to go in opposite directions on the symbolic street.

In traditional Christian marriage catechesis much has been made of the relationship between "the two loves." If human spouses love God strongly, it is argued, they will also love each other strongly. Their faith in God will strengthen their faith in each other, and their love for each other will motivate them to grow in love of God.

It is often hard to tell how serious this catechesis is taken. Does the overarching "story" of God's love affect the emerging "story" of "our" love, and does "our" love for each other rebound back to intensify "our" involvement in God's story?

Does divine intimacy really affect human intimacy, and vice versa? How closely are the two love stories related? Is the relationship merely a matter of conventional piety without any measurable impact on people's lives? Or does it articulate an insight that is latent in the

Catholic imagination and that will have an impact on married life, no matter what the institutional Church may say about the dangers of, to use the term of the Roman document, "unbridled sexual pleasure between husband and wife"?

If one takes prayer as a fair measure of intimacy with God and sexual fulfillment as a fair measure of intimacy with one's spouse, it is possible to fashion a rough and ready empirical test of the nature of the relationship between the two loves. What effect does the prayer life of a young Catholic married couple have on their sex life? Such questions asked in many fashionable and progressive Catholic circles would lead to ridicule. Prayer is nice, one might be told, and sex is nice, but the two really do not mix.

In approximately a quarter of the Catholic marriages both members of the couple pray every day. In 42 percent of those families both husband and wife described their sexual fulfillment as excellent. On the other hand, where one or both of the spouses do not pray every day only 24 percent described their sexual fulfillment as excellent. Moreover, the association between husband's and wive's prayer increases with the duration of marriage. As "your" story and "my" story become "our" story, both of us are more likely to get involved with God (though not necessarily together, since the question merely revealed whether the respondent and the spouse pray every day, and not whether they pray together).

Those who have sacramental images of the cosmic personages are also more likely to communicate with them. Hence, prayer, sexual fulfillment, and GRACE-ful religious images intercorrelate with one another. The more a husband and wife pray, the more likely they are to have sexually fulfilling marriages, and the warmer the imagery, the more likely they are to have sexually fulfilling marriages. Furthermore, both of these variables, while they are related to each other, also make an independent contribution to each other and to sexual fulfillment. The greatest probability of sexual fulfillment comes in marriages in which there is both daily prayer by the two spouses and warm images in the religious fantasy of the two spouses. Indeed, it is precisely among those marriages in which both spouses pray every day and both spouses have warm images that the difference in sexual fulfillment occurs. More than half of them report excellent sexual fulfillment (by both husband and wife), twice as many as in the other three categories. In the technical parlance of social science, daily prayer specifies the difference in sexual fulfillment between those families that share warm imagery and those that do not. It is precisely the combination of the two that accounts for the difference in sexual fulfillment in a young Catholic family.

The proportion of Catholic families in which both husband and wife pray every day increases as the marriage goes on. It is not merely, then, that "your" story and "my" story become more closely related, and that "your" story of "your" relationship with God and that "my" story of "my" relationship with God tend to converge. It is also true that "our" joint relationship with God improves through the years of the marriage, just as "our" relationship with each other is improving. As "our" story gets better—warmer, more exciting, more fulfilling—so does "our" involvement in God's story become more active.

It is impossible with our present data to sort out the influence flow between the two loves. Saint Paul's difficult syntax as he shifts back and forth manifests the same problem that the researcher faces: the two loves are so closely connected that it is hard to chart their ebb and flow. However, if one assumes at least some influence of prayer and warm images on the changing level of sexual fulfillment in young Catholic families, one can say that prayer makes an additional contribution to the explanation of the rebound between the middle and late years of marriage and sexual fulfillment. The difference between the third and the eighth years, on the one hand, and the ninth and the tenth years, on the other, is twenty-two percentage points. When the warm imagery is taken into account the difference diminishes to nine percentage points—in other words, three-quarters of the increase in sexual fulfillment can be accounted for by changes in the religious imagery of the spouses between the middle and the end of the first decade of their marriage. When one adds to that the daily prayer of spouses the difference diminishes even more to six percentage points, and one has accounted for three-quarters of the change in sexual fulfillment. Whether religion influences sexuality or sexuality influences religion may be hard to determine. That they both have an extraordinary impact on each other is beyond any doubt.

A final comment is in order about whether the influences described are perceived by the husbands and wives involved. Do men and women know that they are being influenced religiously by their mates? One of the questions in the survey asked the respondent to rate a number of potential religious influences on a four-point scale (mother, father, friends, priests, etc.). If correlations exist between the conscious rating of the spouse's influence and the family religious styles analyzed, then it would follow that not all the husband-wife,

wife-husband influence is preconscious or subconscious (about 18 percent say that their spouse has a "great deal" of religious influence).

In fact, there are statistically significant correlations between the perception of a spouse's influence and the joint imagery, joint prayer, and joint sexual fulfillment measures. We cannot say with certainty that there is a consciousness that the spouse is leading the respondent to pray more or to have a warmer religious imagery, but there is a consciousness that the spouse is exercising influence. This influence seems to wane, then wax during the first ten years of marriage, as do so many other aspects of the relationship. In the final years of the decade the spouse's religious influence is more likely to be perceived as strong than during the earlier years. The correlations between imagery and prayer on the one hand and the perceived influence of the spouse on the other seem to go through the same "U curve": the relationship between the perception of the spouse's influence and the joint imagery and joint behavior is strongest during the final years of the first decade of marriage. Not only do joint prayer and joint imagery increase in the rebound period; so do the perception of the spouse's influence and the relationship between such a perception and prayer and imagery. Not only are "your" story and "my" story become "our" story, but "we" are becoming self-conscious about the fact that it is "our" story.

A possible scenario would look something like this: Husband and wife share warm religious images. This sharing of "stories of God" makes it more likely that the two of them will pray frequently. A combination of the stories and the mutual, if not common, prayer leads them to perceive that they are having more religious influence on each other. All three factors improve their sexual fulfillment. If one adds self-consciousness about religious influence to the explanatory model developed to explain the rebound in sexual fulfillment, then three-quarters of the 22 percent increase between the third and eighth and the ninth and tenth years can be accounted for.

Earlier I noted that 42 percent of those couples, both of whom pray every day and both of whom have warm religious images, report that their sexual fulfillment is excellent. If one adds self-consciousness about the spouse's influence, the percentage rises to 57 percent—ten percentage points higher than those with images and prayer but without the self-consciousness and thirty-five percentage points higher than the rest of the sample. Thus not only is there some self-consciousness about religious influence of the spouse, but this self-consciousness heightens the impact of the influence.

One must ask again whether the leadership of the Church would rather have this intricate, fascinating, and profoundly hopeful story of the relationship between religion and marital fulfillment or a story of blind obedience to official church teaching on birth control. Publicly, the leaders would have to say that birth control is the only important issue and that the relationship between religious images and marital happiness—the metaphor of the two passions in action—is less important than obedience to the pope. One devoutly hopes that many of them would feel differently in private.

An analysis from the General Social Survey at the beginning of this chapter established that there is indeed a different Catholic way of imagining the relationship of religious faith, sexual pleasure, and marital fulfillment. The Young Catholic study data demonstrated how this system of linkages works for Catholic young people. Catholicism has a powerful resource available for its future in the style of linking the two passions that exist among Catholic married people, especially (it would seem) among the young married people. The parish, the parish school, and the family, all profoundly shaped by the Catholic imagination, continue to flourish, although none of them are fashionable with either the elites in the Church or its leadership. For different reasons both groups have despaired of the family as much as they have despaired of the Catholic schools.

If this chapter has proven anything, it has demonstrated how utterly wrong both groups are, mostly because no more than my editor friend can they see any importance in the fact that Catholics "imagine differently."

The analysis in this chapter is crucial to my theory of a "different" Catholic imagination—one that is different from the Protestant imagination and is also different from the "official" emphases of the ecclesiastical institution, one finally that is more faithful to the Catholic tradition of sacramentality, of God lurking in nature and human relationships, than is the official emphasis. Catholic married couples perceive, however dimly, the importance of their religion to their sexual fulfillment, despite the largely negative approach of their leaders to sexual love. Small wonder that at some deep preconscious level they do not want to give up the imagery that helps sustain their marital pleasure and commitment.

If this chapter is crucial to my argument, it is also the one most likely to be dismissed by critics. "Everyone knows" that religion impedes human happiness, especially sexual happiness. "Everyone knows" that religious devotion is a barrier to fulfillment, especially to sexual fulfillment. "Everyone knows" that Catholicism is more likely than any other religion to be a barrier to happiness, fulfillment, and sexual joy. Have I not read the popes on the subject? Have I not read Augustine? Have I not read the books by former or alienated Catholics? Am I not arguing against what everyone knows to be true?

Yeah. So what? What everyone knows to be true is wrong. Let those who wish to disprove my analysis collect their own data or reanalyze mine. Not only have I disproved what everyone knows to be true; I had predicted the refutation on theoretical grounds before my analysis of the data. Catholic religious imagery, I had predicted, would have a stronger influence on people's married lives than the current doctrinal emphases. The tradition of the sacramentality of sex would be stronger than the tradition of sexual repression.

So the theory looks pretty good, despite what everyone—especially the anti-Catholic bigots inside and outside the Church—knew to be true: the graciousness of imagery triumphs over the harshness of dogmatic formulations. It will do so every time.

My analysis—the theory that guided it and the data that support it—has been available for eight years. Not a single theologian or church leader, in fact not a single priest as far as I know, has ever mentioned it. Church leaders are afraid to mention the possibility that Catholic imagery leads to sexual fulfillment because their own responsibility is to repeat the teaching of *Humanae Vitae*. Theologians and clergy cannot admit that any insight can be gained from the lives of the ordinary laity who are corrupt and consumerist and secularist and materialist.

I think they're worse than the anti-Catholic bigots.

11

PRIESTS: HINT OF THE TRANSCENDENT?

HE FOURTH NIGHT of "The Thorn Birds" had just aired on ABC television. I was sitting in the studio of the ABC affiliate in Tucson waiting for a transcontinental panel discussion of the film about a priest who sins (only once, which is not all that bad in a whole lifetime). Ted Koppel, with the usual overkill that marks his program, had assembled a group that included a married priest and his wife, Father Theodore M. Hesburgh, Cardinal Krol,[1] and myself. Father Hesburgh and the cardinal were there as church leaders and I suppose I was present as someone who had the data—and maybe as an example of a priest who had sinned far more often than the character played so woodenly by Richard Chamberlain.

Father Ted explained why he personally was a celibate. The cardinal repeated church teaching and regulation on the subject. The married priest, backed up by his wife, assured the national audience that he was very happy. I kind of felt sorry for the poor woman.

At last Koppel got to me. Usually folks whom he can't categorize as "liberal" or "conservative" have to wait for the end, and they get vague questions like "What did you think of the program, Father Greeley? Should it air the week before Easter?"

I said that I thought it was a great program for Holy Week since it was about sin and redemption and since the priest died to give life to others. Then I added, "The celibate priest is a sign of transcen-

---

[1] I was told that my own archbishop was ready to go on the program till he learned that I would be on it. John Krol was a last-minute choice, according to this source.

dence, a rumor of angels, a man who points to the world beyond this one, a man who fascinates others. Would there even have been a book or a miniseries about a married clergyman? Priests fascinate people. That's why we're here tonight."

You don't usually get a response from an interviewer to a statement like that. Koppel is nothing if not quick under such circumstances.

"What about you, Cardinal?" he asked. "Do you think you're fascinating?"

"I'm not a priest to be fascinating," the cardinal replied. "I'm a priest to be configured to Jesus Christ."

Who I guess wasn't very fascinating, huh? I knew I had one more chance coming. I could play it for laughs and say, "Gee, Cardinal, I think you're fascinating!"

Or I could have played it straight and said that being configured to Jesus should make a priest very fascinating indeed.

Or I could have said that I had data that proved that the celibate priest was fascinating.

Or I could have been responsible and said that I supported the ordination of women.

So I was responsible.

But I still regret the lost opportunity to say that I thought John Krol was fascinating. I might have added—with a bow to Warner Books—that my early novels fascinated readers not because they were by a priest but because they were about priests. For sheer fascination you can't beat a priest in your story, not even with an extraterrestrial. Priests are the most fascinating people in the world—at least until they open their mouths. Celibacy makes them fascinating because no one would live that way unless he strongly believed that there is Goodness and Beauty and Love that transcend this life. So I continue to support celibacy (along with a limited term of service in the priesthood) just as I support the ordination of women. Most people think the position is inconsistent.

However, just as I see woman as a sacrament of God, so I see the celibate priest as a special manifestation of the Sacramental Imagination at work. The celibate priest represents in a special way by his office (which he might not always discharge very well) the God who lurks in the world. Moreover, this is the image that the empirical data seem to support at least in the imaginations of some Catholics.

For which observation I am often rebuked by fellow priests with the comment that so do married Greek priests or Protestant ministers. To which I reply that they don't make miniseries about them.

I can't figure priests out. From my position on the margins of the institutional Church and with my freight-train load of empirical data, priests seem more important than they ever were to Catholicism; but most priests seem to be caught up in a terrible identity crisis that is a blend of very low morale and the conviction that in this era of a wide variety of lay ministries there is nothing left for them uniquely to do.

They are encouraged in this identity crisis by the various lay ministers who often define their own roles in terms of what they *can* do and what the priest *can't* do.[2]

[2] I refrain in this book from trying to discuss the alarming decline in vocations to religious orders of women. In 1962 there were 173,351 women religious. In 1988 there were 106,912 women religious. Moreover, because of the large exodus from the women's communities and the absence of young vocations the median age of nuns now is in the middle fifties. It would appear that the care of elderly nuns will soon absorb most if not all of the sisters who have not yet retired (which seems to be one of the reasons that many younger nuns have already departed from their communities). I am baffled by the phenomenon. Much of the good that was done in the American Church in the first half of the present century was done by women religious. Indeed, much of what is finest is still being done by them and now with rules of life which respect personal freedom, dignity, talent, and privacy—all of which were often not respected by the religious orders in the past.

Why then the decline? Perhaps there was oppression in the communities that had become intolerable. Perhaps the "emancipation" of the orders led to a removal of the rigid life that the personalities of many of the members required. Perhaps the nuns themselves have lost confidence in their vocation, just as I will suggest in this chapter that priests have. Perhaps the feminism of some nuns has seemed too shrill to young women. Perhaps young women see nothing special in the vocation of the "liberated" nuns. Perhaps the special religious garb exercised more appeal for idealistic young women than was appreciated. Perhaps many of those who would have been attracted to the religious life choose such "lay ministries" as youth minister or director of religious education because they see them as forms of dedication that do not cut them off from the possibility of marriage—a way to hedge your bets. Clearly the religious communities of women, which were extraordinarily attractive to young women not so long ago, have lost almost all of their appeal.

I offer the speculations in the previous paragraph as little more than guesswork. I am not a member of one of the religious orders of men (which have fared somewhat better than their women counterparts) and I do not understand the religious life from the inside. Moreover, I find little analytical help in the vast body of research that has been done on women religious—mostly because it is so biased by ideology as to be of dubious scholarly value.

Hence I must be content with saying that I lament the decline of the religious orders of women as a great tragedy and that I do not understand it.

If pushed sufficiently, I would add the following: The purpose of communities of any sort should be to facilitate the development of the persons who are its members. Most of the religious communities with which I am familiar, however, have become an end in themselves and expend much greater energy on restricting and constraining their members "for the good of the order" than they do on freeing the personalities of their members for growth. Supposedly existing for social support, in fact they mostly exercise social control. This "iron law of oligarchy" by which the means (the community) for a larger goal becomes an end in itself is by no means limited to religious communities, but seems to be part of the human condition. Hence strong communities (of whatever sort) always will need reform. *Ecclesia Semper Reformana!* Perhaps reform came too late for the religious orders of women.

A priest complained to me once about the teenage boys who camped on the rectory lawn after their basketball games in the summer evening dusk. They disturbed the people coming to the rectory, he said.

"Invite them in for a Coke, make friends with them, go out and talk to them," I argued. "In many places in the Catholic world it would be impossible to get young men that close to the rectory."

He thought about it. "I'll see what the youth minister says about it."

That, gentlepersons, is an identity crisis if there ever was one.

For many priests, it is my impression that the celibacy issue is the primary cause of the morale crisis—which often sounds like self-pity. In the study NORC did of the priesthood in the late 1960s, the vast majority of priests supported optional celibacy; and of that majority, the majority also said that they would continue to remain celibate even if it was optional—though there was a negative correlation with age in that response as one might expect.

In those days it was widely expected among priests that the change "had" to come. Even the savage blow to postconciliar euphoria by the birth-control encyclical did not lessen the enthusiasm of such expectations. I was dubious. The Roman Curia was digging in, determined to maintain its power at all costs. I was told that "they" would nevertheless be forced to change because of the coming shortage of priests.

I doubted that, too. There were shortages all over the world already, and had been for centuries, and such shortages had not forced a change on the Vatican. Moreover, if priests were overworked and laity underserved, that would not make the daily life of a bishop or a cardinal or a curial bureaucrat or a pope one bit more difficult.

As it turned out, my skepticism was justified by events. But many priests, even if they had no personal plans to marry, have taken this issue as the greatest single justification for their low morale, a symbol of Vatican insensitivity and intransigence and an indicator of just how bad the situation in the Church has become in the last twenty years.

Many simply refuse to attempt to recruit young men to be priests unless and until the celibacy rule is changed. One is forced to conclude from this reaction that the Church has not made a good case in a long time for celibacy—other than the typical argument that it is a rule and it will continue to be a rule because we say so and too bad for you if you don't like it.

I've tried to defend the "witness value" of celibacy in my fiction, a point that critics on both the right and the left have cheerfully ignored.

At the end of *The Cardinal Sins*, for example, Kevin Brennan is asked the reason for celibacy: "I'd hate to see us lose it. The world, Catholic and otherwise, needs the witness of a few people who are living proof that you can intensely and passionately love members of the opposite sex without having to jump into bed with them."

In my new novel, appropriately called *The Cardinal Virtues*, I present in story form the argument I am about to make with regard to the role of the priest as confidant:

"Father McAuliffe." She rose like the convent school girl she was and extended her gloved hand respectfully.

"Nice to see you, Maria." I shook hands with her. "Please sit down."

Maria was not the kind to throw a down jacket over jeans and a flannel shirt to visit the rectory and see a priest—even if any priest would do. She felt obliged to dress as if she were paying a visit to a doctor or a lawyer, a divorce lawyer perhaps. She was wearing a blue checked suit, a black blouse with large white buttons, and a full array of jewelry.

I was glad that I had the foresight to put on my Roman collar.

She gestured nervously with her right hand. "I'm not altogether sure why I'm here, Father."

I waited. Maria had seemed to me to be aloof, reserved, distant—light brown hair in place, makeup perfect, Middle Atlantic diction a little affected in my flat prairie ears. Frigid, I would have insisted once. Perhaps terribly shy, I would have said later. Maybe both, I would guess now. And scared.

"I want to talk to you."

"I'll try to help, Maria."

"Yes, Father." Her voice choked. "The problem is I'm not sure what it is I want to talk about . . . do I sound a little strange?"

"Just honest, Maria."

"I'll try to be honest."

"And a little frightened."

She considered that. "Perhaps. Surely baffled."

I waited again.

Maria was not one of those attractive matrons who, in my argument with God a few days before, I would have pictured as open to the chance of dalliance with their pastor. Nor was she engaged in seduction now. She was rather working up the nerve to be vulnerable.

That made her more attractive than she had ever seemed before.

"As you know," she began carefully, "Ed and I have been seeing Father Keenan periodically. Ed goes all the time. I go some of the time."

I nodded my head.

"As you may also know Ed has resigned from his law firm and is seeing a therapist, about neither of which actions did he consult with me." She frowned, upset by the irresponsibility inherent in such behavior.

"I didn't know that, Maria. We priests do not violate the confidences of the rectory office, not even with one another."

"Sometimes it might help." She smiled briefly. "It would make it easier for people like me."

"Only when we have explicit permission—under ordinary circumstances."

"I see." She tapped her finger lightly on her knee. "Then perhaps I should tell you that Ed has moved out of the house into an apartment in one of the townhouses over near the station."

"I see."

"He did so at my request."

"I see."

"My children are furious at me."

"Children are usually sullen when their parents seem to be separating."

"I don't want to hurt them." She sighed. "I have my own life to lead."

"I understand."

"Do you?"

"I didn't say I approve. I merely said I understand."

"You think, I would imagine, that they are wonderful children . . . Your young aide across the way was most interested in the health of my son Neil."

"She is part of the admiring consensus for your children."

"I daresay." She lifted her shoulders slightly, a deftly controlled shrug. "Does anyone," she burst out, "understand how much of a mother's life goes into raising such young people? How much her own life she must bury in theirs?"

I chose my words carefully. "If I may dare to interpret the consensus about Maria Sullivan and her children, the admiration extends to both."

"You're clever, Father McAuliffe. I suppose you image that I'm just another silly premenopausal woman in a mid-life crisis."

"I would never dare put you in a category, Maria."

She colored slightly. "Indeed? In any event what I want to ask you is whether it would be possible for me, perhaps on only one or two occasions, to seek counsel from you, apart from my husband. There may be once in a great while some matters about which I would wish to consult you if I go ahead with plans for a divorce."

"Certainly."

I suspected that she would never file the divorce suit, about which she would talk for a long time. As I had told Jaimie, Ed might sue eventually to escape the intolerable—and thus be guilty.

"I'm grateful, Father."

She rose to leave.

"Maria!"

"Yes, Father?"

"Sit down."

Her eyes widened in surprise and she sat down.

"You did not get dressed up like a proper product of the Religious of the Sacred Heart and come over to see the parish priest merely to assure yourself that on a possible future occasion you would have a counseling resource available."

She bowed her head and bit her lip.

"No, Father . . . and when the pastor tells me to sit down, like the docile Sacred Heart girl I am, I sit down."

"So tell him why you're here."

Did she already have a lover?

Maria?

No, that would be utterly without class.

"Yes, Father . . . I am frightened and I don't even know why, isn't that strange?"

All my life in the priesthood, women have astonished me by their willingness to trust themselves and their most intimate problems and fears to a priest confidant. Some of them were targets for seduction by priests during the terrible years of the late sixties and early seventies; but that did not seem to have shattered their confidence in us, although now they are perhaps a little more careful in choosing whom to give their trust.

"You can't beat it," Mike Quinlan says, "if you're a woman. The local priest is a man to whom you can give a lot of yourself and still feel reasonably secure that he's not about to take that which he shouldn't take. It's a good argument for women priests. Men should have a similar supply of confidants available."

"I wonder they still trust any of us after all that has happened."

"They'll always trust you, Lar." The Turk jumps into the conversation, looking up from his potatoes. "You're handsome and sympathetic and they understand that if they ever put a move on you, you'd run at a speed only slightly less rapid than light. So a crush on you is fun and safe."

"God knows," Mike concludes. "They may even get a little help in the process."

The New Priest merely laughs.

Thus for Laurence McAuliffe, the last playboy of the Western world.

"Not strange at all, Maria."

"Father . . . are most men afraid of women?"

Had Jaimie planted that idea in her head? If he had, it sure had hit home.

"As a general rule they are."

She shook her head in disbelief. "I have the impression that Ed is trying to tell me something like that, either because of his conversations with the young priest or the therapist, or, arguably, both."

"You don't want to hear it."

"Of course not." She clutched her gloved hands together, fingers working back and forth against one another. "I will not permit him to continue such a line of conversation."

"Why not?"

"I do NOT want to hear such matters."

"Why not?"

She paused, searched my face carefully, and then said, "They are profoundly disturbing . . . arousing even . . . "

"I see."

Which I didn't.

"There is an implication of power that I do not want and won't have."

"What kind of power, Maria?"

She shut her eyes. "When Neil was a tiny baby and I held him naked at my breasts I experienced a feeling of enormous power over this tiny male and"—eyes still closed—"considerable arousal, too."

"I see."

She opened her eyes. "Does that shock you, Father McAuliffe?"

"No, Maria, it doesn't. I would have been more shocked if you had denied ever having such emotions."

"They are not uncommon, then?"

"No more uncommon than women bringing men into the world."

"I see." She sighed with relief. "I had wondered. Logically it seemed to be as you say. I never had the courage to ask anyone."

I was silent again.

"Is my husband afraid of me, Father?" She closed her eyes again, dreading the answer.

"I assume so, Maria. He has no sisters, as I remember. You're a, how shall I say it, a strong womanly reality. It would be most improbable that he would not be afraid of you."

"I don't see myself that way." She opened her eyes. "I'm a little . . . a little nothing. Why would anyone be afraid of me?"

"If you are a threat to men, it would mean you aren't a little nothing and that would, right now, be profoundly disturbing, wouldn't it?"

"Of course it would . . . are you afraid of me, Father McAuliffe?"

"That's direct, Maria."

"I'm sorry if I shouldn't have asked it."

I took a deep breath.

"It's a legitimate question under the circumstances, Maria. I am not involved in anything remotely resembling a relationship as intimate as your relationship with Ed. If I were, I assume that I would be frightened of you. As it is"—I hesitated, searching for exactly the right words and phrases—"what else can I say except that you are certainly a disconcerting presence?"

"I can't believe it!" She threw up her hands in dismay. "I don't want to be that at all!"

"Or you don't want to consider the implications of that?"

"Is it because I am physically attractive—though in truth I can't quite believe that either?"

She was sitting on the edge of her chair, stiff and erect, her hands clutched together as if in desperation.

I continued to tread on eggshells. "I don't like to separate body and character, Maria."

She grimaced. "I want to become someone, my real self. Now you and my husband are telling me that I am someone, someone whom I don't want to be—a . . . a biological symbol or something of the sort."

"You're much more than that, Maria, but you're that, too. Why don't you want to be a person who is a symbol?"

"Because that would change everything, don't you see?" Her hands unclutched and reached out to me in entreaty. "It would close off my last escape hatch."

"I don't quite understand."

"The image of little Neil haunts me. I don't want that kind of power over another man. Ever."

"It's not quite the same."

"I know that! It's even worse when the defenseless little man child is an adult like you, capable of a response besides passive acceptance of mother love! I tell you," she shouted, "I don't want that!"

"That image disturbs you?"

"Tremendously . . . and, since I'm being more candid than I have ever been with anyone in my life, it arouses me terribly, too. It makes me want to find a man and quickly!"

"You're afraid you might close the escape hatch yourself?"

She nodded and bit her lip to hold back the tears. "I do not want my own earth-mother inclinations to trap me."

Maria's problem was that she was sufficiently intelligent to recognize her own emotions—I would not have imagined that before this session— and not yet so brave to trust them. It was likely that she would never be that brave.

On the other hand, recognizing the existence of an emotion and giving it a name does let it half out of the box.

"Why should men be afraid of me?" she murmured, almost in a whisper.

"We men are afraid of you women, Maria, because you have so much of what we need and can't possibly obtain by ourselves."

"Men take what they want!"

"No, Maria, they take what they can, which is infinitely less than what they want."

"We have to give it to them," she snarled.

"Only if you want. That's why you're so powerful against us."

She nodded. "I guess I understand. Maybe I'd figured it out myself, more or less. I needed to have someone tell me what I figured out is right. It's not fair, Father, it's not fair. It puts all the responsibility on us."

"How so?"

"Not only must we be both wife and mistress to THEM, we have to be mother, too."

"It's not possible to separate the roles that sharply. If you want, yes, women play a mother role to their men. How could it be otherwise? Men play a father role to their women, too, but it's not nearly so important."

"That's why it is so unfair."

"If there's one thing I've learned in almost thirty years in the priesthood, Maria, it is that we can never judge the relationship between the sexes appropriately by the norms of fairness."

"You have had all the legal power over us down through the centuries."

"We sure have. And that is changing and has to change even more. You have all the other kind of power over us and that will never change—not as long as women carry men in their bodies and nurse them and then eventually permit them back into their bodies."

A bit of the conversation with Jaimie had come back and was proving useful. He had probably planted the idea in Ed's head. Ed, thinking it was his own, talked it over with his psychiatrist, and then had tried in his inarticulate and clumsy way to share it with his wife. The implications terrified her.

"Dear God in heaven!" she shouted. "How terrible!"

"And how beautiful."

"I suppose so . . . Yes, of course it is. A terrible beauty, to quote Yeats out of context. I'm sorry for shouting, Father."

"That's perfectly all right."

"If you men can persuade us that all of this fear is true, then we will be pushovers for you, just like we are for little boys like Neil."

"That would be so terrible?"

"You'd fuck us to death!" she snarled again. "Oh, Father, I'm so sorry, I didn't mean that. I've never said anything like that before, and certainly not to a priest. I'm so ashamed."

She buried her face in her hands.

I grinned. "To tell you the truth, Maria, I am kind of proud of you for saying that. Realistically, it wouldn't be quite to death. Live women are much more fun than dead women. And in all honesty you might not find the experience completely unsatisfactory."

She removed her hands from her red face. "That's the problem. I might not want my escape hatch."

We were silent again, Maria struggling to assemble her thoughts and I trying to recoup my energy. These kinds of confidant talks were emotionally draining—not unpleasant, God knows, but exhausting.

"He's trying to seduce me again by this power and fear theme."

"You're right but there's more to it. He also has learned more about himself and about his relationships with women than I would have expected Ed ever to learn."

"A complex, intricate, and clever come-on." She reached for her purse and took out her car keys.

"Yes, indeed; and you're not sure you can resist it. Sometimes you're not even sure you want to resist it."

She sighed, deeply this time, and her shoulders lost some of their convent school stiffness.

"You know me better than I know myself, Father McAuliffe."

She rose to leave, sensing that we had said all that we could.

"One more thing, Maria." I rose with her.

"Yes, Father." She actually smiled. "I wouldn't dream of leaving without giving you the last word."

"You'd better not or I'll report you to Reverend Mother. Freud was wrong, biology isn't destiny. It is, however, an important part of destiny. Right now you mostly don't want your new power, or your old power newly discovered. It's not an option. You can stop your exercise and abandon your diets. You can stop reading and let your mind rot. You can break away from your commitments and responsibilities in the name of being your own person; you can't change who and what you are."

"A woman?"

"No. The woman that YOU are."

She stared at me uneasily.

"I'm not sure I believe you, Father . . . I understand you."

We walked out into the corridor.

"I'll get your coat," I said.

I did not want little miss busybody with the green eyes trying to check out Neil's cute mother to see why she had shouted.

"Thank you, Father," Maria said as I helped her on with the mink.
"You're welcome."

"Nice doggy." She patted the now ever-present Norah. "Remember I get one of your first puppies."

Norah arched her back in clear agreement.

I had given up trying to banish her from the front office in the evening. The one night I had locked her in the garage, every single caller asked where the big bitch was. Well, they didn't call her that. I did.

At the door we shook hands. "You've been a wonderful priest to me, Father McAuliffe. Whatever happens I'll always be grateful."

"I'm here to help, Maria. Anytime you want."

Outside, as the fog and the mists swirled around, she turned toward me.

"I frighten my husband?"

"Woman, you scare the hell out of him!"

"You, too?" she said softly.

"After this conversation, a lot more than before."

She turned and ran down the steps.

I glanced at my watch after I had closed the door. No time for a drink before dinner. God knows I had earned it.

I was not hopeful about Maria Sullivan. Other women in the same situation had arrived at the same place to which she and come and then turned and run away. She was more intelligent than the others and hence more articulate about it, not necessarily braver.

There was a net around her, a benign spider's net whose silken cords would bind her through this crisis in her life, a net spun by her husband and his therapist, by her priests and her children. She would have to decide for herself whether freedom was inside the net or outside.

In most such dilemmas these days, the women choose to break out of the cords and find freedom somewhere else.

Whether in a novel or in empirical data, neither side of the debate, I fear, will listen as long as the contest is shaped by an argument about rules.[3]

One must speak first of the transcendent—the world that is to come and is yet somehow present among us, in the Church, in the community, in the tradition, and in the priesthood, a world of whose sight we lose when we disregard the Sacramental Imagination.

[3] Nor is helped by frivolous comments of men like Father Richard McBrien, the chairman of the Theology Department at Notre Dame. In an interview in *Notre Dame* magazine he suggested that the next pope appear on the balcony the Saturday of his election with his fiancée on his arm and announce his marriage. Such foolishness shows contempt for the tradition of celibacy and the many priests who have honored their celibate commitment and served the Church better because of it.

In the Young Catholic study, there are virtually no differences between women and men (whether married or unmarried) in their judgments as to whether their parish priest is very sympathetic, or in their having had a conversation with a priest about a religious problem during the past year and saying that a priest has had a considerable impact on their thinking about the Catholic faith.

The last two items were combined into a scale, which taps both recent conversations with a priest and agreement that a priest has had a powerful religious effect on one's life. (It cannot be argued that the priests are the same person.) The scale correlates positively with marital satisfaction, both for the wife and for the family unit. If a woman is high on the scale, both she and her husband are more likely to say that their marriage is very satisfactory. Far from being a rival to the husband, then, it would appear that the celibate priest is a positive asset to his marriage relationship.

This effect seems to exist only for women. The more likely a woman is to have an influential and recent relationship with a priest, the more likely she is to be very satisfied with her marriage, while a man's relationship with a priest does not increase the quality of his marital satisfaction. However, the woman's relationship does increase the joint satisfaction of husband and wife with their marriage. If the woman has neither had a recent conversation with a priest nor been strongly influenced religiously in her life by a priest, only half the couples will both say they are very satisfied with their marriage. Both recentness and strong influence are required for the effect on joint marital satisfaction (the "high" score on the scale). One without the other makes little difference in marital satisfaction for husband and wife.

The "confidant" relationship also correlates with positive psychological well-being, significantly for women and not significantly for men, but only for married women, a little more than one-third of whom are high on the positive psychological well-being scale if they have no contact with a priest, and almost two-thirds of whom are high on the scale if they have a confidant relationship.

One out of every seven married Catholic women is high on the relationship-with-a-priest scale, which is to say that she has a priest "confidant"—she has had a recent conversation with a priest about religious matters and reports that a priest has had an important religious influence on her life. Such women are likely to be higher on the score of positive well-being and to be involved in marriages in which both the wife and husband are satisfied with the quality of the relationship.

The question naturally arises as to whether this apparently satisfactory relationship happens despite the celibacy of the priest or because of it. Can such relationships be found in other denominations? Since the data in the General Social Survey provide no methods for directly addressing this question, one must use an indirect and tentative argument that is presented as speculative exploration and not as certain proof.

Young Catholic women who have high confidence in their organizational leadership are more likely to say that they are very satisfied with their marriage than those who have low confidence in their religious leadership. However, this seems to be entirely the result of the fact that some such women have a confidant relationship with a priest. Those who lack a confidant relationship and have a great deal of confidence in church leadership are lower in marital satisfaction than those who have low confidence in church leadership and have a confidant relationship. Without the intervention of a priest, confidence in church leadership correlates negatively with marital satisfaction for Catholic women. If you are very confident in church leadership, your marriage is less satisfactory unless there is a priest "confidant" involved who seems to be able to reverse the direction of the relationship.

Returning to the GSS, we find that the significant positive correlation between confidence in church leadership and marital satisfaction for women exists only among Roman Catholics. It is not statistically significant for the other denominations. Since we have already determined that the reason there is a positive relationship between marital satisfaction and confidence in church leadership for Catholic married women is the intervention of a priest confidant, we may speculate that the absence of a significant relationship in the other denominations may well be the result of an absence of an intervening clerical confidant. Minimally, it can be said with confidence that the celibacy of the priest is not an obstacle to explaining the confidant relationship and there are strong hints that it may be a positive asset.

One might further speculate that for young Catholic married women a friendly and trusting relationship with another man in which there is little "danger" and considerable encouragement, social support, and reassurance leaves her more free and less tense for the relationship with her husband. It may well be that the ability to provide such relationships for married women is one of the unperceived but important functions of clerical celibacy. (I would add that those of us who have worked as parish priests have intuitively been aware of this function for a long time.) It also may be that the absence of a counterpart relationship for young Catholic married men could be a pragmatic argument for the ordination of women—though if our speculative reasons about the importance of celibacy for such relationships are correct, then it would follow that this function would be achieved only with a celibate female clergy.

What is there about a confidant relationship between a priest and a young married woman which facilitates the marital happiness of both her and her husband? While the confidant relationship does indeed correlate with "Stories of Grace," it is not the intervening variable that explains the link between a priest confidant and a fulfilled marriage. Nor does a confidant relationship improve the woman's estimate of the sexual fulfillment in her marriage. However, it does improve her husband's propensity to say that the sexual fulfillment is excellent. A confidant relationship correlates not with the wife's sexual fulfillment but with the husband's. Furthermore, when these three variables are considered together, it develops that the sexual fulfillment of the husband is indeed the intervening variable linking the confidant relationship with a priest and the marital satisfaction of the wife. A wife's marital satisfaction is improved by a confidant relationship with a priest precisely because that relationship tends to enhance the sexual fulfillment of her husband.

A possible explanation for this phenomenon is that the young wife receives sufficient encouragement from the priest to be open to sexuality. Because of that support perhaps she abandons some of her inhibitions; then she is able, therefore, to be a more satisfying sexual partner to her husband, a success that makes both of them happier with their marriage. If such be the dynamics of the relationship—and they certainly ought to be examined much more closely in future research—one has an interesting manifestation of a "latent function" of clerical celibacy and also perhaps another pragmatic argument for the importance of a counterpart "confidant" for married men.

What kind of priest do such women seek out for confidant relationships? Those in such relationships are much more likely to rate priest's sermons as excellent, to describe priests as very understanding, to be in parishes where there is a good deal of activity and where priests do not expect laity to be followers. They are also substantially more likely to endorse the piety, concern, and training of their professional clergy. It would appear that the confidant relationships exist in parishes that are active and have democratic leaderships, where the counseling skills are excellent and where the priests are pious, committed, and well-trained. Presumably these are precisely the qualities a young woman would look for in the priest "confidant."

A scale that measures the "professionalism" of the priest correlated positively and significantly with the confidant impact. The women who were high on the scale estimating the "professionalism" of their clergy were twice as likely to have confidant relationships.

There was no relationship between feminism and confidant relationships. Those who are high on the feminism scale (about which much more in the next chapter) and those who were low were equally as likely to have such a relationship. Young women's perception that church leadership wishes to keep them in an inferior status does not seem to have any effect on their propensity to enter into confidant relationships with priests.

The analyses presented here are tentative. We do not know, for example, that the priest with whom the married woman has talked recently is the same priest who has had a notable impact on her life. Nor can we be sure that celibacy is an asset developing the clergyman/woman relationship. Finally, it is possible that it is precisely those women who are in satisfactory marriages and whose husbands are satisfied with the quality of the sexual relationship who would feel free to choose a religious relationship with a priest, so the causal connection may flow in the opposite direction from the one assumed. This seems less likely but certainly cannot be excluded until further research is done.

Nevertheless, despite their antagonism toward higher church leaders, it is clear that young Catholic married women are able to have satisfying relationships with their priests, relationships that are linked to happier marriages.

What effect does a confidant relationship have on young Catholic married women's attitudes toward change in the clerical life? Such women are more "liberal" than those who lack such relationships on the matter of ordination of women. Fifty-five percent of them think such a change is important, as opposed to 40 percent of those without a confidant. On the other hand, they are less likely to support permission for a married clergy—48 percent of the confidant women support such a change, as opposed to 60 percent of those who lack a confidant.

Clearly the confidant women are not reactionaries on the subject of women priests, yet they favor the retention of clerical celibacy, perhaps because they perceive—however dimly—that their own beneficial relationship with a priest is in part the result of his celibate status. Perhaps one of the reasons they strongly support the other change is that they perceive that their husbands might benefit from a similar relationship with a celibate woman priest.

Furthermore—and perhaps astonishingly—exactly the same pattern exists among the husbands. Those with wives in confidant relationships are more likely to support the ordination of women and less likely than those whose wives lack such relationships to advocate optional celibacy—as though they, too, perceive the enhancement to their lives of a celibate priest counselor for their wives, and perhaps even the additional enhancement that would occur if they had a celibate woman priest as their own "confidant."

The final question to be asked is whether it is precisely those husbands and wives who have benefited from the confidant relationship who are the most likely to be in favor of celibacy and also in favor of the ordination of women. Are those whose marriages have been positively affected by a wife's relationship with a priest most reluctant to see celibacy abandoned but also most eager to have women priests (from whom, possibly, men can derive similar benefits as their wives have from relationships with celibate priests)?

This question asks whether the relationship is to be found only among those whose marriages have profited from confidant relationships, and if for others in which there is a confidant relationship the situation will reverse itself. It assumes that if a table is created in which those who are in confidant relationships (or whose wives are) and those who are high on marital satisfaction (or in the husband's case on sexual fulfillment) represent the upper left-hand cell, the proportion in that cell will be higher than in the other cells on the subject of the ordination of women (above half) and lower than those in other cells in support of optional celibacy (less than half).

This is precisely what occurs. The highest support for women priests and the strongest opposition to optional celibacy come from those husbands and wives who seem to have benefited (either in marital satisfaction in the wife's case or sexual fulfillment in the husband's) from a wife's confidant relationship with a priest.

The implications of this phenomenon for the social psychology and sociology of the celibate state are enormous. There is something in the "chemistry" of the relationship between a priest and a married woman which establishes an "electricity" often beneficial to both the wife and her husband and makes both of them more committed to celibacy and to the ordination of women. The phenomenon ought to be studied in much greater detail but will doubtless be ignored. The left wing will not tolerate anything good to be said about celibacy, and the right wing will not tolerate the thought that there is a special "chemistry" between the celibate and the married woman (and possibly between a celibate woman and a married man).

The priest, whether he wants to be or not (and I fear many of us don't want to be), is evidence of the Sacramental Imagination at work. He not only believes that God lurks in the world; he is in fact in a special way[4] himself a sign of the presence of the lurking God.

Alas, the laity are not satisfied with the way these men-who-are-also-signs perform.

The Catholic laity are surveyed every year in studies by Gallup and by NORC and every two years in the biennial Michigan election surveys. The Catholic clergy, however, have not been studied systematically since the National Conference of Catholic Bishops study of the priesthood in 1970. Moreover, because no explicitly Catholic study of the whole population has been undertaken since the NORC parochial school study in 1974, there is a lack of data about Catholic attitudes toward their clergy in the years since then. The exception is the Young Catholic study in 1979, which provided information about their views of the clergy and a single question about confidence in religious leadership taken from the General Social Survey.

I will now attempt to pull together from the 1970 priest study, the 1974 study of Catholic adults, and the 1979 study of young Catholics some data on the condition of the clergy, the attitudes of the laity toward the clergy, and prospects for future vocations to the clergy.

There were four important findings in the 1970 study of the Catholic priesthood in the United States which, in retrospect, ought to have created considerable concern in the leadership of the American Church about the future of the priesthood:

—Between a sixth and a fifth of those who were still active in the priesthood were planning, with varying degrees of certainty, to leave the priesthood.

—More than four-fifths of the Catholic clergy did not insist on

---

[4] The words "special way" are important. Obviously a lay person who is especially kind and loving to fellow humans is a more effective sign of God's presence than a priest who is not kind and loving. The priest's sign value comes from his office. He is *ex officio* a sign—though he may blow most of his sign value by his own personal failings.

acceptance of the official birth-control teaching in the confessional. This represented a change from even five years earlier before the birth-control encyclical and probably an even greater change from ten years before the 1970 study. Few, if any, Catholic priests in 1960 would have been willing to give absolution to penitents who refused to accede to the birth-control teaching.

—Catholic priests were much less likely in 1970 than they remembered themselves being in 1965 to engage in active recruiting of young men to be priests like themselves.

—The occupational satisfaction of associate pastors is no higher than that of semi-skilled workers.

These four findings point to a loss of nerve, a loss of discipline, a loss of sense of identity in the priesthood, and a decline of job satisfaction among younger priests. When any professional group loses interest in recruiting replacements, that professional group is in considerable trouble. Moreover, when in addition to this loss of interest in recruiting replacements a substantial proportion of the group is planning to withdraw from the group and those who remain are not satisfied with their work, and are unwilling to accept one of the major rules that are supposed to govern the activity of the group, then clearly that particular collectivity of human beings has very serious internal problems.

Unfortunately, the concern of bishops in reaction to the findings of the 1970 study of the priesthood tended to focus on the embarrassment of the discovery that priests had rejected the teaching of the birth-control encyclical and the further embarrassment that four-fifths of the priests in the country believed that married men should be ordained priests and the priests who had left the active ministry to marry should be permitted to return (though only two-fifths of the inactive priests actually wanted to return to the ministry and only about one-fifth to the kind of work that they had been doing before they left the ministry).

Such findings attracted considerable attention from the mass media and put the bishops who had funded the research in an awkward position. How were they to explain to Rome that they had funded research that showed that the American clergy were in fundamental dissent from the Holy See on the question of mandatory celibacy, the return to the active ministry of married priests, and the birth-control teaching? It is to be feared that the bishops were so interested in distancing themselves from the project that they missed the underlying warnings that were more serious and more threatening to the effective ministry of the priesthood than the findings on married clergy, celibacy, and birth control.

The only practical result of the study was that a committee was set up in the National Conference of Catholic Bishops to worry about the problems of the priesthood, a committee whose impact on the lives and ministry of priests in the United States seems to have been practically nonexistent.

Therefore, the identity crisis and the loss of nerve in the priesthood, which were clearly indicated in the 1970 study, and which ought to have served as a warning to bishops and priests alike that there were greater problems ahead for the priesthood, simply were overlooked.

All other problems of the priesthood would be unimportant if the recruiting of young men to serve in the priesthood in years to come was proceeding successfully. However, there is no reason to believe that the reluctance of priests to recruit men to assist them and replace them, noted in the 1970 study, has changed in the slightest. In 1962 there were 55,581 priests and 46,189 seminarians. In 1988 the numbers were 53,522 priests and 7,510 seminarians. Because there are still almost as many priests (at a much older average age), some church leaders are not fully aware of the implications of 16 percent as many seminarians as a quarter century ago.

What has happened to vocations? In the Knights of Columbus study we attempted to analyze the problem at great length. For all the attention that was paid to the results by priests and bishops we might just as well have saved our time and the Knights' money.

First of all, young women are much more likely than young men (three times as likely when they are teens) to consider lives of dedication to the Church. While there is little interest at all among young people in the diaconate as a vocation, young women are more likely than young men (twice as likely) to express interest in being a woman deacon. As one might expect, they are also notably more likely to say that they would think of becoming priests if they were able to do so.

These young women probably represent the same religious and altruistic enthusiasms that led their predecessors to join religious orders of women a quarter century ago.

The 1979 Young Catholic study proved beyond any reasonable doubt that there were two important persons in the process by which a young man begins to think seriously of becoming a priest—the young man's mother and his own priest. The study of Catholic adults in 1974 showed that there had been a decline of ten percentage points in the number of Catholics who said they would be proud to have their son a priest—though still half the American Catholics said they would be proud of a son priest. In the 1979 study of young Catholics half also would be proud to have a son priest.

More than four-fifths of the respondents reported that no one had ever suggested to them the possibility of a religious or a priestly vocation. Many of those who said they had thought seriously about a vocation also said that no one had ever encouraged them.

Pride in a priestly vocation in the family is one thing, and active recruiting of young men to the priesthood either by a parent or by a priest is something quite different. Approximately 5 percent of the young Catholic men in the country had seriously considered a vocation to the priesthood; and another quarter in 1979 had at least given it some thought. The analytic models developed in the Young Catholic study suggested that the principal missing ingredient was the absence of encouragement from the mother and the parish priest in pursuing the thought of the vocation.

If either the celibacy rule were changed or there were more encouragement for priestly vocations from priests themselves and from the families of young men, there is every reason to believe that the present crisis in vocations would be speedily eliminated.

The numerical decline of the priesthood, which may be the most serious problem facing the Church in the wake of the Second Vatican Council, does not seem to be properly attributable to a spiritual decline among young Catholics, a very considerable proportion of whom are interested in social and religious problems and even (10 percent) would be willing to consider a life of dedication to the Church. A change in the requirement of priestly celibacy would probably lead to the ordination of fifteen hundred more priests a year than are now being ordained. A modification of the requirement of the priesthood in which priests would continue to be celibate but would be permitted to serve in the active ministry for limited periods of time would produce a thousand more priests a year.

Note that most of the benefit in increased vocations that could be achieved by eliminating the celibacy requirement could also be achieved by the much less drastic change of permitting limited-term service in the priesthood. However, the most serious obstacle to increasing the number of priestly vocations still seems to be the lack of encouragement that young men ought to receive from priests themselves. The celibacy rule is not likely to be changed. If the notion of a limited-service priesthood is not to be taken seriously, then the principal obstacle to the recruitment is among priests themselves. As my colleagues and I have remarked in our report on the 1979 study, in the absence of more enthusiasm for vocations in the priesthood, the problem of diminishing numbers of priests will be insoluble.

My suggestion of a "priest corps" like the Peace Corps, in which men (and women, too, one hopes) would serve in the active ministry for limited terms of service, is normally ignored—although there is no theological reason someone should have to serve in the active ministry all his life. Up until a century and a quarter ago, the average age of a priest at death was thirty-five. Now most priests live to celebrate their golden jubilee, a life expectancy roughly twice as long. A priest who can put up with the many and varied demands of the ministry for his whole life may be unusual. By forcing men to stay in the priesthood when they're worn out, the Church runs the risk of their becoming bitter and cynical and taking out their frustrations on the laity.

Yet these demographic and psychological considerations are irrelevant when the leadership determines to hunker down and discuss nothing.

The usual reaction to the vocation crisis from church leadership is to appoint a young priest (or two in larger dioceses) to "vocation work." Perhaps such recruiters are given an office and even a secretary. Those actions having been taken, the bishop can turn to other matters.

It is often argued that more intense vocational recruiting has been tried and found wanting. In fact, it has been found hard and not tried. As a businessman remarked to a priest who was trying to make the bricks of vocations without the straw of adequate resources of personnel and finances in Chicago, "Your work is simply not important or the cardinal would provide you with a lot more help."

How much help? Well, how much help would the U.S. Navy provide to its recruiters if there was a shortage of jet pilots?

One cannot imagine that the Navy would not institute a crash program in which every possible resource was poured into recruiting. Maybe more serious efforts would not make any difference, but we'll not know that until such efforts are tried.

How many more persons would investigate the possibility of a life of dedication to the Church, for example, if every pastor in a diocese was required to write a personal letter to his bishop each month to report what he had done for vocations during the last four weeks?

"I would not have time to read more than a few of them," a busy bishop said to me. See what I mean about resources?

However, the knowledge that he would read any of them would be sufficient motivation to many pastors to do more than they're doing now.

The vocation problem, in other words, is a priest-and-bishop problem and not a young-person problem. Paradoxically, it would appear that at a time when the preaching and counseling abilities of priests are most important to Catholics, priests themselves have relatively little regard for the importance of their own work. American Catholics may complain about the quality of preaching and the quality of counseling and sensitivity they encounter in the rectory, but they still have considerable respect for the sincerity and the diligence, if not the professional competence, of their priests. While many of them, and among the young adults most of them, thought that priests were too authoritarian and still expected the laity to be followers, rather than colleagues or leaders, and while about half of them objected to priests becoming too involved in politics, the admiration and respect and affection for parish priests was still high. Moreover, as I reported earlier, the most powerful single influence in facilitating the return of someone to the Church who had drifted away—particularly a young Catholic in his/her early or middle twenties—was a relationship with a priest.

Preaching, counseling, and close relationships with young adults were at least as important in the Church of the late seventies and of the early eighties as they were in the Church before the Vatican Council. And yet the overwhelming majority of young Catholics have no contact with and indeed no opportunity to establish contact with priests. Priests are at least as important in the lives of the lay people as they used to be.

Unfortunately, perhaps because of poor communication with lay people, priests do not seem to have as much confidence in the importance of their own ministry as they had in the years before the Second Vatican Council. And because of the lack of conviction of their own importance and of the future importance of their work, they are disinclined to invite other young men to follow them into the priesthood. The decline is not in the importance of priestly ministry but rather, it would seem, in priestly perception of the importance of their own ministry.

Precisely at a time when the quality of Sunday preaching is a powerful predictor both of the strength of religious affiliation and of the development of the religious imagination, and when contact with the priest is the most important element in a young person's drift back to the Church after he or she has drifted away, precisely at this point it would seem that priests are at least as important in the lives of the lay people as they used to be.

The laity are not about to leave the Church. The clergy, however, are in the process of committing collective suicide because they do not have enough confidence in themselves and their work to actively recruit young men to follow them into the priesthood.

The laity, for their part, are much more likely to accept changes in the priesthood than is ecclesiastical authority. In 1974, 70 percent of the Catholic population would accept a married priesthood and 50 percent approved of a married priesthood. For young Catholics five years later, that proportion was even higher. Interestingly enough, there is a strong correlation between willingness to consider a vocation to the priesthood among young adults and antagonistic attitudes toward the church's sexual teaching. Many young Catholics consider an "updating" of the sexual teaching as an essential part of a program to attract more vocations to the priesthood. At first glance there seems to be no connection between sexual ethics and priestly vocation, but perhaps the connection is that the sexual teaching of the Church, thought by the young adults to be outmoded and inappropriate, gives the institutional Church and the priesthood an image that is not likely to make religious or priestly vocations appealing.

One has the impression that in the early seventies the ecclesiastical authorities in Rome and the United States made the decision to "tough out" the crisis in the priesthood and to essentially do nothing to resolve the loss of nerve and identity among priests, to curtail resignation from the priesthood, to think and rearticulate the reasons for ecclesiastical celibacy, to improve the quality of vocational recruiting, or to devise imaginative and creative ways to attract more young men to the priesthood. Perhaps it was felt that attempts in these directions would prove unacceptable to Rome or would require too much effort or would be doomed to failure in the face of the sullen resentment many priests feel toward ecclesiastical authority and toward their own perceived declining status in the Church.

It is difficult to find anything in the evidence available to us, either from studies of priests or studies of lay attitudes toward the priesthood, that would justify optimism about the present condition of the

Catholic priesthood in the United States. The laity seem convinced that priests are important and are certainly not anticlerical, but they do not give priests high grades on professional performance. Priests, for their part, have lost confidence in their ministry and are not actively involved in recruiting young men to the priesthood. And the hierarchy finally, for its part, is apparently resigned to a continuing vocation crisis. It is not prepared to experiment imaginatively or expend substantial resources of money or personnel in the recruitment of young men to the ministry. Nor is it willing to institute changes in the life and work of the priesthood that will make it more attractive to young men. The priest shortage will have to become far more acute than it is perceived to be before any of the three major actors in shaping the future of the priesthood become sufficiently concerned to address themselves to the problem.

The full impact of the vocation shortage will be perceived in the years ahead only when the retirement and death of those cohorts of priests that are large leave the Church with substantially fewer priests—some observers say as many as half of the present number before the end of the century—than are presently available. The shortage of priests in the United States is a problem that is discussed but not felt. By the time it is felt—in the next fifteen or twenty years—it may well be too late to discuss it. The priesthood in the United States, and indeed it would seem in the whole Western world, is in very serious trouble; no one is prepared to do anything about it or even engage in serious research and reflection in response to the crisis.

We do not fully understand the origins of the crisis: Why did so many men leave the priesthood as soon as it became possible for them to leave and still remain in some fashion in the Church? What was there about the change created in the Church by the Second Vatican Council that created not increased confidence and self-respect among priests but rather a deterioration of confidence and self-esteem? Why is it that at a time when all the evidence indicates that priests are at least as important to lay people as they've ever been, priests themselves don't perceive this importance? Why did the changes in the Church, received enthusiastically by most priests, lead not to an increase in vocational recruiting but to a decline? What went wrong in the Catholic priesthood in the United States following the Second Vatican Council?

Even stated as simply as that last question, the crisis in the priesthood remains to a considerable extent inexplicable. The changes of the Second Vatican Council did something to the priesthood from which it has yet to recover. Until we understand better than we do now why the Council was such a severe blow to the morale, the self-esteem, the self-confidence, and the self-respect of priests, we will have to accept as almost inevitable the continued decline in the number of priests available to minister to the Church and the mounting problems for laity and for priests because of that decline.

One possibility is the rigidity and narrowness of the clerical culture in which so many priests are trapped, a culture that causes them to worry more about what their fellow priests are thinking or what the bishops are doing than about the needs of the lay people they were ordained to serve. Has clerical culture become a substitute for religious faith?

Another possibility is the loss of respect for leaders. On my desk as I write (from the morning mail) is a document from the American bishops on priestly morale, written by a committee chaired by Archbishop Thomas Murphy, a fellow West Side Irishman. The committee cannot, naturally enough, address itself to the failings of fellow bishops. I am half tempted to invite Tom and ask whether he thinks the recent appointments in, let us say, Philadelphia and Bridgeport, are a help or a blow to priestly morale.

The Curia, astonished at the independence of the American hierarchy during the Vatican Council, has appointed "safe" and "conservative" bishops ever since—except during the term of Archbishop Jean Jadot as apostolic delegate. Doubtless Rome felt that such appointments would restore order and discipline in the American clergy and laity. In fact, the new hierarchy (except the Jadot appointments) is not only conservative, it is often incompetent and stupid.

It's difficult to sustain morale when you believe that you are not only governed by fools but that their folly in increasing.

Just as the hierarchy of the Catholic Church seems to have lost its ability to influence the attitudes and behavior of its laity on matters of sexual ethics, so it also seems to have lost its ability to influence its clergy on matters of self-respect, self-confidence, professional performance, and recruitment of priests for the future.

Yet Catholics seem to imagine their clergy differently than do members of other denominations. Despite themselves and the crisis in their morale, priests are nonetheless perceived as sacraments of a world that transcends our own. They are the sacramental persons par excellence. They want to be, if one is to credit the passionate assertions of some priests, "just like everyone else." But the Catholic imagination, fully aware of the human limitations of its clergy, still imagines them as "different," as hints of what the ever-lurking God is like, as rumors of angels, as men who point to a world beyond themselves, as signals of the transcendent God.

Apparently that is precisely what most priests do not want to be. They seem to comprehend no longer what the priesthood means.

12

THE WOMAN PROBLEM: WORSE BEFORE IT GETS BETTER?

HEN MY SISTER AND I published our book *Angry Catholic Women*[1] in 1984, the reaction from church leaders—insofar as there was any at all—was that most Catholic women were not angry at the Church. A few radical nuns who wanted to be priests might be angry, and a few militant feminists, and maybe some lesbians; but the typical Catholic woman, the good wife and mother, the solid and responsible member of the parish, the sister or the mother of the bishop (or priest)—why, none of these were angry.

It seemed to both Dr. Durkin and myself at the time that the clergy and hierarchy had to be blind, deaf, and dumb to think they didn't have a major "woman problem" on their hands.

In the last half decade there has been a big change in perception: hardly any Catholic leader in this country now denies that women are bitterly angry. When they try in their bumbling way to tell this to the Vatican and much of the rest of the Church, they are written off as being worried about a "purely American" problem—a reaction that suggests that the Vatican and its sycophants are blind, deaf, and dumb to what is happening all over the world.

No less a person than Cardinal Tomas O'Fiach, archbishop of Armagh and primate of all Ireland (not to be confused with the

---

[1] Chicago: Thomas More Press.

archbishop of Dublin who is merely the primate of Ireland), rose up at the Synod of Bishops, when the "woman problem" was dismissed as an American concern, to insist that it was by no means just an American concern. Yet there was no evidence that those in power comprehended the cardinal's ominous warning.

I don't deceive myself that our report on the anger of women—based on the Young Catholic study and confirmed by General Social Survey data—made any contribution to the change in perception by American Catholic leaders. The cries of protest from Catholic women were so loud that even bishops could no longer ignore them.

Nonetheless, Catholic leaders still do not understand the origins or the complexities of their "woman problem," much less how the religious imagination is involved in its causes and possible cure. They grasp neither the nature of the problem nor their own resources for responding to it.

They must learn to distinguish between the complex of "feminist" attitudes and images that cause some "feminist" women to withdraw from religious practice, and the mix of attitudes and images that are not an obstacle to other equally "feminist" women continuing religious practice.

A "sacramental" approach to the image of the Church and the image of women, I contend, is necessary to understand both the causes and the cure of the "feminist" alienation.

The appropriate question is not why some Catholic women diminish their religious devotion because of the Church's shabby treatment of women; the appropriate question, rather, is why many more don't defect from regular religious practice or even from the Church itself. Is it possible that in addition to the contempt for women which is institutional policy in the Church today there is something else in the Catholic tradition that makes women like being Catholic despite the official attitude toward them?

In the chapter on the two passions, I suggested that a struggle persists between the institution's distrust of sex and the imaginative tradition's insight that if God is present in the world (and not distant from it), then S/He is certainly present in sexual love. I also suggested that there is a parallel struggle between the contempt for women practiced by those with power in the Church and the insight of the Sacramental Imagination that woman is as equally a sacrament of God as is man.

Women continue to like being Catholic, I argue, because they perceive that picture of woman revealing the life-giving, life-nurturing power of God as authentic Catholic imagery. They struggle with the institutional contempt for women precisely because they want the institution to be faithful to its own imaginative heritage.

Approximately half of the young Catholics in the United States (in the Young Catholic study) approved of either the ordination of women or of working mothers, and approximately one-fourth of the men and one-third of the women approved of both. It is this latter one-third that I call "feminist."

Those who are not "feminists" are half again as likely (47 percent as opposed to 30 percent) to attend church regularly. It is this seventeen-percentage-point difference in church attendance which was the measure of the anger of young Catholic women against their church ten years ago. Why do attitudes that might be taken to stand against traditional gender-role definition lead to lower levels of church attendance for Catholic women? (These attitudes do not lead to lower levels of church attendance for members of most American Protestant denominations.)

To project from the sample to the Catholic population between eighteen and thirty at that time, there were a little more than 6 million young Catholic women between eighteen and thirty. Two million of them were "feminists"; 17 percent of that 2 million is approximately 340,000 young women who were not attending church regularly because they believed women should be ordained and because they believed it is proper for mothers of young children to work.

I hardly need observe that for a church that has spoken repeatedly in recent years about the need to "evangelize," this very large number of alienated young women represents a significant evangelistic challenge.

The "feminists" are not significantly different in many respects from other young Catholic women. Their rating of the sermons, of the sympathy of priests' attitudes toward lay people, even of the desirability of their daughters being nuns are not significantly different from the attitudes of the nonfeminists. They are also not different from the nonfeminists in their recollections of a happy childhood and the reports of a happy and sexually fulfilled marriage. They are significantly more likely to approve abortion if a mother wants no more children (twenty-four percentage points more likely) and also significantly more likely (eighteen percentage points) to approve of living together before marriage. Moreover, the feminists are substantially less likely to say that they have a great deal of confidence in church leadership.

There is no significant difference in church attendance between the feminists and nonfeminists who have a great deal of confidence in church leadership, but there is a significant difference in church attendance between the feminists and nonfeminists for those who have less than "a great deal of confidence" in those running organized religion. Thus, to the question of why some feminists go to church as often as nonfeminists do, the beginning of an answer is that feminists go to church if they have, despite their "feminism," a great deal of confidence in church leadership.

Might the image of Church and intense attitudes toward church leaders be affected by whether a young woman has attended college? Clearly college attendance has a considerable effect. There is not a statistically significant difference in church attendance between the feminists and the nonfeminists, but there is (twenty-three percentage points) for those who have attended college. What eliminates the likelihood of a feminist being less devout than a nonfeminist? Both not attending college and a great deal of confidence in church leaders seem to eliminate the negative relationship. If one wishes to discover the reasons for the anger of some young Catholic women, one must concentrate on those who attended college and who have something less than a great deal of confidence in religious leadership.

The theory of the Sacramental Imagination which has shaped the perspective of this book might lead one to expect that the images of Church and religion from a woman's childhood experience might explain the negative relationship between religious devotion and feminism. Might it not be that those college-educated feminists whose mothers actually worked during the respondents' preschool period and would therefore have been expected to have had an image of feminist behavior available to them would be even more angered at the Church's opposition (as they perceived it) to the elimination of old gender roles and hence even less likely to attend church?

Or might it not be the other way around? Might not such young women have learned from the example of their mothers that feminism and religion are compatible and hence see no conflict in their adult life between woman and Church because the images inherited from their childhood experience are not incompatible?

If the mother of a college-educated respondent worked when the respondent was under six, there was no statistically significant evidence that feminism leads to lower levels of church attendance. However, it is precisely among those respondents who attended college and whose mothers did not work during the first six years of the respondent's life that one finds a significant and indeed dramatic difference between the feminists and the nonfeminists. The former are approximately one-third as likely to attend church as the latter. The anger that is the object of our study seems to be specified, i.e., localized, in precisely that population group of college-educated women who did not have available an image of working mother to assure the compatibility of images of woman and Church if the respondent is not committed to feminist positions.

Feminism leads to lower levels of religious devotion when all of the following are true: the respondent went to college; the respondent does not have a great deal of confidence in church leaders; the respondent's mother did not work during the first six years of the respondent's life. If the image of woman that one has acquired as a "feminist," to put the matter differently, is incompatible with the image of woman acquired in childhood, and the latter image is attributed to the Church, the present adult respondent feels conflict between modern woman and Church and therefore has lower levels of confidence in church leadership and is less likely to attend church regularly. There are four forces at work in this incompatibility: the image of woman perceived as child; the image of Church perceived as child; the image of woman as influenced by feminism and enhanced by college education; and the image of Church in the present. The present images are incompatible because the present image of Church is identified with the image of Church one acquired in childhood; that in turn is identified with the image of woman acquired in childhood, and that image, in its turn, is incompatible with the image of woman as defined by feminist principles.

The conflict between feminist positions and the contemporary Church, a conflict manifested in lower levels of church attendance, is rooted in the young woman's past experiences and images and is, in some sense, a function of a conflict she perceives between her own image of woman and the image of woman she observed in her mother. The Church, which was seen as endorsing and as still endorsing that image, is necessarily at odds with the young adult woman's image of woman. The present Church is suffering from the identification of a past image of Church as opposed to the equality of woman with a childhood image of woman.

On the other hand, those young women who are feminists and who perceive feminism as compatible with an image of woman absorbed from their past (because their mothers worked when they were small children) are not offended by the past image of Church and hence are not offended by the present image of Church. They therefore see no incompatibility between their image of Church and image of woman and are as likely to go to church weekly as are nonfeminists.

The weak link in the image incompatibility explanation, as many readers will doubtless have perceived, is that thus far I have been unable to establish that the Catholic feminists who do not go to church in fact attribute the image of woman they observed in their mothers to the Church. Thus far I have not established the compatibility of the image of Church and the image of mother in the previous generation that creates, among college-educated "feminists" whose mothers did not work, incompatibility between the image of Church and the image of woman in the present generation.

A statistically significant difference in church attendance (one of almost forty percentage points) exists only for those college-educated women whose mothers did not work during the first six years of their life, and whose mothers attended church every week. Though the number of cases is obviously very limited in this microanalysis, it would appear that if a woman's mother did not attend church every week, i.e., if she was not very devout, then the woman does not link the image of woman from her childhood with an image of Church from her childhood. If, on the other hand, the mother was both traditional in church attendance and traditional in her exercise of the role of woman, then those two traditionalisms are linked; if her daughter is a feminist, then the daughter's feminism will have a negative impact on her church attendance. The problem for the Church in the present, in other words, has been created precisely because, for the mother of our respondent, there was a high degree of compatibility between religious devotion and the traditional role of woman. When the daughter dissents from the one, there is a propensity for her to dissent from the other.

What are the factors that can reverse the incompatibility of image of woman and image of Church? Can the image of God as present, which is central to the Sacramental Imagination, cancel the less benign images a woman may have inherited from her past?

Can the incompatibility of images of woman and Church be eliminated if a respondent has a powerful image of God, since God is (despite the behavior of many leaders of the Roman Catholic Church) more important than the Church?

A statistically significant difference in church attendance between feminists and nonfeminists (a difference of forty percentage points) among those respondents who went to college, whose mothers did not work, whose mothers attended Mass every week, is to be found precisely among those respondents who do not feel close to God. If you feel close to God, then the incompatibility of your present image of woman with the image of woman in your childhood and your image of Church seems to be eliminated. While you may "blame" the Church for the image of woman with which you were raised and which you now reject, that blame does not keep you away from church attendance because you still like God and you feel that God likes you.

An image of a "God who is present" to the woman negates any conflict she might feel between her present image of woman and present image of Church. This is *because a God who is close improves the image of Church,* a finding that will delight all who believe in the Sacramental Imagination; the Church reveals God and God reveals the Church.

The image of God as a lover also deflects the image conflict a young woman may experience. If the link between traditional woman and traditional Church is broken by the fact that the daughter had a nontraditional image of woman because her mother worked for the first six years of her life, the nontraditional image of God as lover has an enormous effect on church attendance, increasing the proportion of feminists going to church regularly to 69 percent.

Data collected in the National Opinion Research Center's General Social Survey supplement and confirm this "image" explanation for feminist anger at the Church.

A woman was defined as "housewife" if she was not working full-time; even those who were working part-time were placed in the "housewife" category because it turned out, in preliminary analysis, that the phenomenon to be described differentiates between full-time working women and all other women.

The housewives are likely to be angry at the Church. The working woman (the non-housewife) is less likely to go to church than the housewife but her feminism has no statistically significant impact on the likelihood that she will go to church. There is an eighteen-percentage-point difference between feminist housewives and non-feminist housewives in their church attendance. It is those who stay at home, and who are nonetheless feminists, who are less likely to go to church.

Moreover, the statistically significant differences (almost thirty percentage points) between feminist and nonfeminist in church attendance occur only among those housewives with low family satisfaction who, in addition, are less than very confident in church leadership.

If one is dissatisfied and a housewife, there is a forty-percentage-point difference in church attendance between the feminists and the nonfeminists if the mother did not work before the respondent was six. An image of woman from the past compatible with one's feminist image of woman in the present protects the Church from incompatibility with the current image of woman, even if one is dissatisfied with one's family situation.

Feminists are less likely to attend church because they're more dissatisfied with their present situation and because they have less confidence in church leadership. The differences are localized among the dissatisfied and the nonconfident. Combining the mutually reinforcing analyses of data from two independent samples, one could summarize by the following observation: the anger of Catholic feminists is the result of conflict among images of the Church, past and present; woman, past and present; and God and housewife, present.

If the present Church is linked to the past image of woman, then only a strong image of God can protect the Church from anger. If, on the other hand, the link between the present Church and the past image of woman is reinforced by the present image of dissatisfied housewife, then the incompatibility between present Church and present woman, an incompatibility that results in lower levels of religious devotion, is reinforced. Church leadership trying to intervene in this image system will discover that the image of Church is caught up in a delicate system of conflicting images of mother, Real Self and Ideal Self.

If ours is really an age of narcissism, as many have suggested, the conflict between Ideal Self (which is loved) and Real Self (which is rejected) for angry Catholic women may be but one manifestation of a larger cultural phenomenon. Unhappy in their present situation because of rejection of their Real Self, such women may find in the Church a ready and willing scapegoat for their unhappiness. The grass always looks greener in someone else's yard, especially when you can blame the gardener for the blandness of your own yard. Nonetheless, as someone has wisely remarked, in both yards the lawn has to be mowed and no gardener is going to do that for you.

The next question is how the experience of marriage might affect the complex network of image conflicts that seems to account for the lower levels of devotion among Catholic "feminists."

In the 1979 Young Catholic study, questionnaires were administered to the spouses of respondents in the sample, and thus there is an opportunity to investigate the impact of marriage on the religious behavior of Catholic "feminists."

There is, first of all, a modest correlation of .18 between a wife's score on the "feminism" scale and her husband's, about the same as that between husband's and wife's religious imagination. However, while the correlation between imaginations increases with years of marriage, the correlation between "feminism" scores decreases. An analysis that compares duration of marriage with age in their impact on this correlation led to the conclusion that age is the important influence: among younger wives (under twenty-five at the time of the study) there is a much higher correlation with a husband's "feminism" score—.33. Among wives over twenty-five the correlation decreases to an insignificant .07.

And this age effect is not a matter of there being more "feminist" young men available for the younger wives. The younger women "choose" husbands with similar attitudes on the role of women at a rate of more than half again as much as there are such men available in the population of husbands.

The word "choose" is used loosely because the consensus may have come as part of the general struggle for value compatibility which goes on both before and after a marriage begins. The husbands of these younger wives may have been feminists to begin with and hence were more attractive partners to their future wives, or they may have been converted as part of the courtship and early marriage value socialization. Or, finally, they may have been the feminists and may have converted their wives.

There are no effects of a wife's feminism on either the marital satisfaction or the sexual fulfillment of the wife. However, both indicators of marital adjustment are affected by the husband's "feminism." Young women are more likely to be happily adjusted in their marriage if their husbands have a modern view on the role of women—regardless of what the woman's own perspective on women's roles might be. Perhaps a feminist husband is more sensitive to the needs and problems of his wife.

Both husbands' and wives' feminism has a statistically significant impact on the sexual fulfillment of wives under twenty-five, though only a wife's feminism affects the marital satisfaction of women who are older than twenty-five. The higher level of value consensus in the marriages of young wives seems to be related to the importance of the impact on marriage of attitudes toward the role of women.

Thus, despite what one might have expected about the strains that feminism puts on family life, the fact is that for young people it is not a liability but an asset to a happy marriage.

What effect does marriage have, then, on the devotion of a young Catholic woman who is a feminist?

Feminists are less likely to marry devout men—29 percent of their husbands attend church regularly as opposed to 39 percent of the husbands of nonfeminists. However, the devotion of the husband has an overwhelming impact on the devotion of the feminist wife. Three-quarters of the young feminist wives go to church regularly if their husband is also a regular attender—as opposed to two-thirds of the nonfeminist wives married to regularly attending husbands.

The devotion of the husband, then, seems to blot out the effect of feminism on church attendance. The husband is a religious influence so important that past image conflicts seem to become irrelevant.

Moreover, it would appear that devout husbands are especially likely to be chosen by those young feminist women who come from traditional families and whose feminism might have been expected to have the strongest negative effect on their religious devotion. There is no difference in the church attendance of the husbands of feminists and the husbands of nonfeminists, if the wife's mother worked before she was six, but a twenty-percentage-point difference among those feminists whose mothers did not work.

Moreover, it is precisely among women under twenty-five that feminists are especially likely to be married to a husband who is devout, twice as likely in fact as their nonfeminist counterparts, while the reverse is true for those who are over twenty-five, a group in which the nonfeminists are significantly more likely to choose a devout spouse.

It would almost appear that such young women are seeking a husband whose religious devotion will cancel the negative relationship between images of Church and woman from their childhood.

Do husbands influence wives or wives influence husbands in the search for family value consensus? Our young feminist wives are aware of their husband's influence on their church attendance. It is among those women who perceive their husband as a "very great" influence on their religion that the differences between feminists and nonfeminists in religious devotion are eliminated, whereas the difference remains statistically significant among those women whose perception is that their husbands do not have a "very great" influence on their religion.

A combination of feminist wife and feminist husband notably increases the likelihood that a young woman will think of God as a lover. When a woman who rejects the traditional gender definitions joins forces in marriage with a husband who rejects them, too, not only does the Church seem to obtain a better image; so, too, does God. From the point of view of the Catholic tradition, a marriage between two such young people is a highly desirable event. A devout spouse and a nontraditional mother—both independently and together—play important roles in determining whether or not feminism leads to anger and alienation from the Church.

Feminism is a positive asset to a young marriage, and a feminist husband has a direct impact on both his wife's image of God as a lover and on her church attendance. A woman's image of both God and Church, then, is affected by her experience with her husband and by the story of their relationship with each other. Such experiences are especially important for a feminist woman whose husband, particularly if he is devout and particularly if he is also a feminist, is able to be a strongly positive sacrament of both God and Church. God lurks in the person of the beloved for such women, a classic example of the Sacramental Imagination at work.

The anger of Catholic feminists is rooted in their past experience of Church as opposed to their present image of woman. Apparently this image conflict is mitigated by marriage to a devout husband. Is there anything else the Church can do to correct its image problem with those who see the Church as supporting the traditional gender role of women? Can the institution in its ordinary pastoral work expect to undo the conflicts of the past? In particular, can priests make a contribution to the reestablishment of image harmony?

The sympathetic parish priest can play an important role in diminishing the anger of the alienated Catholic feminist. Unfortunately, only a minority of priests seem to be qualified for such pastoral intervention.

There is little difference between feminists and nonfeminists in the proportion who feel that their parish priests are "very understanding" of human problems, the percentage who have had a serious talk with a priest in the past year, and the proportion who say that a priest has had an important impact on their religious lives. Indeed, one-sixth of Catholic young women under thirty responded positively to the last two questions and only one-third to the first question. Many young women (about one-third) are unable to rate the understanding of their parish priests because they do not have the information to make a judgment. However, among those who are able to judge, the sympathy of the parish priests is very important indeed for the feminists who, if they rate their parish priest as "very understanding," are as likely to go to church as are those who are not feminist. If the young woman has any information about her local clergyman, then her evaluation of his human sympathy is likely to be a very important counter to the negative effect of her feminist attitudes on her church attendance.

Similarly, those feminists who say that a priest has influenced them greatly and who have had a serious conversation with a priest in the last year are as likely as their nonfeminist counterparts to attend church regularly (about three-fourths of both go to Mass almost every week).

"Every time I get mad at the pope and the bishops," a young Catholic mother tells me, "I think of Father Jack and then I realize how lucky I am to be a Catholic."

The priest seems to play a role similar to that of the devout husband and the nontraditional mother in opening the mind of a young woman to this image of God. Both the sensitivity of the priest and the intensity of the image of God make their own contribution to the propensity of feminist women to go to church, though the image of God seems to be more important in equalizing the church attendance rates of the feminist and the nonfeminist. Thus, to a considerable extent, the priest's effectiveness seems to be mediated through the image of God which is associated with a woman's evaluation of his skills. The effective parish counselor acts as a sacrament—a revelation—of an image of God which diminishes the inconsistency a woman might perceive between her image of the Church and her image of woman. God lurks not only in the person of the husband but in the person of the sensitive and sympathetic parish priest.

But may it not be the fact that these feminists were devout women to begin with which led them to consult their clergy? Could it not be the case that in fact the priest has little effect on a woman's devotion and that rather the devotion causes her to consult the priest and to rate him highly, whether she is a feminist or not?

I will rely for an answer to this question on a questionnaire item that asked the respondent to locate herself in a series of five concentric circles indicating her closeness to the Church (and to God and parish) at the present time and also five years before the survey. By subtracting the present score from the past, we are able to obtain the respondent's evaluation of whether she is closer to the Church now than she was five years ago.

A conversation with a priest does relate to a greater propensity to have returned to the Church, significantly so for feminists. Again there is a difference of twenty percentage points in the proportion who are closer to the Church between those feminists who have talked to a priest and those who have not.

Finally, which is more important, the fact of conversing with a priest or your evaluation of the clergy's understanding of human problems (an evaluation that does not necessarily result from your conversation)?

A conversation without a high regard for the priest's empathy is not of much help in leading to a return of Catholic feminists (though it does seem to help the nonfeminists). Thus, it does seem very likely that for feminists a return to the Church is greatly facilitated by a conversation with an understanding priest. And in the absence of the actual conversation, an awareness that there are understanding priests in one's parish is a notable help.

There is, then, no iron determinism in the childhood linkage between traditional Church and traditional woman's roles. A devout husband and/or a sympathetic parish priest can help break such a linkage—findings that were anticipated by the theory of the Sacramental Imagination.

Nonetheless, most young women do not give their clergy high grades on their understanding of human problems, and only one out of six has actually talked to a priest in the last year. When feminists do seek out priests with whom to talk, they seem not unsatisfied with the results of their conversations (though perhaps they also select priests who they think will be sympathetic).

The Young Catholic analysis is based on data a decade old, so the question arises as to whether it can be replicated with more recent data in which comparisons with other Americans are possible. Do images of God as present, lurking in the Catholic imagination, constitute a countervailing power against the male chauvinism of the official Church and a resource for Catholics in an age of feminism? Moreover, does this imaginative resource exist in a special way among Catholics, who, I am arguing, imagine social reality somewhat differently—not only the "big" reality of the whole society and the state, but also the "small" reality of the man/woman relationship?

The 1988 General Social Survey provides a new six-item "feminism" scale and special religious questions that enable us to approach the question of whether the image of God as present in women affects Catholic attitudes toward feminism.

(The feminism scale consists of items about harm done to the child if the mother works, weakening of the relationship between child and mother, a woman's obligation to help her husband's career in preference to her own, a woman candidate for President, and a woman's obligation to stay at home.)

Catholics score significantly higher on the scale than do others—sixteen standardized points. But the important question is whether Catholic men experience something in their religious heritage which cancels the chauvinism of their church leaders and makes them more pro-feminist than other men.

In fact, that is what happens. The scores of Catholic and other women on the scale are not significantly different, but Catholic men are twenty-five standardized points more likely to endorse feminism than are other men and, unlike other men, do not differ significantly from women in their attitudes toward feminism. Despite the behavior of their Church, then, Catholic men are more likely to be feminists than other men and as likely to support equality for women as do women. Moreover, it is precisely those Catholic men who are likely to say that they feel "very close" to God who are different from other men—sixty-nine standardized points as opposed to twelve points for those who do not feel very close to God. Thus there is something in the Catholic male's experience of God that opens him to the possibility of equality of women.

I want to emphasize here that this phenomenon is *Catholic.* It is not universal in the American population but happens only among Catholic men, thus strongly supporting the notion that Catholics have a different experience of relational reality than do others.

The Catholic male's experience of intense sexual pleasure as religious also plays the same function. Those who say this happens often are 107 points higher on the feminism scale than non-Catholics who report the same reaction. Among those who do not find intense sexual pleasure as a religious resource, the difference between Catholics and others is only four points.

Finally, the experience of a "very happy" marriage relationship also distinguishes Catholic men from other men in their support for feminism. Forty-five points separate Catholics on the feminism scale from other men who say their marriage is very happy, while only twenty-five points separate Catholics and others who are not so ecstatic about their marriage.

A reader of an earlier draft of this chapter commented that few readers will believe the findings, especially the findings about Catholic male attitudes toward the role of women as described in the past several paragraphs. I am inclined to believe that the reader is correct. The findings are too contrary to the stereotypes among those who are not Catholic, and among many who are, to escape brusque dismissal. That fact, however, does not make them go away; it only dispenses one from considering their implications. The most important of the implications is that if one suspends judgment on the Catholic tradition and looks beyond the doctrinal emphases of the current Catholic leadership to the Catholic religious imagination, one is able to formulate hypotheses of the sort that are confirmed by the analysis in this chapter. A theory of the Sacramental Imagination that (partially) distinguishes Catholics from others would prepare one for the basic finding that Catholic men are more likely to consider women as sacraments of the ever-lurking God than other men; and Catholic women are more likely than other women to look for the lurking God in their lovers and their priests (who also, in a certain way, are special lovers).

"You don't think I married this guy," a Catholic wife protested to me when I reported these findings to her and her husband, "just because he goes to church every week, do you? I married him because he was special and being Catholic was part of his being special. I knew he'd treat me better."

"Damn little choice," her husband muttered *sotto voce* and with a complacent smile.

The answers were on the level of instinct and imagination and they articulated what many other Catholics (my data establish) experience vaguely and preconsciously, albeit powerfully. Their religion does make a difference in their relationships and not merely as a joint trip to the parish of their choice on Sunday. Once the issue of that difference becomes explicit, they have little trouble giving a name to it and describing it.

Moreover, if the wife happens to be Irish, she'll be more than a little impatient with the poor old priest sociologist who dares to state the obvious with a suggestion that he is revealing something that she doesn't already know! Since said poor old priest sociologist would have, in a different life story, probably married someone like her, he understands that such a reaction, however argumentative it may sound, merely means, "You're right. *Naturally.*"

A happy marriage, intense sex with religious overtones, and a feeling of being close to God—each contributes to the extra support for "feminism" among Catholic men. Something in their experience of God and their experience of their woman makes them tend to respect the quality of women more than other American men do. They are therefore more likely than others to picture (preconsciously perhaps) woman and God as correlates with each other, as metaphors, one for the other. If you don't like that finding either reanalyze my data or gather data of your own or remain silent.

This reaction of Catholic men to women is so contrary to the behavior of the institutional Church and so opposed to the image of Catholic chauvinism (caused by the institutional Church) that exists in our society that it can only be explained by a tenacious component in the Catholic tradition which has survived despite the attitude and behavior of church leaders. The theory of the Sacramental Imagination—which led me to anticipate these findings—would suggest that for those who picture God as present in the world there is an instinct that God is equally disclosed by women for men and by men for women.

If your mind is boggled by that finding, either redo my analysis (the GSS data, on which the concluding phase of my analysis is based, are available at every major university computer center in the country) or go collect your own data.

The findings are as surprising as the process for uncovering them is intricate. However, I would not have bothered to try to uncover them if my theory that Catholics "imagine differently"—picture God as present in the world more than absent from it—had not led me to expect them. The process of confirming the hypothesis is necessarily intricate because the religious imagination is a subtle and fluid dimension of the human personality. Indeed, given the complicated analysis that is required and the nebulous state of our understanding of the religious imagination, it is surprising that the differences between Catholics and others are as striking as they are. Woman, God, sexual pleasure as religious, happy marriages—all contribute to the Catholic male's inclination to be more feminist and suggest that he pictures all four realities as related to one another.

The conclusion, then, must be the same as in the previous analyses. Catholic women tend to remain in the Church and to remain devout despite the way that they are treated by the Vatican and by the hierarchy because they have experiences of God and of men (husbands and priests) which make Catholicism continue to be attractive. Moreover, their husbands at any rate are more likely to support equality for women because they picture the linkages among God, woman, and pleasure somewhat differently than do men who are not Catholic.

To what extent is the Catholic image of woman as sacrament of God encoded in the image of Mary the Mother of Jesus? Is the Marian devotion both the cause and effect of the image of woman which is at odds with the chauvinism of church leadership? Is that image in jeopardy now that Catholicism has apparently agreed in practice if not in theory to deemphasize for ecumenical purposes its Marian tradition?

13

MARY AND THE WOMANLINESS OF GOD

HAT DO PROTESTANTS THINK about Mary?" the dark-haired graduate student, one Colleen McBride by name, demanded.

It was one of my more embarrassing moments as a sociologist—and one that persuaded me that a scholar without students to challenge him is in deep trouble.

In the Young Catholic study, I had reported that Mary the Mother of Jesus enjoyed warmer images with young Catholics than did Jesus and Jesus warmer images than God—in line with St. Bernard's words, "If you fear the Father, go to the Son, if you fear the Son, go to the Mother."

"We don't have any Protestants in the sample, Colleen," I assured her.

"Yes, you do," she said with the stubbornness often linked in stories (not excluding my own) to women of her ethnic background.

"No, we don't. The Knights wanted a study of young Catholics."

"Didn't you give questionnaires to all the spouses of your married respondents?"

"Of course."

"And did all your young people marry Catholics?"

I pondered.

"Woman, you flunk! I'm the full professor! I get the bright ideas!"

So I did the required computations that night. Sure enough, the image of the Mother of Jesus was as strong for the Protestants in our sample as it was for Jesus. (The three Jewish respondents, unaware perhaps of the ethnic group loyalty involved toward one of their own and that Mary is a Jewish mother, did not have such a high image of Mary.)

One of the Protestants in class the next meeting observed, "You Catholics don't have a monopoly on her. We may not buy all the doctrines, but we know that she's the greatest woman who ever lived." On the level of symbol, then, Mary may well be an ecumenical asset.

Colleen, in fact, received a well-earned A.

Astonishing evidence for continuity among American Catholics and continuity of their religious imagination, in the years since the Second Vatican Council, is to be found in the persistence of the importance of the Mary image in the religious imagination of Catholics.

Young Catholics who were studied in the Knights of Columbus study of Catholics between fifteen and thirty had strong and influential images of Mary. This Mary image persists, despite the fact that, in a "liberal" victory, Mary was deprived of her own separate document at the Second Vatican Council, despite the fact that many in the Catholic elite find Mary an embarrassing ecumenical encumbrance, and, finally, despite the fact that formal devotions to and sermons about Mary seem to have declined in the American Church. The survival of Mary is an interesting example of the strange blend of change and stability, continuity and discontinuity that marks the postconciliar world.

However, if one approaches religious behavior from the point of view of the sociology of the religious imagination, the persistence of the power of the Mary image despite rejection of the Church's sexual ethic makes a great deal of sociological sense even if it seems theologically inconsistent.

More than 75 percent of the young adults said they were "extremely" likely to think of Mary as "warm" or "patient" or "comforting" or "gentle"; 65 percent of the respondents chose all four images as "extremely likely," while 50 percent rated Jesus as high on all four images.

Nor were the Mary images irrelevant. Our MADONNA scale (one point for each of the four words checked as "extremely likely") correlated positively with social commitment, frequency of prayer, concern for racial justice, and sexual fulfillment in marriage. Mary is not only still fashionable but, it seems, also still "relevant."

Several years ago I attended with a crowd of friends a performance of John Powers's play *Do Patent Leather Shoes Reflect Up?* During the May Crowning by the second grade in the play, the entire audience seemed to join in for the chorus of "Bring Flowers of the Rarest"—"O Mary, we crown thee with blossoms today/Queen of the Angels, Queen of the May." At intermission I asked John whether this was the first night the congregation (my slip of the tongue) had joined in.

"Every night since the first performance," he replied. "I think even those who are not Catholic sing."

The song is neither good music nor good poetry, but it is eminently singable. And sing it we did, in fond memory of what the clergy have tried to take away from us. They may not want May Crownings, but we still do.

How can this be? one is asked. Have not the Catholic schools deemphasized Mary. Has not the Church played down the doctrine in a quest for ecumenical understanding? Is not much of the old-fashioned Marian piety outdated and unappealing?

To begin with, there is no correlation between number of years of Catholic schooling and the MADONNA scale (or years of CCD either). Second, we are not dealing with religious doctrines. Third, however outdated the "lovely lady dressed in blue" piety of the past may be, it was and is peripheral to the attractiveness of Mary as, to use John Shea's words, a "story of God."

To try to explain the Mary phenomenon I developed the following hypotheses:

—The MADONNA scale would correlate with positive experiences with motherhood as a child.

—It would also correlate with positive experiences with a spouse, particularly in the most intimate aspect of the relationship—"sexual fulfillment," as our questionnaire called it.

—Positive experiences of motherhood as a child would further correlate with sexual fulfillment in marriage and be channeled through (in whole or in part) the Madonna image.

—The Madonna image would correlate at a much higher level with personal prayer than would doctrinal orthodoxy.

—Arguing from history and from anecdotal evidence, I expected Hispanics and Poles to have the highest scores of any Catholic ethnic group on the MADONNA scale. Our "maternity" measure was composed of four items: a description of mother's approach to religion as "joyous," frequent Communion on the part of the mother, mother involved at least as an equal in family decision-making, and mother reported to have a strong religious effect on respondents. Sexual fulfillment was one of a list of dimensions of marital satisfaction ranked from "excellent" to "poor." The doctrinal orthodoxy scale was composed of such matters as papal infallibility, papal primacy, mortally sinful obligation to attend Mass every week, existence of the devil and of hell.

The first four hypotheses were all true at a statistically significant level for both men and women in the United States and Canada (women have higher scores on the MADONNA scale than men, but there are no important differences in the correlations or any of the other findings).

A positive experience with your mother while growing up leads to a positive experience with your spouse (the relationships are hardly strong enough to be determining). Your image of Mary is the conduit linking these two experiences. Mary connects the story of your childhood with the story of your marriage. Small wonder that she's important.

There is no statistically significant relationship between doctrinal orthodoxy and prayer (in fact, the relationship is .07 in the opposite direction). But the MADONNA scale correlates with frequency of prayer at a .37 level, quite high in most social research. Images lead you to prayer, not doctrinal propositions.

On the ethnic group prediction I was dead wrong, although the hypothesis did not flow from my theory of the religious imagination but from a misreading (perhaps) of the history of Marian devotion. The Irish are most likely to score high on the scale, "significantly" higher than the rest of the population, perhaps because of their tradition of strong mother figures.

Neither the Jesus nor the God scale correlates with experiences in either family of origin or family of procreation. Mary is the story of God that links the two aspects of "my" story.

She also plays a role in the process by which "my" story and "your" story fuse into "our" story. When husband and wife are both high on the MADONNA scale, it is half again as likely that they will both say that their sexual fulfillment is excellent (questionnaires were, of course, filled out independently, not that anyone would be likely to conspire on the image of Mary). Furthermore, among those families where both husband and wife are high on the MADONNA scale, the correlation between one spouse's description of the quality of the sexual relationship in marriage and the other's description of it becomes higher as the years together increase. If we both share a common story of God in the Mary image, we come to share more and more a common story of our own sexual relationship.

Some feminist critics of devotion to Mary have argued that the Mary symbolism traditionally was used to support a "conservative" approach to the role of women, emphasizing fulfillment in the home and family to the exclusion of all else and placing a high value on passivity and fertility. They have also contended that this tradition has "spoiled" the image for contemporary women. I am in no position to discuss the historical impact of Marian imagery on women; however, it does not seem to play any such conservative role for modern young men and women.

"I am furious at the very mention of Mary," an angry woman snapped at me. "She's responsible for my enslavement. You men have used her to imprison me."

The problem with that argument coming from her was that she knew enough about symbols and enough about history to realize its weaknesses. Yet she was so angry she would not reflect on her own knowledge or listen to my data.

With such people, however much reason they have to be angry, you can't win because they can't listen.

There is no difference between those who are high on the MADONNA scale and those who are low in attitudes toward birth control or divorce or abortion in the case of likely handicapped children. They marry at about the same age, have the same number of children, expect the same number of children, and have the same estimates of ideal family size (low, but higher than non-Catholics). Nor does a strong Marian image impede college graduation or work after marriage or economic success or propensity to reject the idea that a working mother harms her children.

Those who are high on the MADONNA scale, however, are more likely to reject abortion on demand and to disapprove of living together before marriage. Only the most rigid ideologue will insist on the "conservative" nature of such responses, especially since the MADONNA scale also correlates with various measures of social commitment such as concern for the environment and for racial justice and emphasis on social activism as a source of life satisfaction.

Two questions are asked by colleagues with whom we have discussed our findings: Can the young people be fairly said to be "devoted" to Mary? Where did they get the story of God and Mother from if they did not learn it in the schools or CCD class and are not likely to pick it up from Sunday sermons?

We do not know whether our respondents pray to the Mother of Jesus, nor do we know whether they are aware of the impact of the Mary story on their lives. We hope in further research to explore both these issues. However, it must be observed that preconscious imagery need not be conscious to have an impact, although the impact may be greater if it becomes conscious.

We presume that young people learn about Mary from their mothers. From whom else? We also speculate that they learn it very early in life as they are told the Christmas story. The woman by the crib, they are told, is God's "mommy," a proposition with which the child has no difficulty. Everyone has a mommy, doesn't he? From such an insight it is but a small jump to say that God loves like a mommy. The story is born again.

Obviously, Mary is an enormously useful resource for the Church. Our teachers and thinkers and leaders, official and unofficial, should make much more of her than they do. They are wasting an opportunity. The waste is not going to cause Catholicism to lose the story of Mary. It's too good to be lost, ever.

To return to Colleen McBride's pertinent and pertinacious question, we have no way of knowing how non-Catholics in general react to the Mary symbol. However, we can investigate the reactions of the non-Catholics who were married to our respondents. Rather surprisingly, Mary's image is almost as good with them as it is with Catholics: 62 percent say they are "extremely likely" to think of her as "warm," 67 percent as "gentle," 52 percent as "patient," and 56 percent as "comforting."

Two-fifths of the non-Catholic spouses endorse as "extremely likely" all four items on the MADONNA scale, not quite as many as the two-thirds of the Catholic spouses, but still an astonishingly high number. There is also a correlation even among non-Catholic spouses between a high MADONNA score and frequent prayer; 52 percent of the spouses high on the MADONNA scale pray almost every day, as opposed to those who are low. (More than half of the Methodists and Baptists endorse all four MADONNA items as do 37 percent of those spouses who report no religious affiliation.) Perversely, the

Catholic ecumenists seem willing to sacrifice an image which turns out to be a powerful ecumenical resource.

Moreover, *men need the image of God-as-woman more than women do.* The most striking image of the womanliness of God in recent years was presented in Bob Fosse's film *All That Jazz*, a story of Fosse's brush with death during a massive heart attack. The death experience, however, turned out to be an interlude of grace. Death itself seemed to be very much like a woman—a tender, sensuous lover who sees through the phoniness of Joe Gideon (the fictional Fosse) and loves him anyway. Indeed, Angelique (Jessica Lange) is a summation of all the women in Gideon's life. She gently wipes the sweat from his hands as he is dying, as would his wife, threatens to absorb him with a passionate kiss at the very end as have his mistresses, and playfully mocks him as does his daughter (indeed in the final sequence the identification between Angelique and his daughter is heavily emphasized—the daughter's tears make Angelique sad).

Demanding, sexy, a bit sinister, inescapable, tender, and passionately loving—that's what the angel of death is like, Fosse tells us. The angel may also be God. Fosse is not sure, yet twice in the movie he brackets scenes with Ms. Lange in references to God; and at the end he gives us a choice: either life ends with a lifeless corpse being zipped up in a plastic bag or in the consummation of a love affair with a beautiful spouse.

According to *All That Jazz*, then, death is a beautiful woman, and the beautiful woman may be God. Fosse doesn't insist. Like any good poet he merely suggests . . . yet what if he's right?

It seemed to me as I reflected on the film that in principle we men ought to have more invested in the image of God as someone like Jessica Lange than women might. God, we are told, is love. Our relationship to God is a love relationship. Normally, the most powerful love experiences we have are cross-sexual relationships. It is hard to fit these experiences into an imagery of God which is predominantly male.

The usual reaction (even with college students, I find) to a comparison of human love with divine love is to insist that it is utterly different from sexual attraction ("not at all physical," my students tell me). Thus, to use scholastic terms, the word "love" is predicated equivocally on intimacy with humans and intimacy with God.

I do not believe, however, that such an equivocal predication will stand the tests either of good spirituality or of good exegesis—or good Catholic tradition. If love with God isn't really like human love at all, then it can hardly be very appealing, since human love is the most powerful emotion of which we are capable. Moreover, the sexual imagery of the Scriptures is washed away if the usage is equivocal.

Thus we must conclude that the use of "love" is analogous. God does passionately desire us in a way similar to how an attractive member of the opposite sex might desire us. And we desire God in a way similar to the way we might desire an appealing member of the opposite sex.

Of any analogy one must inquire how the two uses differ. There can be only one answer: divine love is more passionate than human love. God's desire for us is greater than that of any human spouse; and God's appeal is more powerful than that of any human bedmate. God is different from Jessica Lange mainly in that God is more attractive, more demanding, more tender, more passionate, more gentle.

It would follow that men who have a womanly image of God will find it easier to think of God as a lover, will pray more often and more intensely, and will be more deeply committed to the social concerns that should come from intense religious devotion. Moreover, precisely because they are involved in a love relationship with a womanly God, they should have better relationships with human women. Finally, it seems not unlikely that their womanly image of God will be affected by their relationships with their mothers and by strong, womanly images of Mary.

These predictions would substantiate my theory only if they did not also apply, or at least did not apply to such a great extent, to women's imagery of God-as-woman. It is possible to test these hypotheses against data collected in the Knights of Columbus study of Young Catholics. All the hypotheses are sustained.

Some 10 percent of young American Catholics say that they are extremely likely to imagine God as a "mother." There are no differences between young men and young women in this proportion. However, men with a womanly image of God are significantly more likely than men who do not have that image to picture God as a lover, to pray often, to offer prayers of gratitude, to consider a life of social concern and involvement to be important, to say that their sexual fulfillment in marriage is excellent, and to be in marriages in which both husband and wife report the sexual fulfillment excellent. They are also more likely to say they were very close to their mothers and to score high on a scale which measures their image of Mary as "patient" and "comforting." In only two of the variables are there significant relationships in the same direction for women—the image of God as lover and closeness to mother.

Women who think of God as a mother are twice as likely to think of God as a lover as those who do not imagine God as mother, but men with the picture of God as mother are *three* times more likely to imagine Her also as a lover than are men without that picture.

Such men are also half again as likely to be in marriages in which both they and their wives say that sexual fulfillment is excellent. Picturing God as a mother is not only good for the prayer life of a man; it is also good for the sex life of his wife.

So the Fosse/Gideon experience of the womanliness of God is not as rare as one might have thought. While a tenth of the Catholic men under thirty is surely a minority, it is by no means a trivial number of young men who imagine God as a mother, and who are likely to benefit in their spiritual and sexual lives from that image.

One is forced to wonder where the image comes from; surely it does not originate in any educational or spiritual direction they have had. Perhaps it results from experiences with women in which they sense that God has disclosed Herself to them.

Confirmation of this explanation can be found in the data. Men who say their mothers had a strong impact on their religious development are almost three times as likely to report that they imagine God as mother as do those who do not report such maternal influence. Furthermore, men who say that their wives have a powerful impact on their religious development are more than three times as likely as are other men to imagine God as mother. There is no parallel effect on the religious imagery of women respondents.

Women, then, seem to mediate on the womanliness of God for men; they are sacraments of God's womanly love for their men. Apparently they do so without seeking permission from the official Magisterium. Religious imagery, with its profound effect on human life and human religion, is shaped with little attention to, and little support from or awareness of, the institutional Church.

The implications of these findings for spiritual and pastoral theology as well as for prayer and spiritual direction are enormous. They are also shattering and revolutionary. A woman may well imagine herself as a bride of Christ (and a married woman or an unmarried laywoman has as much right to that image as does a religious woman). But a man imagine himself as the husband of God? Or God as his paramour? Or God as a woman pursuing him with passionate desire?

How shocking and scandalous! God may desire women but certainly not men.

Yet, however scandalous and shocking the implications, the findings are hard to dispute. Some young men do benefit from cross-sexual images of God, and so do their spouses. And as we discovered in the last chapter, some young women do benefit from cross-sexual confidant relationships with priests. And so do their spouses.[1]

In the mind of the church leadership there may be a strong link between devotion to the Mother of Jesus and sexual "purity"—which is defined by the leadership as the absence of erotic emotion (which, it is much to be feared, is often absent in their crabbed, power-hungry lives). They would be mistaken, however, to think that this link is psychologically or sociologically necessary whatever its theological validity may be. The image of Mary continues to be enormously important even after some of the key components of the sexual ethic have been rejected.

The Mary Myth's powerful appeal[2] is to be found, I think, in the marvelous possibility that God loves us the way a mother loves her baby, the way all those Madonnas love all those little *bambini*, the way the Mother loves the Child in the crib scenes. If such tender passion is indeed a sacrament of what the universe means and what life is all about—and the Sacramental Imagination of Catholics insists that it is—then there is very good news indeed.

As a woman of my generation remarked to me, "If you've ever held in your arms a child you have just given life to and been filled with love for that wondrous little being, you know that's how God feels about us."

Oh, yes, *very* good news indeed. Perhaps even too good to be true, but still the news that Catholicism is all about. An image that hints at that possibility will never be obsolete. The laity, apparently, feel quite at ease not only in appealing to God from church leadership but also in appealing to Mary from church leadership.

These research findings do *not* suggest that institutional leadership will any time soon change its attitudes toward women—for such attitudes are not based either on imagery or on sophisticated theology but on a determination to protect a power base. However, the countervailing image of woman, which persists in the Catholic imagina-

---

[1] I take consolation in the hope that God, when finally encountered, will be even more spectacular than Jessica Lange. She'd better be.

[2] My book *The Mary Myth* was published in 1977 by Seabury Press. In it I discuss the origins and functions of the Mary symbol at much greater length.

tion, suggests that church leadership will continue to offend the sensibilities not only of their women followers but also their men followers as long as they treat women like second-class human beings. The image has struggled with institutional power for a long time and has managed to survive and make a difference in attitudes. Now Catholic men and women are no longer content to ignore the official image of women; they have chosen rather to actively oppose it.

From the point of view of church leadership those who are no longer regular in their devotion are not the problem. They're not around anymore. Rather the problems come from the women and the men who are still around and who now explicitly reject the orientation toward women of their leadership.

Curiously enough—and paradoxically enough—the leadership adheres to its chauvinism in great part because it fears that change will weaken its influence with its own people. In fact, just the opposite is what is happening: the intransigence of church leadership is diminishing its influence and credibility. The power base remains secure because women are excluded from it; but the base grows smaller and smaller.

Despite them, Mary is the "defining image" for the Sacramental Imagination, that image which most sharply distinguishes the analogical imagination from the dialectical imagination, the Catholic tradition from other Christian traditions. No one else has Madonna statues in church. Mary is essential to Catholicism, not perhaps on the level of doctrine but surely on the level of imagination, because she more than any other image blatantly confirms the sacramental instinct: the whole of creation and all its processes, especially its life-giving and life-nurturing processes, reveal the lurking and passionate love of God.

How can you say such things? I am asked after lectures. How can you be a "liberal" on such matters as the rights of women and still support an image that has been used to keep women in their place by a chauvinist, patriarchal church for two millennia?

I always reply that it is precisely because of the image of Mary that I support full equality for women and especially their ordination.

The one who has asked the question has not listened to or at least not heard my discussion of religious imagery as prior to and more powerful than propositional religious doctrines. I do *not* endorse all the forms of Marian piety and doctrinal articulations, particularly those that make the Mother of Jesus sexless (which she was not) and subservient (which on the basis of the Scripture she certainly was not). I argue rather that the obvious functional role of the image of Mary the Mother of Jesus in the Catholic tradition is to reflect the mother love of God.

A symbol is dense, multilayered, polysemous. It emits many different signals. A given culture at a certain time in history may concentrate on some signals for the source of its propositional articulations; these signals can become so important in the propositional explication of the symbols that other, and more basic and fundamental, signals are not heard. The point of the analysis of this chapter is that even in an era when propositional Mariology tends to be sterile, life-denying, flesh-denying, woman-hating patriarchalism, imaginative Mariology continues to emphasize the mother love of God and the equal sacramentality of woman.

To pose a pointed question again at church leaders: which is more important—a male picture of woman as an equal sacrament of God, or male acceptance of the papal rule that women can't be ordained priests? Mary as a symbol of furious, aroused divine passion or Mary as a symbol of sexual abstinence?

Again the public posture demands that leaders choose the latter set of options. Despite their pose of fervent devotion to Mary the Mother of Jesus—whose function is to reflect the womanliness of God in a special way—many church leaders are themselves so afraid of women that even in private they are unlikely to approve of the triad of woman, intense sexual pleasure, and God which lurks in the Catholic imagination.

It is, they will doubtless tell you, "inappropriate." In fact, they are the ones that are inappropriate because, in the wonderfully expressive language of adolescents, they are "out of it." Totally.

14

YOUNG PEOPLE:
JUST LIKE THE
FORTIES

HEN TV INTERVIEWERS run out of all other subjects (and they certainly don't want to talk about the book that is your reason for being on the program because they haven't read it), they turn to the subject of young people.

"Do you find young people today to be more conservative?" they ask with a show at thoughtfulness. Anyone who reads the national press or watches national TV knows that the question is trite and the thoughtfulness fake.

"Young people are always conservative," I reply. "They have much to conserve, especially their own future. They turn radical when it seems the only way to conserve their future."

"But the radical sixties . . . ?"

"Most kids were pretty conservative in those days, too. Maybe a little more radical on the average because of the war, but the activists were a small part of the population, as they always are."

"Campus unrest . . . ?"

"More of it then than now, but it exists now, too, and there wasn't all that much of it then."

"But young people today aren't like those in the sixties?"

I'm tempted to say "Thank God"; but this interviewer is a product of the sixties, living an affluent, upper-middle-class life with some pangs of guilt for deserting the ideals that he thought he once had because he'd marched on a protest line.

"More like the forties."

"Pretty bad, huh?"

"That's when I grew up. Pretty good."

The point of the conversation was that, while there are changes, continuity is more important than change. The sixties was at most a blip.

There is more divorce today than there was forty years ago and (perhaps) more premarital sex—both because of the easy and safe methods of contraception available. Human passion, however, is no stronger than it ever was; nor is human ingenuity for finding sexual pleasure during the most passionate years any more clever. Finally, the propensity to settle down with a spouse and raise a family shows no sign of declining.

The demonstrations at Berkeley, the confrontation in front of the administration building at Columbia, the takeover of the administration building at Chicago—these create the images of a generation, but most young people then as now were more concerned about career and family than they were about politics. Such is the nature of the human condition that even activists become tired. And marry and worry about raising families, as was obvious when all the Weather Persons came in from the cold.

Older generations assume that younger generations are different— probably since Adam and Eve complained about the behavior of Cain and Abel. In fact, the differences are often not as great as they might at first seem. The dictum that apples do not fall very far from their trees is often a very good summary of research evidence. Priests, nuns, and parents may well be prepared to insist that Catholic young people today are "different," or not as "loyal," or not "different from others" as they used to be. After all, are they not more likely to use drugs, to engage in premarital sex, to live together before marriage, to refuse to attend church, to reject important Catholic doctrines, and to be critical of and disrespectful toward ecclesiastical authorities?

In fact, a careful consideration of the young Catholics studied in the 1979 project for the Knights of Columbus suggests that the apples are much closer to their trees than many people are prepared to admit. If young Catholics are more likely to engage in premarital sexual intercourse, it can hardly be said that their parents did not engage in premarital behavior that stopped just short of intercourse or that their parents now disapprove strongly of premarital sex. If Catholics in their teens and twenties reject the Church's teachings on birth control and divorce, they are not in those respects very different from Catholics over thirty.

If their church attendance is not what the church attendance of Catholics was twenty-five years ago, neither is the church attendance of any other age group of Catholics what it was a quarter of a century ago. If the younger generation are committed to "selective Catholicism," how are they different from the rest of the Catholic population? If some of them use marijuana or cocaine, do not many of their parents drink more than they ought to? If they are not at all times devout, socially concerned, responsible Catholic young adults, how many of their parents can be said to be at all times devout, responsible, and socially concerned Catholic older adults?

Have not the changes in the Church, both the ones officially approved by the Vatican Council, such as the English liturgy, and those unofficially approved by the local clergy, such as "selective Catholicism," weakened the ties of loyalty that bind young people to the Church? Has not the experience of growing up in a Catholicism where the "old rules" are not imposed made them somehow less loyal and indeed less Catholic than previous generations have been?

In the absence of "Sister's" stern warning and "Father's" drawing the hard canonical line, in the absence of compulsory confessional and compulsory Mass and compulsory Communion, are not the ties that bind the next generation of Catholic adults to the Church substantially weaker than they would have been a generation ago or than they ought to be today? Having lost all the quick and ready answers which religion teachers and parents had before the Second Vatican Council, is not the Church now faced with a new generation of young people who don't "know what it means to be Catholic"?

The best answer to all these questions is "no!"

There is nothing in the empirical data available to us to suggest that the generation of Catholics who have grown up since the Second Vatican Council are any less loyal, any less committed, any less devout than their predecessors—once one takes into account the changes that have occurred in the whole Catholic population that I have reported previously in this book. Granted, for example, the "one shot" decline in church practice in the late sixties and the early seventies, the curve that projects the religious path of young Catholics through the life cycle, is no different than the curve for the age cohorts over thirty. When Catholics in their early twenties today are in their early forties, at the beginning of the next millennium, they will be as likely to attend church weekly as are those in their early forties today, unless something happens to affect the trends. That they would be less likely to attend than Catholics who were in their early forties twenty years ago is a result of the single-jolt decline after the birth-control encyclical, which established a new and lower level of church attendance for Catholics, and NOT the result of the younger generation of Catholics being inherently less religious or less loyal to the Church than their parents.

Another way of saying the same thing is that the rules and the customs and the regulations and the practices and the styles of the immigrant Church are more likely to have been the result of loyalty to the Church instead of the cause of it. Loyalty is transmitted across generational lines by parents and reinforced within generations by spouses, even if "Father" and "Sister" no longer rule with an iron hand, even if indeed "Father" and "Sister" have run off with each other to play house and proclaim their own "relevance."

Or to say the same thing yet another way, projections[1] based on the available data about Catholic young adults would indicate that as far as the essentials of practice and commitment to Catholicism are concerned, the picture in the first decade of the next millennium will not be greatly different from the picture today—save presumably that there will be fewer priests and nuns.

Many readers will resist this projection. They will say that my empirical data do not take into account all the energies and forces and factors that are at work. Perhaps they do not. But unless one is to go beyond the boundaries of empirical evidence and make projections by wetting one's finger and holding it up to the wind, or investigating the entrails of slain chickens, one must do serious data collection and analysis to confirm that the impressions that contradict the data that I have gathered are correct.

Anecdotes about what happened to a family down the street or about what the kids in your parish have done or about your own children or grandchildren or the children of your friends, however interesting and powerful and poignant, are no substitute for systematic and disciplined investigation and cautious professional analysis.

It might be argued that the problem will appear not with the generation in its teens and early twenties today, but with younger Catholics raised and educated after the rigorous boundaries of the immigrant Church had completely disappeared. Such a prophecy may well be correct, but it will nonetheless be prophecy until that still

---

[1] Made by Michael Hout and myself and reported in Chapter 2.

younger generation begin to reach maturity and establish religious patterns of their own. However, the fact that loyalty to Catholicism survives as vigorously among young people in their twenties today as it does in people who are twenty years older indicates that Catholic loyalty has displayed remarkable durability through very trying and difficult times. If it has survived the last twenty years, then it may survive a long time to come.

There are, however, two important differences in the younger generation of Catholics which may well be the result of the Second Vatican Council.

In the earliest studies I did of American Catholics, back in the first half of the 1960s, there was much less of a life-cycle correlation with church attendance. Young people went to Mass less than older people, but the age slope was not so steep. Is the life-cycle phenomenon the result of the Council or is it the result of more young people going away to college and living in their own homes as soon as they can afford to and long before they're married?

I incline to the latter explanation. Mass attendance rates are higher for young people who live with their families.

Second, younger Catholics, especially those born after 1959, have a sharply different religious "sensibility" than older Catholics, different from those over thirty and forty and even on the average different from those who are just a few years older than they are, born in the early and middle 1950s. This new sensibility seems to be an intensification of the Sacramental Imagination. The younger generation of Catholics, those at present under thirty, are considerably more likely to picture God as a lover, a spouse, a friend, and a mother than are either their non-Catholic counterparts or older Catholics. This religious sensibility correlates positively with frequency of prayer, marital fulfillment, respect for the rights of women, consideration of the possibility of a religious vocation, happiness in marriage, and even disapproval of premarital sex. The religious imagination, as we have said earlier, is not a fluffy, pretty, artistic luxury; it is a powerful energy that has considerable impact on the lives of Catholics, a greater impact indeed than does any doctrinal conviction. That more younger Catholics have this "gracious" religious imagination suggests not perhaps a change in the years ahead in the ordinary quantitative measures of religious behavior but a change in the quality of Catholic life as it is lived by at least some members of the present young generation as they move through the life cycle. There is a hint in the data—at the present it is only a hint—that this generation may even, precisely because of their more gracious religious imagination, be more likely to attend church and engage in other traditional religious practices as they grow older.

This new religious sensibility seems to be acquired from three different sources—from a mother (particularly if she went to a Catholic college and is a frequent communicant), from a spouse, and from a priest (if one has a close relationship with a priest). As Archbishop Jean Jadot used to remark after being informed of these findings when he was apostolic delegate to the United States, "How else would one expect an ecumenical council to be implemented—through husbands, wives, priests, and mothers!"

The thesis of this chapter bears insistent repeating because it flies in the face of so much conventional wisdom. There is no evidence that Catholics born after 1945 or after 1955 or even after 1960 are inherently less religious than Catholics born during the Second World War or the Great Depression. Nor is there any evidence that they are inherently any less loyal to the Catholic tradition (which of course is a way of saying that some are more loyal, some are less loyal, but that the average does not seem to have changed greatly). There are some faint traces of evidence which ought to be pursued in subsequent research that Catholics born after 1960, who certainly have more benign and gracious images of God, may also be more devout, more religious, and more loyal than any cohort of Catholics that has been observed in the last fifty years.

The most notable declines in Catholicism we have described thus far in the book—selective Catholicism (particularly with regard to sex and authority) and decreased church attendance—have not disproportionately affected young people. These phenomena are population-wide and have had no greater impact on those who matured after the Council than they did on those who matured before it.

Has not the number of young people living together before marriage increased in the last quarter century? Doubtless it has, though the custom is hardly new in the human condition. Data from the Knights of Columbus provide information about the practice.

Approximately 11 percent of the young people in our sample who were not "single" were living in "out-of-wedlock" relationships. Approximately the same proportion of out-of-wedlock relationships was reported in English and French Canada. Moreover, in 1989 some 40 percent of Catholics under forty reported that they had "lived" with their spouse before marriage, an increase of twenty percentage points over those who were between forty and sixty, approximately the same rates as for Protestants. Such cohabitation was not, it would seem, unheard of in the past.

It is possible to speculate before the analysis that a number of different factors might go into the decision to enter such a relationship. First of all, the person involved might not believe that the relationship is wrong. Second, the person might perhaps be young and experimenting before settling down and marrying. Third, the person might be less interested in traditional family values than those Catholics who have contracted a marriage. Fourth, there might have been strain or tension in the family of origin which would make the young person somewhat more hesitant about entering a permanent or quasi-permanent commitment to marry.[2] Finally, Catholic education and a religious imagination might play a role in explaining the propensity of some young people who enter into such unions.

Nearly all of the expectations were sustained. A number of different influences seem to go into making the decision about entering out-of-wedlock unions, and the factors relate to one another in a fairly complex fashion, suggesting that there is no simple explanation of such a choice.

Those in such unions are much more likely to be younger (under twenty-six) than those who are married, to come from families where the relationships between the parents and between the child and the parents are strained, to come from religiously mixed marriages, and to report an unhappy childhood. Those who had more than eight years of Catholic education were three times as likely to be in married unions as in unmarried unions, and there was a twenty-percentage-point difference between the two in their willingness to say that children were very important "in their life." Those who are in out-of-wedlock unions were also thirty percentage points more likely (80 percent versus 50 percent) to say living together before marriage was never wrong but they were also substantially less likely (31 percent versus 43 percent) to be high on a scale of religious imagination which measured their images of God as a mother and lover. The "new" religious sensibility represented by this scale does not seem to lead to greater sexual permissiveness but rather to less sexual permissiveness,

---

[2] My colleague Robert Michael tells me that his research indicates that the majority of such relationships are viewed by the young people who engage in them as a preparation for marriage, especially for those who are uneasy about a permanent commitment in marriage (often because they come from divorced families).

perhaps because if God is perceived as a mother and lover one is more careful about the love relationships one enters.[3]

In dealing, then, with the dramatically increasing phenomenon of out-of-wedlock unions, the Church is faced for the most part with forces over which it can have little influence. It cannot protect young people from the difficult years between twenty and twenty-six—years of loneliness, confusion, and uncertainty. Nor can it undo the effects of a strained and unhappy childhood. It could indeed build more Catholic schools to affect this life-style choice in the future but it cannot provide for Catholic education that was not available in the past. Nor is it likely to be successful in persuading young people that children are more important than they think they are or that living together is not wrong. Perhaps the only way the Church can deal with this life-style among young people in their early twenties is to stress even more vigorously than it has the "story" of God as a mother and lover.

In fact, all the Church seems to be interested in doing is condemning such young people when they come to arrange for a marriage and on occasion even refusing to marry them.

Just what Jesus would do, huh, guys?

The religious practice of those in out-of-wedlock relationships is low. Less than 10 percent of them go to Mass every week, though 5 percent receive Communion every week—rather against regulations of the Church. However, almost 40 percent pray at least several times a week. Twenty-five percent view themselves as very close to God, 28 percent say that they are either very close or somewhat close to the Church, and an amazing 27 percent say they are either very close or somewhat close to their parish (and in this matter, they are very similar to those who are in wedlock relationships).

The parish continues to be important, regardless of what is happening in your life.

Those who are living together without the benefit of marriage are certainly alienated from church devotional practices and sexual ethics but are less likely to feel alienated from God, or from the Church, or from the parish. They may not feel as close to God or as close to the

---

[3] Cohabitation is not necessarily a good preparation for marriage. Those who had cohabited were less likely to say they were "very happy" and that their marriage was "very happy." Moreover, as the years since a marriage which had been preceded by cohabitation increased, satisfaction levels went down even more. Finally, those who were not happily married (not "very happy") and who had cohabited were significantly less likely to recommend such behavior to young people. Obviously these data fly in the face of the conventional wisdom, but that does not make them any less accurate.

Church as those who are married, but they do not seem to have given up on the Church either.

They see considerable value in Catholicism. Indeed, they are more likely than those who are married to say that Catholicism gives them a sense of identity, and they show little difference from the married in seeing in Catholicism values to communicate to children, a way of understanding life, and a way of worshiping God. Despite their temporary alienation from devotion because of their violation of what they think to be "church rules," they still see Catholicism playing an important role in their future.

They are remarkably similar to those in wedlock relationships in their Catholic activities. Although they are less likely to have read a Catholic periodical or a Catholic book recently, there are only relatively small differences between those out of wedlock and those in wedlock in having talked to priests, made a retreat or day of recollection, and watched a Catholic television program, and they are more likely to have participated in a religious discussion group. One-third of them have participated in at least one such activity (as opposed to 43 percent of those in wedlock), and 16 percent of them have participated in three or more of these activities (as against 13 percent of those who are in wedlock). Once again, those the Church would consider "living in sin" do not seem to be all that alienated from the Church. Indeed, many of them seem almost to be leaning over backwards to leave open the paths by which they might return.

Youthfulness, problems in the family of origin, conviction that premarital experimentation is not wrong, the tendency to minimize the importance of children, lack of Catholic education, and a religious imagination that does not stress the role of God as a mother and lover—these seem to be important factors contributing to the decision of many young Catholics to enter nonmarital liaisons. Their devotional practice suffers as a result of these liaisons as does to some extent their sense of being close to God and the Church. Yet they still rate Catholicism as highly as those who are married in its value/identity/worship function and are as likely to engage in a number of Catholic "linking" activities. They are surely not a group of young people the Church can take for granted; but neither are they a group about which the Church ought to despair. Moreover, they have the right to be treated by their clergy with compassion and affection and not to be denounced or read the rules when they come to the rectory seeking to normalize their relationship. They know what the rules are. The critical question is to ask them why they want to convert their liaison into a marriage. The answers to that question are as good a beginning as any I know to "premarital" instruction.

Do I really think that the young people with whom I water-ski every summer are not much different from those with whom I grew up forty years ago?

Not much different at all. They have more freedom, more options, more responsibilities to choose from. They are, however, at least as religious as we were, if in different ways. They are also at least as Catholic as we were and maybe more Catholic.

Does this mean I am optimistic about the young—as Mr. James O'Gara of *Commonweal* accused me long ago of being an optimist because I wanted to be a bishop?

By temperament I am a moody, melancholic Celt. My views of Catholic young people are not shaped by optimism but by the empirical data. I say that they are no worse than we were not because of bias or mood but because that is what the evidence establishes.

The choice for them may be more difficult than it was for us, but it's pretty much the same choice. Caught as we were in the Sacramental Imagination in the very earliest years of life, they like being Catholic as much as we did.

Maybe more than we did.

15

ONLY IN AMERICA?

AM TOLD by almost everyone whom I encounter outside the United States that the phenomena I describe in this book are purely American. It is not the situation in Western Europe, they insist, nor in the Second or Third worlds. The birth-control encyclical was not as important in Western Europe, and the "loyalty" of which I have written simply does not exist. There is no Sacramental Imagination in these countries to protect the Catholic tradition from declining.[1]

I have already established that the Catholic Sacramental Imagination exists in all the countries about which data exist in the two international surveys currently available. Do the other image factors I have described also tend to operate in the other countries? Or is Catholicism surviving only in America?

The inevitability of religious decline seems to be an accepted fact by both nonreligious intellectuals and religious leaders. The former are confident that "secularization" is eliminating religion from the modern world, save as German sociologist Thomas Luckmann contends, in the private segments of life. The latter argue that while the number of Catholics, for example, is in decline, those who remain in the tradition will be better Catholics. Both positions view the "secularization" process as an irresistible and indeed almost mystical force which dominates the modern world and to which religion must adjust if it is to survive at all.

In the literature that emerged from the 1981 International Study

[1] In this chapter I draw on an essay that Michael Hout and I wrote for the London *Tablet*.

of Values, the emphasis was on social change and the decline of religion, particularly as the decline is manifested in the absence of religious interest in young people. If the young are not interested in religion, the argument seemed to run, what hope is there for religion when the young become older?

The appropriate answer, of course, is that there is no hope unless the young become more religious as they grow older. Since youth in the North Atlantic world is a time of experimentation before permanent decisions are made about occupation, career, employer, dwelling place, sexual partner, and political affiliation, might it not also be a time of religious moratorium? When the other life-shaping decisions are made (or are in the process of being made), might young people also drift back to religion?

Mike Hout and I decided to try to replicate our American findings in Europe, using the ISV and ISSP surveys. In addition, for five countries—Great Britain, the United States, Australia, Italy, and the Federal Republic of Germany (BRD)—we were able to obtain data sets from election surveys in the mid-1970s and mid-1960s to measure change over time.

Our first finding is that in all the sixteen countries we studied, *the relationship between age and church attendance is the same*. The intercept of the curve (the level of churchgoing when men and women are in their twenties) differs from country to country as the various religious cultures differ, but the shape of the curve is the same. Ireland is a country with a high level of religious practice, Great Britain is a country with a low level of religious practice. But the relationship between age and church attendance is the same in both countries. If one places the curve on the proportion attending church when they are under twenty-five in either country, one obtains a precise prediction of the proportion who will be attending church in their middle forties and late fifties.

It must be emphasized that the increase in church attendance is not a phenomenon of the late stages of aging. Rather the increase is most dramatic between twenty-five and forty years old.

The one partial exception is Hungary, where the return to religion—if one may tentatively call it that for the moment—begins not in the late twenties but in the forties; however, the upswing is sharper in Hungary, so that for people in their fifties and sixties Hungarian church attendance—the lowest of any of the countries—is actually slightly above what the curve would predict.

The uniform relationship between age and church attendance is a striking phenomenon. It suggests either a universal "secularization" or a universal life-cycle phenomenon in all the countries. The question remains as to which explanation is valid.

If "secularization" is the explanation, then one would expect it to be most pronounced among those who are better educated—most likely to be exposed to the scientific critique of religion. However, neither in the ISSP nor the ISV is there a negative relationship between education and churchgoing; indeed, in the ISSP the relationship is positive (and the education measure in the ISV, like much else in the project, is problematic).

Moreover, the relationship between age and church attendance can be accounted for statistically in all countries (except Hungary) by much more ordinary and mundane processes than great historical trends—marriage, childbearing, and child-rearing. In both the ISV and the ISSP the relationship between age and churchgoing is explained statistically by marriage and children. Young people increase their church attendance as they marry and have children at the same rate in all sixteen countries studied. The curve is the same in every country because the processes of marriage and family formation are basically the same.

One wonders why the analysts who reported on the ISV project did not address themselves to that possibility.

It should be noted that the connection between increased religious devotion and family development—a connection that exists in all the countries studied except Hungary—indicates that the return to religion that comes with maturation goes on quite independently of anything religious institutions do or don't do. The churches cannot prevent the return and apparently they cannot accelerate it either, reason for a humility that church leaders might not find appealing.

The critical test of our replication was the analysis of the five countries about which we were able to collect data from studies done ten and twenty years ago (the most serious methodological flaw of the various ISV reports was their failure to attempt this "longitudinal" analysis).

While levels of religious behavior are different among the United States, Great Britain, BRD, Italy, and Australia, the processes at work seem to be the same in all five countries: there has been no decline in non-Catholic churchgoing (whether weekly or monthly are measured) in the last two decades. Catholic attendance declined sharply between the late 1960s and the mid-1970s and has not declined since. Moreover, the rate of Catholic decline (the downward slope of this curve) is the same in all five countries. Catholics continue to be approximately the same proportion of the population in all five countries that they were twenty years ago—nine-tenths in Italy, two-fifths in the BRD, a quarter in the United States and Australia, and a tenth in Britain.

Finally, we asked whether for either Catholics or non-Catholics in all countries there was a change in the age relationship over time: in effect, are young people less likely to go to church than they were twenty years ago in all or any of the five countries, given the decline of Catholic practice between the mid-1960s and the mid-1970s. We found no change in the correlation between age and attendance. The age curve does not show generational change or long-term secularization change, but only life-cycle change, as our demographic explanation described earlier suggested it would. Young men and women will become more religious as they mature and at the same rates as they did twenty years ago.

It also follows from this finding that the decline in Catholic practice that occurred between the mid-1960s and the mid-1970s was uniformly distributed throughout the Catholic population and not concentrated in any age group, just as in the United States.

Since the slope of decline is the same in all countries and since we have proven that this slope can be accounted for in the United States by reaction to the birth-control encyclical and that the decline has been arrested by "tenacity of affiliation," it is not unreasonable to postulate that the same dynamics have been at work in the other three countries.

Young people become more religious as they become older (or, if one wishes, as they mature). So what else is new? one might be tempted to demand. Everyone knows that people become more religious as they mature. All we can claim to have done is to have stated precisely the shape of the maturation effect, to have demonstrated that in sixteen countries the maturation effect is the same (given the level of religious culture in the country), that in five quite different countries the maturation effect does not prove that "secularization" has occurred, and that, in conclusion, the dynamics at work in the United States are also at work in the other five countries for which we have longitudinal data.

Succinctly: the only change in church attendance during the last twenty years in the five countries was the Catholic decline that occurred at the same rate in all five countries; the Catholic decline ended ten years ago. To repeat the finding about young people: in all five countries they are no less likely to attend church today, given the general Catholic decline between 1965 and 1975, than their predecessors were twenty years ago.

The similarity in the dynamics of Catholic behavior strongly provides that the oft-heard cliché that the birth-control encyclical created problems only in America is not true. The problem seems more serious in America because it is the only country where the impact of the encyclical on Catholic religious behavior has been carefully monitored.

It is often said (and I was told in so many words by a Curial cardinal) that the faith has been lost in the North Atlantic world but that the Church will survive in the Second and the Third worlds. That assertion is never stated in a form that can be tested operationally, but it implies a total or near-total alienation of Catholics from religious behavior.

What is the religious condition of Catholicism in the countries Michael Hout and I have studied? As a rough indicator of how people relate to their religious heritage (tenacity of affiliation) we propose the proportion of men and women over thirty-five who attend Mass at least once a month. By that indicator one can hardly find reason for the despair that seems to possess many clergy and religious leaders: Ireland, 95 percent; Northern Ireland, 93 percent; Spain, 77 percent; the United States, 75 percent; BRD, 67 percent; the Netherlands, 67 percent; Canada, 66 percent; Great Britain, 60 percent; Australia, 60 percent; Belgium, 60 percent; Italy, 53 percent; Austria, 49 percent; New Zealand, 46 percent; France, 45 percent; Hungary, 12 percent. (The sixteenth country analyzed was Denmark, where there were not enough Catholics to estimate a churchgoing rate.)

Why, then, do Catholic theologians and leaders seem so eager to describe the present situation as a "diaspora" (Karl Rahner), a time of decline in religious faith?

Those who are older tend to see the world as a worse place than it was when they were younger, a phenomenon that may tell more about selective memories than social change. Moreover, some men and women may find themselves in situations where there is a great change from conditions when they were young. A priest whose origins are rural or small-town may be horrified by the lack of devotion in urban slums, for example. But the pertinent question for social-change analysis is whether the slums are in fact any less devout than they were a quarter century ago.

Some "progressive" analysts tend to portray the present situation in colors as stark as possible in the hope that church leadership will be frightened into change. Unfortunately, perhaps, such stark colors seem to enable the leaders to say that it is too bad the people have lost the faith but that the future of Catholicism is in the Second and Third worlds anyway.

Finally, if what one is watching is the inevitable and necessary working out of vast and glacial social changes that cannot be resisted, then one is justified in throwing up one's hands in despair. If, on the other hand, certain specific declines have resulted from certain policy decisions—and perhaps the way the decisions were made—then one is fated to hard work, reevaluation, and listening to what one's people say. The first explanation justifies, the second challenges. Justification has traditionally been easier to accept than challenge.

The "secularization" theory often becomes a fallacy of misplaced concreteness—a label turned into an irresistible and mystical reality, a force that has a life of its own, an excuse from thought, analysis, and action.

Then it becomes not an empirically grounded phenomenon but a dogma. Dogmas are all right in religion (so long as they are open to deeper and richer interpretation as our understanding grows), but they should be anathema in social science.

Thus in outline, at any rate, the hold of Catholicism on its members seems to be the same in the other four countries (Britain, Australia, Italy, Germany) as it is in the United States. The elaborate data on priests, parishes, women, and young people do not exist in these other countries. But it is not unreasonable to expect that should such data exist, the patterns would be roughly the same. The Catholic tradition may have a stronger hold on its people in some countries than in others, but the tradition is not appreciably weaker than it was twenty-five years ago.

An exception may well be Holland, where it appears on preliminary investigation that the decline continues. It is worth noting that it is precisely in Holland where the Curia has been most ruthless in its attempt to restore order and to prevent further loss to the Church. One need only look to Holland to see how counterproductive the Curial agenda is—which is apparently that of the present pope. The goal of less chaos and confusion is surely appropriate. The technique to achieve that goal—the appointment of reactionary and semiliterate bishops—has been counterproductive in Holland.

That it has not been counterproductive in the other countries studied is not proof of the wisdom of the Vatican but only of the tenacity of Catholic loyalty and the power of the Sacramental Imagination to prevent the institutional leadership from causing disaster.

16

THE QUEST FOR GRACE

HE THESIS of this volume is easily summarized: Catholics remain Catholic because they like being Catholic—that is, because they are loyal to the poetry of Catholicism—even if they might not use quite those terms to describe the reasons for their continued affiliation.

Poetry is used here in the broad sense of the word to include everything beyond the prose and propositional articulation of that heritage, which, I argue, is the result of reflection on the poetry—the experiences, the images, and the stories of the Catholic tradition. The poetry is broader, deeper, and richer than the prose heritage, but not opposed to it. Rather it envelops and embraces the prose tradition.

Let me illustrate by an example of the Sacramental Imagination at work, an example suggested to me by art historian Charles Scribner III: Bernini's statue *The Ecstasy of Saint Teresa*.

An affectionately smiling angel withdrawing an arrow from the breast of the saint. She is overcome with pleasure, a woman in a swoon after ecstatic love. So satiated is the saint and so delighted the angel that a contemporary critic accused the sculptor of "dragging that most pure virgin . . . into the dirt, to make a venus not only prostrate but prostituted."

Yet Teresa herself used language that justified the metaphor: "In his hands I saw a golden spear, at its tip, a point of fire. This he plunged into my heart several times so that it penetrated into my entrails. When he pulled it out I felt he took them with it and left me utterly consumed by the great love of God. The pain was so severe it made me utter several moans . . . this not a physical but a *spiritual* pain, though the body has some share in it—even a considerable share."

The point is *not* that the saint's ecstasy was erotic (though it probably was that, too), but that both the saint and the sculptor used erotic images to describe what it is like to be caught up in God's love. Human passion is a sacrament (as Saint Paul had said long before) for divine passion. Bernini's masterpiece (he thought it was his best work) is a perfect example (a classic in David Tracy's sense of that word) of the poetry of Catholicism at work, a poetry that no prose prudery can ever undo.

This model of a religious tradition, poetry enveloping prose, may seem odd to those whose perspective on religion, especially their own religion, is purely reflective. However, they must understand that for most of Christian history, most people had very little prose religion and very much poetic religion. Even today, reflective religion is probably less important in the religious lives of most people than are the prior and more powerful components of a religious tradition such as experiences, images, and stories.

To repeat a caveat from the beginning of the book, I do not deny that it is the function of reflective religion to critique imaginative religion. I do assert, however, that it is also the responsibility of reflective religion to listen closely to imaginative religion. When it fails to do so, it loses its ability to critique because it does not know what it is talking about.

Let me illustrate what I mean about poetic religion: The notion of a "novena"—nine days (or weeks) of prayer for a special intention—is or at least was very much part of the poetry of Catholicism, though it occupies little place in its prose compendia. The idea of "nine" as a special number is not part of Christian doctrine at all, but has been appropriated from occult and cabalistic traditions. Yet, properly understood, it has been approved for centuries as a form of Catholic devotion. Catholicism has appropriated a pagan notion and reinterpreted it for its own uses. One expects not that the number itself will produce magical results but rather that nine days of prayer will be pleasing to God, who will consider graciously the petition that goes with the period of prayer.

We do not buy God with powerful numbers; we appeal to him with our prayers.

Consider, for example, a staple religious devotion of thirty years ago—the novena to Saint Anne for unmarried women in the middle of the summer. While it was never said explicitly, the purpose of such novenas was to pray that such women would be able to find a husband (not an irrelevant issue even today when two-fifths of the women born in the 1950s are unmarried and with very low morale).

Harmless Catholic poetry, an instinct that God lurked in the world and would answer our prayers—if that for which we prayed would ultimately be in our best interests.

There were, however, two problems with the novena to Saint Anne which illustrate nicely the risk of Catholic poetic religion.

—Saint Anne, the name given to the Mother of Mary, hardly seemed an appropriate saint for unmarried women, unless one postulated a legend that she married late in life. In fact, the real patron of unmarried women was the pagan Irish goddess Ana, who was somehow assimilated into the Catholic Saint Anne and became thus a patron saint instead of a goddess. Catholicism, in its confidence that God lurks in the world, has never been afraid to appropriate and transform pagan religious practices. The transformation, however, often takes time. Hence touches of paganism remain. Catholicism does not worry greatly about those touches of paganism so long as it considers them to be "good paganism."

—Confidence that Saint Anne would hear the prayer was not necessarily magical, but the approach of many women to the powerful number nine often bordered on the magical—as has confidence in the number nine in other Catholic devotions. Superstition and folk religion, with elements of paganism threatening to take over the devotion, are an inherent risk in Catholic poetry, since Catholicism seeks to find God disclosing Himself in the world wherever it can.

The Catholic tradition sees no harm in appropriating whatever is good, true, beautiful, and useful in paganism for its own purposes, so long as the paganism is reinterpreted to have a solidly Catholic meaning. The Indo-European sun symbol, called by the Irish the Brigid Cross, was once the symbol of the pagan goddess of spring and has become the symbol of the Christian patron saint of spring—both Brigid by name. Now the cross stands for Christ the Light of the World and represents a prayer that Jesus and Brigid will see us through the harsh cold of winter into the warmth of spring.

Sweet, innocent, harmless?

Right. Except that the early Irish Christians had not shed completely their pagan belief in reincarnation. So when they hailed Saint

Brigid as the Mary of the Gaels, they meant it quite literally—she was the Mother of Jesus reborn into the world!

As it searches for metaphors of God, signs of God's self-revelation, Catholicism has wrestled with three tendencies which operate powerfully within its tradition. The first is to expropriate everything in sight. The second is to reject most expropriations as dangerous flirtations with paganism. The third is a cautious but determined adaptation to its own poetic purposes of the good, the true, and the beautiful that it finds in the created world and the religious of the world.

Thus stated, it is obvious that the third option is the one to be exercised. The trouble is that it is often hard to tell at a given time, or even over centuries, which policy one is in fact following. The early missionaries to Ireland were able to "baptize" almost everything in sight. Saints Cyril and Methodius adapted Catholicism to the Slavic culture, but only after overcoming opposition. The Church forbade the adaptations to India and China attempted by two great Jesuit missionaries, Matteo Ricci and Roberto de Nobili. It is clear now that all three adjustments to pagan cultures were brilliant exercises in the Catholic imagination and that the destruction of the efforts of the Jesuits in Asia was one of the great disasters of Catholic history.

It's easy to be wise with hindsight. Yet such wisdom does not tell Catholicism how to react to the African cultures with which it now interfaces. Should they be completely rejected? Or completely accepted? Or should some cautious middle course be followed? What, for example, about polygamy, not forbidden by the divine law and part of African culture? Should it be condemned? Encouraged? Tolerated?

The leadership, especially with the resources that the prose tradition makes available, must decide such issues. That's what the structure of the community which passes on the tradition is for. But the decisions are effective only if they are accepted by the people involved and often only after years or even centuries.

Is there anything that can be salvaged for Catholicism from what seems to be the mostly pagan folk religions of Brazil with their mixtures of Christianity and African and Native American symbols and stories?

How Christian is devotion to Our Lady of Guadalupe, a pagan goddess in Spain, lightly baptized before she moved to Mexico?

My inclination is to say that novenas and the Brigid Cross are surely Christian (though still subject to possible superstitious interpretation), that the Macumbe cult is certainly pagan but perhaps no more so than the Irish folk religion of the fifth century, and that Guadalupe is somewhere in between but acceptably Christian.

And crawling up on your knees to her shrine? Or to Patrick's in Ireland?

You tell me.

The poetry of the Catholic tradition, one realizes, is rich and powerful and fertile; it is also a mix of various components, some of which are more immediately acceptable than other components.

Would it not be more simple to reject everything that was not explicitly Christian? To abandon all attempts to baptize paganism?

Sure it would. That's what the Vatican thought when it terminated the Jesuit experiments in Asia, with tragic results. But such rejections violate the Catholic instinct that God lurks everywhere and that we must find his self-disclosure wherever we can.

The logic of rejecting everything is the logic of the dialectical imagination, of an absent God, of a God revealed only in the crucified Jesus, of a bleak and God-forsaken world. The Catholic attempt to absorb paganism on its own terms—because it believes it can use any good metaphor for the lurking God—looks bad only when you consider the alternatives.

I have argued in this book that the parish, the priest, the local community, and especially the lover are metaphors for God which have great power and durability in the Catholic tradition; when one approaches Catholicism from the point of view of these metaphors one can fashion seemingly incredible hypotheses that are sustained by the data (such as devout Catholic men being more pro-feminist than devout Protestant men, especially if the marriage of the former is "very happy"). I have further contended that it is the power of this poetry, of this system of metaphors, which—at the level of the preconscious—is the basic reason Catholics like being Catholic.

If a religious tradition commits itself to metaphor (for which another word is analogy) then it has to be open to all possible metaphors and to be willing to judge each one as it comes along, aware that some unsuitable metaphors cannot be resisted, and that the suitability of others will be certain only after the passage of time, and that finally the rejection of still other metaphors may be a catastrophic mistake.

Catholicism is a religious tradition that is enthralled by metaphors and at the same time constantly uneasy about the metaphors that it finds itself using.

This is a very different notion of Catholicism than the one that is contained in the catechisms or in *New York Times* dispatches from the Vatican. Nonetheless, once one realizes how important the poetic envelope is for Catholicism, one comprehends how apposite such a description is.

I offer this model not as a subtitle for other—and more "prosaic"—models of Catholics but as a complement to them. This "poetic" model, I contend, is particularly useful today both because it explains why Catholics remain Catholics and it also challenges the Church (in its institutional manifestation) to be more aware of its poetic dimensions and indeed of the power and riches of its poetic tradition.

It also serves to remind church leadership that the imaginative tradition continues to work and continues to be powerful, even if the leadership temporarily forgets it or cannot find much to support it in its documentary sources and compendia.

Despite Augustine and the Roman Curia of the present, Catholics still picture the erotic lover as a metaphor for God. The Curia will never change that, so perhaps it ought to seek to understand it.

If one can force oneself to adjust to the complexities and confusions of this "wider" model of the Catholic tradition as prose encapsulated in poetry, one discovers some fascinating and perhaps critically important issues.

Such issues were raised for me recently by my colleague Donna Swaim of the Humanities Department at the University of Arizona, by the Madonna video "Like a Prayer," and by the phenomenon of the Sila-na-gig in early medieval Ireland. All three encounters forced me to reflect on the extent to which Catholicism can use womanly eroticism as a metaphor for the life-giving, life-nurturing vitality of God.

Ms. Swaim is interested in the survival of pagan decorative motifs in the church architecture of the late Romanesque period, especially erotic symbols in the art of small parish churches. She told me at lunch in Tucson that such symbols were widespread on the Continent even up to the eleventh century (a time closer to us than it was to Jesus). Many authors dismiss the erotic images, particularly of women, as witches or demons against which the congregants were praying for protection (a less refined version of the later demons on the Gothic cathedrals). However, Ms. Swaim rejects that explanation because some of the symbols can be found on the altar as well as the church. She believes it much more likely that the symbols played the same role as they did in paganism: they represented vitality warding off morbidity, the powers of life protecting the church and its congregants from the powers of death.

Deeply concerned about the divorce of the Christian tradition from sexuality, Ms. Swaim wondered if rediscovering the insights which supported the use of such symbols in church construction might help young people cope with the difficulties of sexual maturity and provide a religious dimension to their sexuality.

I reflected that, according to Vivian Mercier in his book *The Irish Comic Tradition,* the Irish used to make love in the fields around the house where a wake was occurring with the same grotesque and defiant symbolism: "Screw you, Death! Life is stronger than you are!" A pagan custom, it continued into the first half of the nineteenth century and was one of the reasons the Church opposed wakes. It does not follow, however, that the insight that life is stronger than death is not Christian.

Did the Church ever approve of such symbolism and customs?

The answer to that question is easy if you look for prose approval in the documentary compendia of the Church. You will not find a word on the subject. But, as I have tried to argue in this book, the Catholic tradition is much wider than its prose articulation. At various times in various places in ancient and medieval Europe, pagan survivals existed alongside mainline Christian piety. Some of these pagan survivals had become thoroughly Christian (like the novena and the Brigid Cross), some of them had become semi-Christian, and some were tolerated as harmlessly pagan. Still others were condemned but not always too vigorously.

Moreover, what was once condemned could at a later date be rehabilitated. In early-nineteenth-century Ireland, church leaders were preoccupied with fighting against the "patterns," holy wells,[1] and wakes. "Patterns" were patron-saint festivals marked not only by pilgrimages to shrines but also by dancing, buying and selling, matchmaking, and especially drinking. Holy wells were condemned as pure paganism. Wakes, of the sort commemorated in the ballad about Tim Finnegan (later providing the title for James Joyce's novel), were wild drunken brawls with, as the Irish would say, a lot of "focking in the fields."

---

[1] Wells whose water was supposed to have healing powers.

Now in Ireland the "patterns" are fashionable again (*without* the poteen, I am assured) and so are the holy wells, and the wakes are under reconsideration.[2]

One hears often that "wicca," the alleged "old religion" of witches, survived underground through the Christian era. But this model assumes that everything that is not covered in the prose documents of the Church belonged to a distinct "underground" religion. In fact, the pagan components existed—and continue to exist—as completely or partially or barely absorbed components of the Catholic imaginative tradition, Christian metaphors trying to find God wherever S/He lurked.

Ms. Swaim's symbols, therefore, were certainly considered as legitimate Christian decorative motifs at certain times and certain places. Eroticism, even female eroticism, was thought to be a valid symbol by some clerics, some artists, and some architects, of the enormous divine vitality that overcomes death. God was not identified in their minds, one presumes, with the forces of fertility. Rather S/He was considered to be revealed by them.

The issue of womanly eroticism arose the same week as my long conversation with Ms. Swaim in the controversy over Madonna's album. Some preliminary comments about the audio- and videotapes of "Like a Prayer":[3]

—Virtually all the rock music critics agree that technically the music and singing of "Like a Prayer" are the best that Madonna has ever done. *Rolling Stone* said that it is "as close to art as pop music gets . . . proof not only that Madonna should be taken seriously as

---

[2] Presumably with the "focking in the fields," though in the present state of Irish Catholicism there would probably be no objection so long as the people were married and the matter was "decently done." As one inexperienced in such matters I am not altogether sure how they could occur in the muddy fields, but I will leave that to others to worry about.

I know of a couple (Irish and Irish American) who determined that they would conceive their first child in a potato field in Ireland. They were successful in this scheme and nicknamed the boy child who resulted from this union "Spuds." I wondered aloud how they would explain this name to the young man as he grew up. I encountered the family when he was fourteen. "Spuds," his mother said, "tell Father Greeley why you're called 'Spuds.' "

The young man beamed proudly. "I was conceived in a potato field in Ireland. Isn't that neat?"

You betcha.

[3] Parts of this section of the chapter originally appeared in an article in *America*.

an artist but that hers is one of the most compelling voices of the eighties."

—The lyrics of the album run from harmless to devout. In the title song God's voice calls the singer's name and it feels like home. That "Like a Prayer" is in fact a prayer is evident from the lyrics themselves, from the singer's interpretation of them, and from the critical reaction. In the words of Edna Gundersen in *U.S.A. Today*, "Lyrically 'Prayer' is a confessional feast, with Madonna's Catholic upbringing as the main course. Songs are rife with religious overtones, spiritual and hymnal arrangements and a host of references to joy, faith, sin and power." The *Arizona Daily Star* noted: "It is largely a story of renewal and self-determination and it speaks with authority. You can dance, if you want to, but this time there's a heart and a brain behind the beat." Only those who come to the music and lyrics with a grim determination to find prurience and blasphemy can miss—and then with considerable effort—the God hunger that animates them.

—The music video is utterly harmless, a PG-13 at the worst, and, by the standards of rock video, charming and chaste. More than that, it is patently a morality play. In the singer's own words, it is "a song of a passionate young girl so in love with God that it is almost as though He were the male figure in her life."

The girl in the story witnesses a crime, she sees a black man falsely accused of it, she flees the criminals and hides in a church, she prays to a black saint (Martin de Porres, one presumes), and falls asleep. She dreams that the saint comes alive and represents God as her lover. She awakens from the dream and realizes that in the power of God's love she can run the risk of doing right. In Madonna's words, "She knows that nothing's going to happen to her if she does what she believes is right." She goes to the police station and obtains the release of the innocent man.

To emphasize the religious themes of the album, it comes steeped in the smell of sandalwood, recalling the church incense of the past and implicitly (if unintentionally) the sandalwood themes of "The Song of Songs."

That this is the meaning of the video is clear from its obvious sense, from the testimony of the singer, and from the virtually unanimous reaction of the young people who have watched it. (In my Sociology of Religion class of 150 students, before any comment from me, 30 percent rated the video PG, 68 percent rated it PG-13, and 2 percent rated it R or X.)

This is blasphemy? Or satanism, as the Catholics who want to boycott Pepsi-Cola will tell you?

Only for the prurient and the sick who come to the video determined to read their own twisted sexual hang-ups into it.

Only for those who think that it is blasphemous to use religious imagery in popular music.

Only for those who think that sexual passion is an inappropriate metaphor for divine passion (and thus are pretty hard on Hosea, Jesus, Saint Paul, Saint Bernard of Clairvaux, and Saint Teresa of Avila).

Only for those whose subconscious racism is offended at the image of a black saint revealing God's love.

The line between blasphemy (the abuse of the divine) and sacramentality (the search for the Creator in the created) may sometimes be thin. One person's blasphemy may be another person's sacramentality—a May Crowning is blasphemous for a fundamentalist and sacramental for a Catholic. Fundamentalists may well believe that the use of sexual passion as a metaphor for God's passion, especially in a work of popular art, is blasphemous. Catholics, dedicated as they are to a search for the Creator in creation, can hardly think so.

"Like a Prayer" is not even close to the dividing line between sacramentality and blasphemy.

Even the most rigid fundamentalist or Catholic Jansenist must search desperately to find prurience in "Like a Prayer." Madonna's low-cut dress (or slip)? The tender kiss of the (black) saint (God)? The brief image of sensual satisfaction on the face of the woman in the dream as she's caught up in God's love? These would be an "occasion of sin" for young people?

Someone has to be kidding!

An immensely popular and now critically acclaimed singer tells a morality story filled with Catholic imagery, and her Church responds to it with threats of boycotts against Pepsi-Cola (for whom she has made ads and which has lost $5 million because of its cancellation of the ads). Such a response tells more about those who respond than it does about the work of art itself.

In her interviews about "Like a Prayer" and previous songs, Madonna Louise Veronica Cicone has repeatedly described the importance of Catholicism in her childhood and the remnants of Catholic guilt that continue to haunt her life—"If you enjoy something it must be wrong." In the rock video, when the girl grabs the knife and cuts herself, causing stigmata-like wounds on her hands, the wounds represent guilt, Madonna tells us. However, it is not guilt but love which leads the girl to do what she knows is right. Madonna seems to be saying that the guilt that obsessed her Catholic childhood is not enough to produce virtue.

She has been less explicit about the love imagery and the sense of sacramentality she has also carried with her from her Catholic childhood. Perhaps she is unaware of this second part of her inheritance. Nonetheless it permeates her work. She says she is not sure whether she is a Catholic or whether she would raise a child as Catholic. That is her own personal problem. In fact, she sings "like a Catholic" (especially in "Like a Prayer") and for our purposes in this article that's what counts.

Perceive the paradox: Catholicism in its present formulation passes on to its children both obsessive and imprisoning guilt and a liberating sense of God's love as sacramentalized in creation and especially in human love. It is a paradox struggling to become a contradiction.

The Catholic tradition teaches sacramentality and forgiving love. The Catholic institution, assigned to hold the tradition together and to transmit it, does so despite its obsession with guilt—sometimes just barely.

In a guilt-obsessed leadership culture, there is no room for, indeed no possibility of, tolerance toward any contamination (as it would be seen) of religious images by sexual images. Sexuality cannot be imagined as vitality, as a promise of the strength of the powers of life over the powers of death, as a hint of the power and goodness of the Source of life. All the religious symbolism found in sexuality down through human history must be rigidly suppressed. It is because she has contaminated religion with sex that Madonna must be condemned, say her detractors.

In the present climate of Catholic leadership, the Irish monks would not have dared to convert an Indo-European intercourse symbol into the Celtic cross representing Jesus and Mary and the union of male and female in God. If she wanted to keep clergy and hierarchy happy, Saint Teresa would not have dared use the powerful erotic imagery of her mystical writings (nor would Saint Bernard have dared to write his commentary on "The Song of Songs" the way he did). Fourth-century Roman liturgists would have risked condemnation by inserting the pagan fertility ritual of candle and water into the Easter Vigil service.

Cornelius Jansen is alive and well and triumphant.

The best example of this pervasive Jansenism, I have argued, is the bowdlerization of the Easter Vigil. Anyone who has taken an introductory course in religious symbols knows that the lighted candle represents the male organ and the water the female organ. The repeated plunging of the former into the latter represents an act of fertility and vitality. In the Latin service it was prayed that the candle might fructify the waters. Now, in the name of protecting the laity from shock, the candle need not be plunged into the water, and the prayer is merely that God may visit the water. Like Madonna, the fertility imagery at the center of the service has been boycotted.

As Father Herman Schmid explained the ceremony to me, the liturgists who borrowed the ceremony from their pagan neighbors understood that when Christ rose from the dead he consummated his nuptials with his bride the Church and that we who are baptized with the life-impregnated water are the first fruit of this union. This interpretation has apparently been boycotted, too.

Contemporary liturgists, who know what the ceremony means, deliberately cut the heart out of the Easter Vigil rite. I almost said that they emasculated it, but I think they have done rather the opposite. Their fear was not that the candle would contaminate the water but that the water would contaminate the candle—that the female would contaminate the male. The bowdlerization of the Easter Vigil manifests a fear of women and proves that church leadership can be simultaneously homophobic and anti-heterosexual.

If latent homosexuality may be defined as revulsion against the sexual appeal of women (and not be taken as a sign of sexual orientation), then the Jansenism of church leadership is a classic manifestation of institutionalized latent homosexuality.

Madonna must be denounced and Pepsi-Cola threatened with boycott because she is a sexually attractive woman who dares to link her sexuality with God and religious images: that, gentle persons, is the heart of the matter.

At one and the same time, the leadership elites celebrate life and the right to life (which they ought to do) and condemn both the bearers of life and the process by which life continues.

The link between vitality and fertility, between life and sex, has been so obvious that, until the Reformation and the Counter-Reformation, humankind had no doubts about the pervasive religious imagery of sex and the pervasive sexual imagery of religion. Contemporary Catholic leadership rejects this human experience out of hand. Sex may be necessary for the continuation of the species, but please, lay folk, don't talk about it, don't let its influence seep into your life outside of your bedrooms, don't enjoy it too much, don't let it into your artistic works (especially if they happen to be religious), and don't suggest that the allure of a woman's body in a rock video staged in church can hint at the allure of God.

The novelist Bruce Marshall observed four decades ago that Jansenism is the odd notion that God made an artistic mistake in ordaining the mechanics of human procreation.

The matter is not subject to discussion, as I have learned to my dismay. History, theology, art, archeology, exegesis—all are simply dismissed as irrelevant when they challenge the deep-seated antipathy toward sexuality that permeates Catholic leadership elites. The laity will be shocked, they tell you, refusing to listen to any other idea. In fact, they are projecting their own reactions into the laity, the vast majority of which are not shocked. Married lay people shocked by the sexual imagery of the Easter Vigil?

Again, someone has to be kidding!

There probably has never been a time in the history of the Church when the institution has been so obsessed with guilt, so hung up on sex, and so rigid and repressive in its attitude toward religious imagery and religious art than it is today.

A few weeks after my conversation with Ms. Swaim and the controversy over Madonna, I went to Ireland and discovered the Sila-na-gigs (Sheila-na-gigs).

It was the thirty-fifth anniversary of my ordination and, with little consent on my part, I was dragged by my colleague and friend Mihail MacGriel, S.J., to visit the shrine of Ma Main, two thousand feet above Galway Bay. As we began to walk up the path to the top of the mountain, Father MacGriel said, "Pilgrims were walking this path at the time of Abraham." He paused to consider. "Well, since the time David was king anyway."

No trouble here about baptizing pagan customs.

Mihail told me that the shrine, also called Kileen Phodrag (the little Cell of Patrick), was once a rival to the shrine of Cro Patrick forty miles away and that English travelers had described the great "patterns" that were once held there—complete with seven tents full of poteen.

"There'll be none of that poteen in our revived shrine," Father Mac-Griel, who had rebuilt much of the shrine, assured me. I didn't ask about the matchmaking because he would preside the next day over the marriage of two young people who had met on a pilgrimage to the shrine. The more things change, the more they remain the same . . .

After saying Mass in the little oratory at the top of the mountain, under a cloudless blue sky, and being deeply moved by the traditions behind the shrine, I descended to Galway city and supper with my friends Danno and Mary Heslip.

During the meal, in a Norman restaurant on the shore of the bay, golden in the spring sunset, we fell to discussing Christian symbolism. Well, said Danno, I had an experience not so long ago that astonished me. A friend took me to see an old church that had a Sila-na-gig on the wall. I couldn't believe it, but there it was . . . ah, a statue of a woman ready for, er, sex and on the wall of a Catholic Church! Can you explain it for me?

Danno wasn't shocked. In fact, he was kind of pleased.

Courtesy of Donna Swaim I could indeed explain it. She had wondered about Ireland. Now I had an answer. Even in Ireland! As a matter of fact, it would turn out as I learned more about the Sila-na-gigs, especially in Ireland!

Mary Heslip added another story. During the celebration of the millennium of Dublin, it was discovered that the woman who had designed the official poster had used the Sila-na-gigs as a border decoration. When "the priests" had discovered it, the poster was withdrawn from circulation.[4]

"And the decoration was just beautiful, just beautiful!" she added. "There was nothing wrong with it at all, at all."

About Mary's Catholic devotion there could be as little doubt as there could be about her feisty intelligence; "the priests" might not have liked the artistic display of a woman's genitalia, but it didn't bother women, not at all, at all.

As another woman would remark to me later, if God made something to be beautiful, then it must be good. Not satanic, as the adversaries of Madonna would doubtless say about the Sila-na-gigs.

I pondered this conversation through the meeting in London which had brought me to the British Isles and my trip home. The Sila-na-gig art was not exactly like a *Penthouse* pictorial, but it was not all that different either. The context and the meaning were religious; the art contained a meaning beyond itself; it was a symbol, a metaphor: it pointed toward God.

---

[4] Another version is that it was withdrawn only from Catholic bookstores and disappeared rapidly from others because so many people bought it!

Yet we would not tolerate it in our churches today. Indeed most of us would gasp with dismay at the suggestion that Catholic Christians ever did tolerate it. However, they did, even Irish Catholic Christians.

If we are right, they were wrong. And if they were right, we are wrong. Did they know something about Christianity that we did not know? Or have we discovered something that had been forgotten?

Or, to transcend such questions of historical comparison, is a sexually aroused woman's body, ready, willing, eager for a lover (with a complacent smile on her face) a proper metaphor for God? Is there in God's love something of the same openness, vulnerability, and need? Surely a sexually aroused body of a woman is beautiful, even bishops (well, some bishops) would admit. But does that kind of seductive beauty disclose God or is it a satanic trap?

Surely the God of the Hebrew prophets (as Rabbi Abraham Joshua Heschel demonstrated in his second volume on the prophets) is a God of "pathos," a vulnerable, loving, open, suffering God who needs his people. Is not one forced to say after the prophets that the metaphor of a tumescent woman errs only by defect? The God of pathos needs us (according to His own biblical testimony) even more than such a woman needs her lover.

Art historian Leo Steinberg sees a similar image in certain Renaissance paintings of a risen Christ in which the folds of his loincloth suggest an erection—a sacrament of the enormous power and strength of the God manifested in the risen Jesus.

Both these images are shocking to many Christians today—so shocking that they do not want even to hear about them. Yet the question remains: are we wrong or were those who reveled in such metaphors wrong?

Church leaders today would probably insist that the question is "inappropriate" and would "shock the laity." However, backed into the wall, they would have to admit that the vitality and power of human sexuality is of course a sacrament, even if it is one about which we ought not to talk.

On balance, then, while those who put the Sila-na-gigs (and similar decorations) on eleventh-century churches may not have been able to explain theologically what they were up to, they may well have understood Catholic sacramentality better than we do. I do not intend to suggest that we should return immediately to such forms of decoration. The rediscovery of forgotten metaphors is a more subtle matter than that. Rather, I submit that in time in this post-Freudian age, Catholicism will discover (or rediscover) that the only adequate response to the "sexual revolution" (whatever that may be) is not continued repression of sex but its sacramentalization, or more properly resacramentalization. If God is the lover and if human love is a valid metaphor for divine love, then does it not follow that human sexual arousal is potentially a metaphor for God, a hint of what God is like, of the power and the need and vulnerability and the beauty of God?

Grace in the broad sense of that word is nothing more than the self-disclosure of God in the world. The search for metaphors of God, no matter how wild they may be, is nothing more than the quest for grace wherever we can find it. The analogical imagination seeks for grace everywhere. The dialectical imagination recoils from such a search as reckless and dangerous. Neither imagination is better than the other. Both need each other. Catholicism is a religious heritage that emphasizes the quest for grace, in its best moments surely but, because of the power of poetic religion, even in its rigid and obdurate moments like the present one.

How can I avoid the following conclusion from the preceding chapters: it may take the institutional Church a long time to recapture the metaphor incarnated by those who made the Sila-na-gigs, but the Catholic people, preconsciously perhaps, know it already.

That's one of the reasons they like being Catholic.

APPENDIX

CATHOLIC, CAPITALIST, SOCIALIST, AND ANARCHIST IDEOLOGIES

T HE emerging consensus," said my friend who works in a private organization concerned with international economic problems, "is that food aid is at best only a short-run solution. Over the long haul, the LDCs [lesser-developed countries] are going to have to acquire the capability of producing most of their own food. Only when that happens will they achieve a sufficient level of prosperity to deal with the birth-rate problem. And so there's no way of getting around it: it may not be sexy and it may be hard to see, but there's no substitute for rural development."[1]

I wondered from my urban perspective what he meant by "rural development."

"The only solution is to improve the productivity of the peasant farmer. It turns out you don't do that by pulling him out of his village and putting him into some collective commune; and you don't do it by trying to sell him a tractor. A tractor doesn't do him much good, and it will put at least ten others out of work. What you've got to do is to find out what he needs on his few acres, listen to his problems, and help him to improve his skills, his techniques, and his work. You'll have a hard time changing his worldview, so you've got to adapt your innovations to fit into his world. It may be a difficult process, but there is

[1] This appendix is based in part on a chapter in my book *No Bigger Than Necessary*.

289

no peasant in the world who will resist increased productivity when he finds that it's no threat to his values or to his village."

My head whirled with a combination of vertigo and *déjà vu*. I was back in the late 1940s and early 1950s. Everyone was reading Maritain and Mounier, admiring the work of Eric Gill, and insisting that Hilaire Belloc's distributism was a viable alternative to capitalism and socialism. The National Catholic Rural Life Conference was proclaiming salvation through the family farm; and the Baroness Catherine de Hueck and the Grail movement were proclaiming the survival of Christian community. Here, within a stone's throw of the Brookings Institution, I was hearing the very same line.

Consider:

"If the nature of change is such that nothing is left for the fathers to teach their sons, or for the sons to accept from their fathers, family life collapses. The life, work, and happiness of all societies depend on certain 'psychological structures' which are infinitely precious and highly vulnerable. Social cohesion, cooperation, mutual respect, and above all self-respect, courage in the face of adversity, and the ability to bear hardship—all this and much else disintegrates and disappears when these 'psychological structures' are gravely damaged. A man is destroyed by the inner conviction of uselessness. No amount of economic growth can compensate for such losses—though this may be an idle reflection, since economic growth is normally inhibited by them."

Doesn't it sound substantially like something a Catholic personalist or distributist would have written before 1960? It is in fact taken from a book by the former chief of planning for the British Coal Board, E.F. Schumacher. The great wheel has swung around again, only Catholics aren't there to welcome it back.

Sometime between 1955 and 1970, Catholic social theory vanished from the scene, and Catholics with social concerns were forced to choose between capitalism and socialism. Since the latter is by far the more fashionable of the two ideologies, Catholics have opted for soft-core socialism and have allied themselves with revolutionary forces. Of course, most of these would-be revolutionaries are college professors, bureaucrats, or clergy persons, and their revolutionary activity never goes beyond talk. They issue statements, write articles, and testify at USCC (United States Catholic Conference) hearings, but they never *do* much of anything. They also engage in the "fundamental option for the poor" and continue to pay their employees poverty wages, behavior that in lesser men than Catholic bishops would be damned as hypocritical.

Those who are the legitimate heirs of the Catholic social movement sit complacently by and watch their tradition being replaced by shallow and pathetic imitations of the current radical chic.

I have argued in this book that Catholics imagine social reality differently than do others. The traditional Catholic social theory, articulated especially in papal encyclicals at the end of the last and the beginning of the present century, is an articulation of the Sacramental Imagination and an application of it to contemporary social problems.

Although the bishops and their "peace and justice" staffs don't seem to realize it, there are alternatives to the two allegedly competing economic philosophies and systems of capitalism and socialism (which, in fact, share the same set of basic assumptions). American Catholics used to argue that there was a "third way"; we have abandoned the argument that there was a "third way" just as others have taken it up.

"It is far better," said one of my non-Catholic Christian colleagues, "to oppress the people in the name of the people than to oppress them in the name of greed." To which I found myself instinctively responding, "Damn it, you shouldn't oppress the people in the name of anything." "But," he said, "how else can you amass capital for economic development?" My only response was to admit that, historically, capitalism and socialism seem to have been the only two economic systems capable of storing up capital required for economic development. "But," I insisted, "that doesn't mean there aren't other ways that it could have been done, or other ways that it could be done now." Between agribusiness and the collective farm, for example, there is an alternative. The family farm and the peasant on his plot of land are likely to be more efficient in the long run than either agribusiness or the collective farm, as responsible, reasonable, sensible international economists are now beginning to argue. I am not competent enough in economic history to be able to discuss the processes of capital formation in various countries during the last century. Surely there was massive oppression of the poor in England during the Industrial Revolution—an oppression for which even now England is paying in its self-destructive class conflict. How the oppression of the robber barons in the United States will compare to the oppression of the commissar of the Soviet Union is beyond my ability to judge, though it turned out to be a lot easier to get rid of the robber barons than the commissars.

There are seven points on which there is a fundamental agreement between capitalism and socialism but with which Catholic social theory must vigorously disagree. Obviously, such an outline can be only sketchy, and greatly oversimplified at that, but it should serve as a basis for discussion.

1. Both capitalism and socialism assume (after Thomas Hobbes and Adam Smith) that human nature in its present form is fundamentally selfish and destructive. Capitalism assumes that this is the way humankind has been always and always will be. Yet through some marvelous disposition of nature, or providence, or someone or something, the conflict of selfish, aggressive, destructive individuals (moderated by their self-interest) can combine to produce a healthy, harmonious social unit. The socialist accepts the capitalist description of human nature as it is, but argues that humankind doesn't have to be that way always, that if the constraints of the present economic and social class structures are destroyed, human nature can be changed.

Capitalism and socialism agree that in its present version, human nature is selfish and individualistic. Socialists would disagree that this is the way things have to be, but if anyone doubts their agreement with this as a description of the way things are, he should consult Herbert Marcuse's *One-Dimensional Man*.

2. Given such a view of human nature, one can make some immediate and obvious conclusions about human society. Social organization exists to constrain the unbridled exercise of selfish irresponsibility. The state is established by individuals acting in enlightened self-interest, knowing that only the raw power of institutional force can keep them from completely destroying one another. The state exists to impose constraints. From the capitalist viewpoint, only those constraints that are necessary to establish rules of the competitive marketplace game are tolerable. Socialists respond by saying that all constraints necessary to create a situation in which nature can be remade are required. The selfishness imposed by the present social structure must be extirpated from the human condition. For the capitalist, society will necessarily be permanently oppressive to selfish individual freedom—though hopefully the oppression will be as little as possible. For the socialist a maximum of short-range oppression is justified on the grounds that human social

structures and human nature can be so modified that at some unspecified point in the future all social constraints can be dispensed with when an unselfish, generous, cooperative human nature will have been produced. In both cases, however, the present function of society and of society's political arm, the state, is to restrain and oppress; and in both cases such restraint and oppression are to be imposed on individuals for their own good—in the one case for the continuation of the competition game free from strife and turmoil, and in the other for ensuring a future society in which generosity and unselfishness will produce authentic, responsible freedom.

3. Both capitalism and socialism agree that economic development must be scientific and rational. Both agree that there must be economic planning in which the principles of scientific and rational planning must be utilized to program future economic development. The capitalist will want to limit the planning to the individual corporate structure; the socialist will want to extend it to the whole society; but both would agree that the technically trained, rational, scientific planner must make decisions about the future. "Scientific" and "rational" have very specialized meanings in this context, however. "Scientific" means the maximization of technical efficiency, producing the highest output for the least cost. The capitalist justifies such an approach in terms of his obligation to the shareholders, the socialist in terms of his obligation to the people, but both are interested in production. "Rational" means that one considers the individual members of the corporate body as collections of productive skills. The capitalist entrepreneur is completely uninterested (at least in principle) in the life of his worker off the assembly line or even in his conversations and friendships on the assembly line as long as these do not impede his productivity. The socialist—particularly the totalitarian socialist— claims a much broader interest in the activities, thoughts, and feelings of his workers; but nonetheless it is work and work skill that earn a person a place in the socialist society. Indeed, in Red China one must validate oneself even if one is a college professor by putting in a certain amount of time in rural communes.

The rational and scientific approach to economic development for both capitalism and socialism, then, means the maximization of productivity in a work system in which the individual's primary contribution is taken to be his productive skills. There may be all sorts of enlightened personnel policies or management counsels with labor representatives, but in fact the productive enterprise is organized either on an assembly-line basis or with little concern for other aspects of the personality of the worker besides his productive skills.

Thus farms in China, in the Soviet Union, and, more recently, Tanzania (which, although headed by Catholic convert Julius Nyerere, does utilize the communal farm approach) could be uprooted from their peasant villages and forced into collective farms in the name of economic rationality, whereas on the capitalist side of the fence the assumption of a more or less completely mobile labor market is taken for granted. Does your meatpacking plant close in Chicago? Well, you can always move to Omaha. Does your firm decide to transfer you from Rochester to Rotterdam? You'll probably find a comparable upper-middle-class suburb in either city. The more sensitive of the socialists will lament the suffering of the recently collectivized peasants; the more sensitive capitalist will be sorry about the family disruption caused by the move from Rochester to Rotterdam; but both will shrug their shoulders. There simply isn't any other way.

4. Both the capitalist and the socialist will agree that what they both might call "feudal social styles and patterns" are evolving out of existence or collapsing in the face of the advance of "science." The greats of the sociological traditions—Tonnies, Weber, Durkheim— all noted, not without melancholy, the collapse of the archaic order. However, this collapse would be considered by the contemporary capitalist or socialist (or liberal humanist, for that matter) as not merely descriptive but normative, not merely the way things are, but the way they should be. The particular should give way to the universal, ascription should give way to achievement, the sacred should give way to the secular, the diffuse should give way to the specific, the informal should give way to the formal, and the heterogeneous should give way to the homogeneous.

All the archaic, outmoded, and perhaps superstitious ties of localism, tradition, loyalty, rootedness, "irrational" differentiation (meaning differentiation based on anything other than economic class) simply do not belong in a modern, scientific, enlightened world. Transient man is the explicit goal of contemporary society in the view of the capitalist and socialist alike. For the capitalist, mature man ought to be bound only by the commitments the state requires of him until, when human nature is remade, he may freely choose for himself. But the capitalist and socialist together reject as obsolete and superstitious the ties of membership and loyalty that bind one at birth. The family may persist, but the clan, the extended family, the neighborhood, the locality, the village, the church all have no place in the modern world.

5. Both capitalism and socialism are future-oriented. The socialist is perfectly willing to impose sacrifices in the present so that prosperity and freedom can be enjoyed in the future, if not by the one who now must suffer, then at least by his successors and descendants. Similarly, the immigrant laborer in the United States would work long hours for low pay as long as he had the promise that the money he saved up and the education financed by his taxes would make a better life possible for his children. As Peter Berger points out in his book *Pyramids of Sacrifice,* both China and Brazil have mortgaged the lives of their people in this generation for the future. In China political freedom is sacrificed so that the future may be free; and in Brazil economic poverty is imposed on large groups in the society so that in the years ahead the whole country might be prosperous. The sensitive capitalist and the sensitive socialist may lament this suffering, but, again, how else is one to build for the future except to impose suffering in the present?

6. On the subject of the lesser-developed countries, there is also a fundamental agreement between capitalism and socialism. Neither sees any way in which poverty, ignorance, and hunger can be overcome unless the archaic social structure and the superstition culture of the indigenous people are eliminated. Revolution must destroy the old structure and culture, must wipe the slate clean so a new, modern, rational, scientific social order can emerge. In the capitalist view, revolution is accomplished gradually and normally without violence by the technician of the multinational corporation, whereas in the socialist view revolution is usually both more abrupt and more violent, and is carried out by a technician who may be more guerrilla leader than businessman. But both the Moscow-trained terrorist and the Harvard-MIT–trained corporation executive firmly believe that they know far better than do the untrained citizens of the target country what is necessary to eliminate misery, the injustice, the hunger, and the poverty that afflict the country.

7. Finally, both capitalism and socialism believe in large size and centralization. The socialist assumes that the Politburo and the planning authority are responsible for the politics and economics of the whole country. The capitalist makes no such theoretical assertions, but still seems driven by the logic of his system to build ever-larger corporate combinations such as conglomerates and multinationals to max-

imize efficiency and to minimize "destructive" competition. And all competition, it turns out, is destructive—particularly if it is price competition. It seems to be built into the logic of the scientific and rational approach to production that organizations should get bigger and bigger and bigger. Whether you are a socialist or capitalist, the argument for "economy of scale" seems to be unanswerable. It often turns out, of course, that an increase in size does not make for an increase in efficiency, but such results normally lead neither capitalist nor socialist to question the need for both expansion and centralization.

Obviously, I have greatly oversimplified. There are many differences between capitalism and socialism both in theory and in practice. Peter Berger, in his *Pyramids of Sacrifice*, has done a masterful job of outlining these differences, but Berger sees the two systems converging in their agreement that the present generation must be called on to sacrifice for the good of future generations. In the previous paragraphs I have tried briefly to elaborate on this insight of Berger's and to root it in a prior view that capitalism and socialism owe to their common Calvinist and Hobbesian ancestors of the nature of human nature, human society, and of human social and economic progress.

The most critical Catholic dissent has to do with human nature. Unlike the socialist, the Catholic is profoundly skeptical about remaking basic traits of the human personality. In the Catholic view of things, one does not cease to be wary or afraid of other human beings; one rather loves them despite one's fears. But while Catholicism is skeptical and reserved on the subject of remaking human nature, it takes a much brighter view of humankind in its present condition than does Protestantism. Humankind is deprived, perhaps, but not depraved. There is more that is admirable in man, as Camus said, than is contemptible. The flesh wars against the spirit, and the outcome is generally a toss-up, but Catholicism is inclined to bet on the spirit. Humankind is not fundamentally destructive, selfish, individualistic. There is a selfish, aggressive, destructive aspect to our nature; but there is also a generous, trusting, and cooperative aspect to it, and Catholicism is more aware of and has far more confidence in that aspect of the human personality than does Protestantism. Though under no illusion about the present condition of human nature, Catholicism still sees a sufficient amount of goodness and generosity to call people to virtue rather than to compel them to virtue.

The Catholic social theory, then, makes the fundamental assumption that you create social order by an appeal to humankind's cooperative disposition and not by force or by Hobbesian constraints. You sometimes have to back up pacific appeals by force, but society is not created by violence or maintained by force or even by formal social contract. It exists by definition when you have more than one social animal in the same physical environment.

Since it has a relatively more benign view of human nature, Catholicism can also take a more benign view of society. Social constraints, which in the Catholic view exist to reinforce and support the cooperative tendencies of social beings, are not so oppressive that one must keep them to an absolute minimum (as in the capitalist view of things) or that one need impose them to a maximum in order that they may eventually wither away (the socialist view). Catholicism is under no illusion about oppressive states and oppressive societies; it has fought some and, lamentably, has allied itself with others; but it would deny that society or the state are necessarily or fundamentally oppressive. Society exists not so much to restrain human selfishness as to facilitate human growth (though in the process it must restrain some selfishness). And the state is not the arm of oppression to remake human nature or to keep the competitive system going; it is simply society's arm for ensuring an atmosphere of peace and tranquillity in which flawed but basically good human beings can create and share common enterprises and activities by which they may stumble through life a little more easily. Such a view of state and society is relatively modest. The state is neither the necessary evil of capitalism nor the temporary evil of socialism, but a mixture of good and evil, like everything human; and under the proper circumstances, it is often more good than evil.

There is about this Catholic view of society and of the state something that may seem just a bit cynical. It is clearly utterly lacking in idealism, but it is also relatively free from disillusionment. The Catholic social theory expects more of both humankind and human society than does the capitalist and substantially less than the socialist. It never expects to see a paradise on earth, but neither does it feel the need to remain content with life in the jungle. It has been around for a long, long time; it modestly expects to be around for a long, long time to come.

The Catholic stands in utter horror of "scientific" or "rational" economic progress. He does not believe in Adam Smith's rational economic man. You never encounter people like that in the villages, the parishes, the neighborhoods, or, the Catholic social theorist suspects, anywhere in the world. Neither does he believe in economic man's first cousin, the *homo faber* of the large corporate bureaucracy. You conceptualize a human being, the Catholic social theorist argues, as a set of economic needs or productive skills only if you fundamentally misunderstand what human nature is all about. Furthermore, if you organize human enterprise in such a way that your theory and your structure assume that you have combined a group of productive skills for the maximum efficiency of output, you are not likely to do terrible things to the human persons involved, but you are also likely to defeat your own goals in the long run. You may try to ignore or to eliminate or even to destroy the nonrational and nonscientific residues that cling to you or corporate bureaucrat and industrial worker. You can take him out of his village and put him on a collective farm, you can move him from Rochester to Rotterdam and back, you may even get him to parrot an abstract universalistic ideology of the left or the right; but in the real world you and he will still be caught in the web of intimate, informal, particularistic, diffuse relationships rooted in biology and shared beliefs. The sensitive capitalist or socialist will say that of course he understands that the human being is a total person and not just a collection of economic needs or productive skills, but the rational or scientific organization requires only economic needs and/or productive skills. One does not deny the other aspects of his personality, and one may be peripherally interested in doing what one can to see that his other needs are satisfied, but when push comes to shove, there is no particular reason to think that they are important either in satisfying the demands of the profit-hungry stockholders or the goals the planning board set up for the five-year plan.

Catholic social theory obviously dissents. Human life is both an organic and differentiated unity. Human beings live in dense networks of overlapping commitments, relationships, loyalties, involvements. There is a pluralism of relationships in human society that constitutes, in Jacques Maritain's words, "organic heterogeneity in the very structure of civil society." To ignore that organic heterogeneity even for the purpose of drawing up an organizational chart is not only to do violence to the people whose jobs appear there but also to risk the ultimate collapse of one's effort, because abstractions are not to be found on the assembly line or in offices of the bureaucracy. One cannot abstract human beings caught in relationships, committed in loyalties, and absorbed in beliefs, viewpoints, and prejudices. To forget that is to misunderstand everything.

Catholic social theory, then, has a profound respect, one might say reverence, for the informal, the particular, the local, the familial. It does not believe that this delicate and intricate web of primordial ties that bind human beings together in dense and close relationships should be ignored or eliminated. It does not believe that evolutionary progress is moving the human race from particularism to universalism. Its definition of human nature as social and relational does not permit it to see intimacies as temporary or transient or easily replaceable.

The Catholic social ethic does not believe that you should try to destroy the web of personal intimacy that every human being spins around himself. More than that, it also believes that you cannot destroy it. Abolish *Gemeinschaft* if you will, but it will reassert itself in the giant factory or the mammoth collective farm. Before you know it, it will be in control again, and its influence will be all the harder to deal with because your ideology forces you to deny its existence.

This argument is perhaps the most telling point that the Catholic social theory can make against both socialism and capitalism, for it is both an ethical and an empirical point. You should not try to destroy *Gemeinschaft*, says Catholic society theory, and besides, you cannot. It is a judgment that admits of empirical falsification or verification, and as we shall see shortly, the evidence is overwhelmingly against those who think you can dispense with or ignore the primordial, the particularistic, the local, the intimately interpersonal.

Catholic social theory categorically rejects the notion that one can or should sacrifice the present for the future. It is outraged that anyone should suggest that you should. The end does not justify the means, however noble the end. A future material paradise of peace, prosperity, plenty, and freedom does not justify slave-labor communes, hunger, misery, torture, repression. Catholic social theory takes this position in part because of its view of the nature and destiny of the human person created in God's image and called by Him to grow in knowledge and love. A creature who hungers for the absolute in the roots of his personality is not to be a pawn in a planner's program for economic development. For Catholic social theory also knows that this benign future paradise cannot be counted on to appear.

Because of its beliefs about human nature, about the organic and heterogeneous pluralism of human society, about the critical importance of the web of primordial relationships in which each person is enmeshed, and because of its convictions about fundamental dignity and the value of each individual person, Catholic social theory must be profoundly skeptical of all attempts at "modernization" or "development" that purport to improve the material lot of people by destroying its culture and its social structure. Doubtless some cultures and structures are more open to growth and development than others. Doubtless, too, there must be changes in some societies if poverty and hunger are to be eliminated; but the Catholic social ethic has too much respect for the tenacity of tradition, the power of custom, the resistance of inertia, and the strength of fundamental belief and values to think that a collective farm, a multinational corporation, a giant steel mill, or a fleet of tractors can enjoy anything but short-range success when imposed on a people who view these innovations as fundamentally alien to their way of life. If you can integrate innovation into the culture and structure of a community, then the innovation may prosper, but if you tell them to jettison their values and forget their customs and embrace new technology for increased food production, for example, they may elect customs and values in preference to food (much to the astonishment of the Peace Corps volunteer, the socialist bureaucrat, or the industrial technician, no doubt). You may dispense medical services in the Himalayas, New Delhi, and the southwest side of Chicago, and in each place you may use the most modern and advanced techniques of preventive and curative medicine; but you must never forget that you are delivering your services to an individual who is not an isolate, bereft of values and convictions. You are delivering them to a person who has value and worth in his own right and who is caught up in an intricate web of human relationships, commitments, and loyalties. Any attempts at social change, the Catholic theorist must argue, that disregard these facts about human nature are both morally and intellectually wrong—and they won't work.

Finally—and this may be the easiest way to tell the Catholic social theorist from the socialist and the capitalist—he is profoundly suspicious about size. Just as the capitalist in principle and the socialist in practice think larger is better, so the Catholic theorist can only respond that small is beautiful.[2] Of course, one must avoid the ro-

---

[2] E. F. Schumacher, *Small Is Beautiful*.

mantic temptation to assume that small is invariably beautiful or better. A hundred people cannot support an airline, a country of small farmers cannot produce enough food to feed the world—or even one large industrialized society. "Too big" is not an absolute matter but a relative one, and from the perspective of Catholic social theory something becomes too big when it is bigger than it has to be to do the job. The principle of "subsidiary function" is perhaps the central theme of Catholic social theory. It vigorously argues that nothing should be done by a larger organization that could be done as well by a smaller one; and nothing should be done by a higher bureaucratic level that can be done just as well by a lower level.

Perhaps the mistake of much Catholic social theory in the past was to argue as though the principle of subsidiarity were a philosophical deduction rather than an empirical observation. You keep things as small as you possibly can because they work better that way, there is more flexibility, better communication, more room for innovation, adaptation, and quick response to new problems. You decentralize decision-making as much as you can because those who are responsible for carrying out decisions participate in the decision-making process and because their motivations to see successful implementation will be much stronger. These are not merely ethical principles; they are empirically documented facts. Such facts are ignored today in the organization and administration of corporate bureaucracy, which merely proves that the blinders of ideology and habit can filter out critically important information. In the short run, giantism is efficient. You can maximize production quickly with "economies of scale." The only trouble is that the corporate organization is made up of more than just machines; it is also composed of human beings, and in the long run, economies of scale easily lead to diseconomies of human effectiveness. This fact has been proven time and time again, but it still does not seem to have sunk into the thinking of the theorists of either corporate capitalism or corporate socialism.

Catholic social theory would also argue that no matter how large the organization, it is immoral, erroneous, and foolish to treat it as though it were made up of atomized, isolated individuals. Even if you bring a group of complete strangers together to operate your plant, those strangers will set up informal social networks during the course of the first morning. Soon they will run the factory, not you. Also, you may drive the peasant out of his old village and set him up in a clean, new, efficient agricultural commune, and you may even threaten him with death if he doesn't live up to your standards of productivity, but that does not mean friendship networks will not emerge to sabotage deftly and subtly the goals set for you by the central planning board in Peking, Havana, or Moscow.

Catholic social theory differs from capitalism and socialism, for example, in its view of individual and class conflict. Capitalism and socialism assume that in the natural state of things individuals and classes are in conflict. In the capitalist society the state is the organ of the ruling class (though capitalists would be reluctant to admit that quite so explicitly); in a socialist society the state allegedly becomes the instrument of the oppressed class against the ruling class (though in fact it usually becomes simply a tool of the new class). Both theories are uneasy about conflict within their own societies. Social and political unrest, or even too much diversity, is viewed by the capitalist as a threat to the stability of his society and the maintenance of high levels of productivity. The socialist, once he has gained power, considers political opposition to be counterrevolutionary and vigorously represses dissent. Both socialist and capitalist applaud conflict and competition in theory and do their best to repress it in practice—perhaps because both are impressed by the inherently unstable nature of human social institutions.

The Catholic theory, on the other hand, is much more relaxed about the stability of human institutions because it views them as based on the dense and intimate interpersonal networks of "lesser groups," which it takes to be the raw material of society. Since these lesser groups (family, local community, friendship circle, local church, neighborhood, etc.) are normally more cooperative than competitive, the Catholic social theory assumes a matrix of much greater social cooperation than do its two individualist social theory adversaries. Of course, even within much smaller groups there is competition (between husband and wife, parents and children, poker players and bridge players), though the competition rarely destroys the cooperative structures. Catholic social theory assumes that such competition is normally more healthy than not and is not greatly disturbed by it.

Precisely because it has much greater confidence in the positive and constructive forces that are at work—or at least can be at work—in society, Catholic social theory is less worried about the society's capacity to deal with diversity, competition, and conflict in its "greater groups." It realizes that such competition can lead to instability and societal breakdown, but it does not necessarily do so. Hence,

Catholic social theory, unlike its socialist counterpart, sees no reason to repress dissent (however much it may have been repressed in certain Catholic states). Unlike capitalism, Catholic social theory is not worried that conflicts between labor and management, for example, will destroy the industrial enterprise. After all, the Catholic theorist notes, labor and management do have common interests as well as diverging ones.

But if it takes conflict and competition for granted (even viewing them as good), Catholic social theory is deeply suspicious of those who deliberately set out to stir up conflict between classes—especially when this conflict seeks to make the opposing class the scapegoat, the enemy to be destroyed, the evil cause of all one's trouble. Thus the Catholic theorist must reject in principle the current epidemic of romantic scapegoating of certain "oppressor" groups—men, whites, older people, the Northern Hemisphere. For all his respect for societal networks, the Catholic theorist is absolutely committed to the worth and dignity of the individual person and cannot tolerate the arbitrary assignment of guilt or nonvalue to anyone because of a characteristic acquired at birth. Furthermore, such scapegoating ignores the mutuality of interests that such falsely opposed groups obviously have. Finally, Catholic social theory observes that in the lesser groups the normal state of relationships is a mixture of cooperation and competition, with the former predominating for the most part. To pretend that such relationships are not the raw material of all society seems to the Catholic social theorist to be foolish posturing.

At the grass-roots level, then, is competition between men and women, between young and old, among various ethnic groups. It has ever been thus, and the Catholic theory accepts as fact that it always will be. Yet for the most part the individuals involved relate to one another with tolerance, affection, and even love. You can compete with people, Catholic social theory observes, and still love them. In fact, love and conflict are correlates as well as contradictions. Those mass-movement leaders who think you can have effective conflict and competition only when you stir up hatred against an opponent (or class) that must be destroyed are quite literally, in the view of the Catholic theorist, doing the work of the devil. Furthermore, in the long run their strategy won't work, for it is not natural for women to view men as enemies all the time, or for the young to view their parents as enemies all the time, or even for one group to view another as enemies all the time. But the propagandists of class conflict demand total enmity against the oppressor.

The three ideologies differ in how they imagine the triangular relationship of self, state, and society. The capitalist self is private but also essentially economic and subject to the laws of the economic marketplace, which unfortunately may on occasion (or frequently in underdeveloped countries) impose heavy burdens on the self. The state is distinct from society and exists principally to see that the rules of economic competition are honored and fairly imposed within the society. The state may occasionally intervene to protect the individual self on the premise that it is necessary for the utilitarian purpose of promoting the health of the society.

The socialist view is almost exactly the opposite. It believes that, effectively, there is no difference between society and the state. The state speaks "for the people" and is identified with the people—or at least with that segment of the people sufficiently free from false consciousness to know the true needs of the people. Since the state is merely society organized or the advance guard of society, it follows logically that there is no aspect of society that is independent of state responsibility and supervision. The whole of human life, the socialist argues, is political and hence it must all be politicized. The state may yield to the self certain areas of privacy, but only because those private areas are not presently essential for achieving the goals of society, particularly its economic goals, or because the state is too busy with other and more pressing demands to worry about certain private areas. In principle, however, everything is liable to state control—the arts, music, literature, radio, television, newspapers, religion, family life—all in the name of the ultimate good of the people.

In the capitalist scheme the state works for the economy; in the socialist scheme the economy and everything else in the society work for the state.

Catholic social theory believes that the state is a tool of society by which certain aspects of the general welfare are promoted and facilitated. The state exists as an agent of the whole society, of the lesser groups within the society, and of the individual persons who make up both the lesser groups and the society. The state urges, exhorts, coordinates, facilitates, reinforces; it does not dominate. However, it does far more than just enforce the rules of the political game. It not only regulates competition, it also sustains, supports, and facilitates cooperation. A state operating within the Catholic ideology might intervene less than do the massive welfare states of the North Atlantic world, but it would intervene, I suspect, in ways that they do not to promote reconciliation and cooperation. It would play the "honest broker" role in a much more formal and self-conscious way than do most of the welfare states. The facilitation of collective bargaining by various government mediation and conciliation services in the United States would be an example of the kind of activity one would expect in a state more strongly influenced by Catholic political and social ideology.

The word "anarchist" is still capable of striking terror into the hearts of many middle-class Americans. It calls to mind images of bomb-throwing radicals, political assassins, crowds rioting in the streets, barricades going up, black flags flying over churches, priests and nuns being massacred and mutilated, and social order collapsing on all sides. Occasionally, perhaps, we also have the image of the brave Asturian coal miner attacking a fascist tank with a Molotov cocktail during the Spanish Civil War. We middle-class Americans may not like communists, but at least the Marxist stands for law and order even though it is his law and his order. But the anarchist believes only in chaos, it seems to us.

Yet anarchism has a respectable intellectual tradition, including such adherents as Godwin, Proudhon, Bakunin, and Kropotkin. Only a tiny minority of the anarchists were men of violence. Anarchism steadfastly resisted Marxist socialism, to which it always and inevitably lost, primarily because its theory prevented it from imposing the discipline that Marxist socialism demanded of its followers. The anarchist tradition, though it has in practice fought the Catholic Church many times, has much in common with the Catholic view of society. Both Catholicism and anarchism, for example, believe in the social nature of human beings and reject in principle the centralizing tendencies of the modern world. They differ, of course, in their view of the reformability of human nature. A Catholic is not as pessimistic as the capitalist about human nature or even as pessimistic as the socialist about the present state of human nature, but he cannot accept the easy optimism (or so it seems to him) of the anarchist about the ease with which spontaneous cooperation will occur when the shackles of oppression are tossed aside. Human nature may not be depraved, according to the Catholic, but it still must be treated with caution. Sinfulness does not make us totally evil, but it does leave us with strong propensities to evil, propensities the anarchist doesn't seem to understand. Indeed, the Catholic might remark that it is precisely the failure of the anarchist to understand the strong predisposition to evil in the human personality that has led him to make self-destructive mistakes in his conflict with the Marxist socialist. This failure has also led to the collapse of his communitarian experiments even in places like Andalusia, where the only really large-scale anarchist social experiment had some success before it was wiped out by Franco's invading army.

The anarchist believes that human personality contains within itself all the attributes necessary for living in peaceful social concord. Human nature is naturally social, indeed social even before it became human. Because of its social nature, no man-made laws or positive institutions, and certainly no social contract, are required to create society. In fact, these positive institutions are the real enemies of society. Hence the anarchist opposition to Marxist socialism with its proletarian dictatorship and rigidly constructed utopian vision. The anarchist argues that human nature is perfectible, but he does not mean that it can be made perfect according to a neatly planned and executed program. Godwin contended that perfectibility did not mean that human nature could be made perfect but merely that it was capable of indefinite improvement, a notion that, he said, "not only does not imply the capacity for being brought to perfection but stands in express opposition to it." In the good anarchist society, then, there is to be no compulsion at all.

While the anarchist may look to other societies for examples of what human nature can do, in fact he is not rebelling in favor of the past as much as he is "in favor of an ideal of individual freedom which belongs outside the present." The anarchist dreams of a society that comes into existence as a result of the spontaneous will of all the members. Under such circumstances, social and economic affairs are administered by small, local functional groups. After an existing society has been decentralized, debureaucratized, and simplified, individuals will spontaneously federate themselves into communes and associations, and these in turn will spontaneously federate into regional units and overriding authorities. In this organic network of balancing interests, based on the natural urge of mutual aid, the artificial patterns of coercion will become unnecessary.

The anarchist is vigorously antidemocratic, for democracy insists on the sovereignty of the people and anarchism insists on the sovereignty of the person. Parliamentary institutions are wrong because in them the individual has abdicated sovereignty to an elected representative. Furthermore, the majority has no right to inflict its will on the minority.

The principal difference, then, between the Catholic social theorist and the anarchist is that the Catholic is much more cautious about human nature and much less likely to be convinced that all restrictive or coercive human authority is necessarily bad. Furthermore, the Catholic may not like much of what he sees of the world, but he cannot accept the anarchist vision of destruction (peaceful or violent, depending on what kind of anarchist you are) as a prelude to a new beginning.

For while the anarchist would admit in principle that the only growth that matters is organic growth, he argues that the political, industrial, and scientific world in which we find ourselves is so corrupt that one must begin almost from the beginning to construct a new social order. The Catholic theorist is skeptical about any "fresh new starts," believing that one begins not from the beginning but from where one is; hence he finds it very difficult to conceptualize the utopian visions or to utilize utopian rhetoric.

Still he runs the risk of being dismissed as utopian by those who rigidly hold to the left-right paradigm. There are, after all, only two ways to solve modern human problems: the state control of socialism or the independent marketplace of capitalism. A third way is merely a compromise somewhere between the two, and it is impractical if not impossible to derive a third way that is not a middle ground but is rather the result of introducing another vector. The Catholic social theorist is told that he is trying to turn the clock back by re-creating a feudal society with its organic and dense networks of human relationships. Impossible, the modernist contends. These dense networks either no longer exist or are no longer relevant to the organization of modern industrialized society. Therefore, we must choose between the tyranny of the corporation and the tyranny of the state or hew out some middle ground.

Three of the four ideologies we are considering would claim to favor individualists—capitalism, anarchism, and Catholicism. The socialist position is that a rigid communitarianism in the present is necessary for freedom of individuals in the classless, communist society of the future. But the other three positions are unwilling to sacrifice the individuals of the present for those of the future. The capitalist insists on the economic freedom of the individual at least, even if often such legal and economic freedoms are not very meaningful for the masses at certain stages of development of the capitalist system. The anarchist rejects all authority, other than that which emerges from spontaneous cooperation, as oppressive to the freedom of the individual. Hence the attempts to find an achievement of the

Marxist ideal in Mao's China or Castro's Cuba indicate a total misunderstanding of that ideal by present-day "anarchists." Anarchism may be communal, but it is surely not communitarian.

Catholic individualism dissents from capitalist individualism in that it rejects the capitalist vision of the individual as isolated, egoistic, and pursuing his own enlightened self-interest. In such a ruthlessly competitive social jungle, the Catholic theorist would argue, one has freedom and vast wealth for a few individuals and misery and slavery for many others. It categorically rejects the immolation of individuals in the holocaust of a pyramid of sacrifice of the present in order that individuals of the future may enjoy a socialist utopia. It comes closer to anarchism in believing that human nature is communal but not communitarian and that the individual achieves most effective personal development as part of a dense network of cooperation, support, and affection—though it dissents from the anarchist by arguing that sometimes, given the propensities of human nature to evil, some individuals must be restrained from taking advantage of others. It also believes that political authority can facilitate, reinforce, and promote the functioning of the subsidiary social and political networks. It concedes that oftentimes civil authority does not do this, but argues that it can and should.

Thus the Catholic social theorist would argue that there is no contradiction between individual and society, between person and community. It would contend that the propensity of many modern observers to see such conflict is merely the result of their looking at human society from a very narrow, rigid, and insensitive perspective. For the Catholic theory the goal of society is ultimately the enrichment and fulfillment of the individual person. The person does not exist for society, society exists for the person; but the person enriches and develops himself only through cooperative social interaction. The community and the larger society are not, in Catholic theory, necessarily obstacles to personal development and freedom (as they often become in the anarchist theory) but the absolutely necessary conditions for and the matrix of such development and fulfillment. You cannot become fully human by yourself, Catholic theory would argue. Of course, both the community and the society often become obstacles to the development of full humanity; they must be reformed. Such is the nature of human nature and its propensity toward evil that community and society need reform, but it does not follow that they are necessarily evil; it follows only that they are part of the flawed, frail, but still improvable human condition.

In principle the Catholic social theory can coexist with a wide variety of governmental forms. However, a number of Catholic theorists in the 1930s and 1940s, particularly Yves Simon and Jacques Maritain, argued that there was a special affinity between Catholic social theory and liberal democracy (of the North Atlantic variety). For the Catholic, insistence on pluralism, decentralization, personal freedom, and limitations on the power of the state seemed to have special affinity with notions of civil liberties, pluralistic governments, and the limited authority of the state that emerged from the Anglo-Saxon political tradition. Unfortunately very few American Catholics have bothered to reflect on the interpenetration of Catholic social theory and American political practice, which has been at the core of the American Catholic experience. The wards, the precincts, the neighborhoods of the urban immigrant world were the places where this interpenetration occurred; and with the exception of Jesuit scholars John Courtney Murray and more recently, John Coleman, very few American Catholics have any respect for this fascinating event.

INDEX